Information Technologies and Economic Development in Latin America

Information Technologies and Economic Development in Latin America

Edited by Alberto Chong and Mónica Yáñez-Pagans

ANTHEM PRESS

Anthem Press
An imprint of Wimbledon Publishing Company
www.anthempress.com

This edition first published in UK and USA 2020
by ANTHEM PRESS
75–76 Blackfriars Road, London SE1 8HA, UK
or PO Box 9779, London SW19 7ZG, UK
and
244 Madison Ave #116, New York, NY 10016, USA

British Library Cataloguing-in-Publication Data
A catalogue record for this book is available from the British Library.

ISBN-13: 978-1-78527-199-1 (Hbk)
ISBN-10: 1-78527-199-7 (Hbk)

This title is also available as an e-book.

CONTENTS

ILLUSTRATIONS

Figures

Tables

EDITORS

Alberto Chong is a professor in the Department of Economics at the Andrew Young School of Policy Studies at Georgia State University and also holds a faculty position with Universidad Del Pacifico in Lima. He is a Fulbright Scholar and pursued graduate studies in Economics at Cornell University and Harvard University and received his MA and PhD degrees from Cornell. Dr. Chong is also Director of Development Research Strategies, a nonprofit organization that seeks to use formal empirical methods to better guide public policy. His publications include more than 80 papers in peer-reviewed journals and several books. Previously he held faculty appointments with the University of Ottawa and George Washington University and spent about a dozen years working in multilateral organizations in particular, the World Bank and the Inter-American Development Bank. He is currently an associate editor with Economics Bulletin and Heliyon.

Mónica Yáñez-Pagans is a senior economist in the Latin America & Caribbean Unit of the Education Global Practice at the World Bank. She works in the provision of technical assistance to governments related to the design of dissemination strategies for large-scale student assessments to promote improved education outcomes, strategies to strengthening school management, strategies to improve education public spending and financing and policies to evaluate education policy, among others. She worked as an economist in the South Asia and Middle East and North Africa, East Africa and the Horn and Global Anchor Units of the Poverty and Equity Global Practice at the World Bank. Before joining the World Bank, she worked as an associate economic affairs officer at the United Nations Conference on Trade and Development and in the Research Department of the Inter-American Development Bank. She holds a PhD in Applied Economics from the University of Illinois at Urbana-Champaign.

CONTRIBUTORS

Ana Balsa holds a PhD in Economics from Boston University. She is Professor of Microeconomics, Econometrics of Impact Evaluation and Health Economics at Universidad de Montevideo, Uruguay and Researcher Level 2 at the Uruguayan National System of Researchers (SNI). Her areas of academic interest include Health Economics and Economics of Education. She has conducted research on the implications of social interactions on behavior and human capital—focusing on statistical discrimination, relative deprivation and peer effects and on the economic impact of health and education programs and policies, including prenatal care, anti-tobacco campaigns, drug prevention and treatment, charter schools and parenting programs. Her projects have been funded by the National Institutes of Health (NIH) in the United States, the Inter-American Development Bank, the Uruguayan National Agency for Research and Innovation (ANII), the Uruguayan Ministry of Public Health (MSP) and the Latin American Development Bank (CAF).

Mariana Blanco holds a PhD in Economics from Royal Holloway College, University of London. Currently, she is an Associate Professor of Economics at Universidad del Rosario, Colombia where she set up the first Experimental Economics Lab in Bogotá, which is today known as REBEL (Rosario Experimental and Behavioral Economics Lab). Mariana is an experimental economist working in many areas, such as labor economics, education economics, development, political economy among others. She is mainly recognized for her contributions on social preferences and belief formation. Her papers have been published in journals such as Journal of Economic Theory, Experimental Economics, Games and Economic Behaviour, Management Science, among others.

Ana C. Dammert is Associate Professor of Economics and International Affairs at Carleton University. Her main research interests are motivated by welfare issues in developing countries. She has considerable research experience in evaluating policies in different countries including Colombia, Ethiopia, Guatemala, Nicaragua, Peru and several others. In particular, her recent work is concerned with the effects of public policies on child labor, schooling and health. She teaches courses in development economics and has published extensively in peer-reviewed journals. She holds MA and PhD degrees from Syracuse University.

José Galdo is an Associate Professor of Economics and Public Policy at Carleton University, Ottawa and a research fellow at the Institute for the Study of Labor (IZA). His research lies at the intersection of applied economics and the evaluation of public policy using both experimental and non-experimental approaches. He has substantial research and field experience in evaluating public policy in countries as diverse as the United States, Canada, Peru, Colombia, Ethiopia and Mongolia. Professor Galdo has published his work in peer-reviewed journals. He is currently an associate editor for two peer-reviewed journals, Economía and the Latin American Research Review. Professor Galdo is a Fulbright Scholar and holds a PhD degree in economics from Syracuse University.

Virgilio Galdo is a research analyst in the Chief Economist Office of the South Asia Region at the World Bank. He has contributed to the preparation of major reports on issues related to the rural–rural transformation of the region. He is coleading the effort to assemble a spatial database for South Asia that brings together into a single platform with granular data from both traditional sources of information and modern sources (satellite, big data). Prior to that, he was a team member of the *World Development Report 2013: Jobs* and worked in the Independent Evaluation Group of the World Bank. His research interest lies on development issues associated with rural– urban transformation, economic geography and geospatial impact evaluation. His work has been published in several peer-reviewed journals. He has a MA degree in Economics from Michigan State University and is an ABD in Economics after completing all his doctoral work at Syracuse University.

Néstor Gandelman holds a PhD in Economics from the University of Rochester. Since 2002 he directs the Department of Economics of Universidad ORT Uruguay. Gandelman is a researcher level III (highest level) of the Uruguayan National System of Researchers (SNI). His research focuses on applied microeconomics and economic development. He has 50 academic publications, mostly in classified in firm level studies (such as the effects of financial constraints on investment decisions, the costs of adjusting factors of production, productivity and the dynamics of work and capital), studies on gender differences (in access to housing, in judicial processes, in academia, in the labor market and in subjective indicators of happiness) and analysis of income and expenditure surveys (studies on microeconomic differentials in savings rates, differentials in spending on education, transport and culture). Gandelman has served as a consultant for the Inter-American Development Bank, the World Bank, the United Nations, International Food and Policy Research Institute and state agencies and is a columnist for the El País newspaper's Economy and Market supplement.

Laura Jaitman is head of International Affairs at the Ministry of the Treasury of Argentina. She is responsible for the representation of Argentina in international economic meetings and for international relations at the Treasury. She joined the Treasury in 2017 as G20 Finance Deputy to lead the Finance Track under the Argentine G20 Presidency. Previously she was an economist at the Research Department of the Inter-American Development Bank. Her main areas of research are the economics of crime, development economics and political economy. She has more than a decade of working experience at various international institutions like the World Bank, the IDB and MIT J-PAL in the evaluation of public policies in different countries of Latin America and the Caribbean. She holds a PhD in Economics from University College London, UK. Her work was published in international peer-reviewed journals such as the Economic Journal and the Journal of Economic Behavior and Organization, among others, and featured in international media.

Dean Karlan is the Frederic Esser Nemmers Distinguished Professor of Economics and Finance Kellogg School of Management and codirector of the Global Poverty Research Lab at Northwestern University. He is the founder and president of Innovations for Poverty Action, a nonprofit organization dedicated to discovering and promoting solutions to global poverty problems, and working to scale-up successful ideas through implementation and dissemination to policymakers, practitioners, investors and donors. His research focuses on development and behavioral economics, and he is on the Board of Directors of the M.I.T. Jameel Poverty Action Lab. His received a PhD in Economics from M.I.T., an MBA and an MPP from the University of Chicago, and a BA in International Affairs from the University of Virginia.

Florencia Lopez Boo holds a PhD in Economics from the University of Oxford. She is currently a lead economist in the Division of Social Protection and Health of the Inter-American Development Bank (IDB) and associate researcher of *Young Lives* at the Department of International Development (University of Oxford) and at IZA (Bonn). Her work focuses on the design, implementation, monitoring and evaluation of public policies on child development and social protection in Latin America. She currently leads an initiative on behavioral economics and social policies and is the chair of the LACEA-BRAIN network. She has been the main advisor in child development issues for the G20 meetings under the presidency of Argentina, achieving the historical inclusion of ECD in the final presidential communique. She has published in specialized journals and has written books on education and child development. She is also a member of various boards, including the Investing in Young Children Forum of the National Academy of Sciences, the UNESCO's Measuring Early Learning Quality and Outcomes technical consortium and the Brookings Institution's Costing ECD group.

Eduardo Nakasone is an assistant professor in the Department of Agricultural, Food, and Resource Economics and the Department of Media and Information at Michigan State University. He holds a concurrent appointment as a Non-Resident Fellow at the International Food Policy Research Institute (IFPRI). Nakasone holds a PhD in Agricultural and Resource Economics from the University of Maryland. His research primarily focuses on how to better use Information and Communication Technologies to induce behavioral changes that can improve agricultural, nutritional and educational outcomes in developing countries.

Rafael Porzecanski is Director of Public Opinion and Social Studies at Opción Cosultores. Bachelor of Sociology, Universidad de la República Uruguay. Master in Sociology, University of California, Los Angeles. He has a long career as a consultant in applied social research for institutions of civil society, public sector and international organizations. He has several academic publications on topics related to areas such as political sociology, social development and cultural identities. He taught at the Universidad de la República and Universidad ORT Uruguay.

Máximo Torero Cullen is the Assistant Director-General, Economic and Social Development Department of the Food and Agriculture Organization (FAO) since January 2019. Prior to this he was a World Bank Group Executive Director and before he led the Division of the Markets, Trade, and Institutions at IFPRI. His experience encompasses Latin America, Sub-Saharan Africa and Asia. Dr. Torero holds a PhD and a Master's Degree in Economics from the University of California, Los Angeles (UCLA). He has published in elite peer-reviewed journals. He is a professor on leave at Universidad del Pacífico (Perú) and a von Humboldt Fellow at University of Bonn. In 2000 he received the Georg Foster Research Fellowship and awarded Outstanding Research on Development given by The Global Development Network in 2000 and 2002. He received the Chevalier de l'Ordre du Mérite Agricole in 2014.

Martin Valdivia holds a PhD in Applied Economics from the University of Minnesota. He has worked as a senior researcher at GRADE since 1993. His fields of interest include health, poverty and social policy, microfinance and rural development, with publications in top peer-reviewed journals. He has carried out research projects and consultancies for international organizations such as the Inter-American Development Bank, the World Bank, the World Health Organization, the Pan-American Health Organization, the Food and Agriculture Organization, the International Labor Organization and USAID. He is currently researching the relevance of soft skills and socio-emotional drivers for the financial inclusion and economic empowerment of women in urban and rural areas of Brazil, Peru and Dominican Republic.

Juan Vargas is Distinguished Professor of Economics at Universidad del Rosario, Colombia. He holds a PhD in Economics from Royal Holloway, University of London (2007) and has held visiting academic positions at Harvard University, UCLA, the Institute of Development Studies, the IADB and University of Bergamo. From 2015 to 2018 he was affiliated to CAF-Development Bank of Latin America. His main interests are on the causes and consequences of violent armed conflict, the economics of crime and the interplay between political and economic, formal and informal institutions in the process of state-building. Juan's research has appeared in top peer reviewed journals. Juan is the network director of Lacea's *America Latina crime and Policy Network* (AL CAPONE). He shared the *2018 Juan Luis Londoño Prize*, awarded every two years to the Colombian economist under 40, as judged both his/her academic contributions and their impact in improving the well-being of Colombians.

ACKNOWLEDGMENTS

The editors and authors would like to thank the following individuals who provided truly generous time and effort in the preparation of the different chapters of this book: Gonzalo Aceijas, Tania Alfonso, Miguel Almánzar, Angela Amaya, Fernando Barberi, Arlette Beltrán, Fernando Bonzi, Yezid Botiva, David Bullón Patton, Matías Busso, Giancarlo Cafferata, René Castro, Bruno Chong, Marco Chong, Angelo Cozzubo, Sandra Darville, Cecilia de Mendoza, Luciana Delgado, Diana Domenech, Maribel Elías, Oscar Farfán, Thais Forster, Rita Funaro, Sebastián Galiani, Luis F. Gamboa, Alejandro Garnica, Megan Greiving, Claudia Gutiérrez, Adam Kemis Betty, Christopher Ksoll, Minoru Higa, Patricia Katayama, Jeffrey Kubik, Diego Lamé, Laura Llambí, Antonio López, Eduardo Lora, Alvaro Margolis, Natalia Miranda, Susana Maggiolo, Elisa Martínez, Natalia Miranda, Manuel Moresco, Carmen Mosquera, Claudia Mutter, Mike Murphy, Yamile Palacios, Abi Pandey, Miguel Paredes, Amitia Pérez-Gold, Giorgina Piani, Ximena Querol, Clara Ramírez, Manuel Ramírez, Vanessa Ríos-Salas, Eugenia Rivas, Anna Serrichio, J. Scarel, Yuri Soares, Benniamino Savonito, Miriam Vásquez, Graciela Vitarella and Luisa Zanforlin.

Chapter 1

INFORMATION TECHNOLOGIES IN LATIN AMERICA

Alberto Chong and Mónica Yáñez-Pagans

1.1 Introduction

The dramatic surge in technological innovations in recent years has led researchers to think hard about the linkages between technology and its effects on society. The expansion of technology has increased the capacity to capture, communicate, compute and store information. This has led to a profound restructuring of the economic and social organization of societies (Webster, 2006). In fact, information and communication technologies have become key factors contributing to economic growth in advanced economies and developing countries alike.

There are compelling reasons to expect significant economic development from the adoption of information technologies. The most obvious way in which these technologies can help achieve economic improvements is by reducing asymmetric and imperfect information in markets, which can help in tasks related with search and coordination, and this in turn may lead to increased market efficiency (Chong, 2011). In particular, individuals and firms can use these technologies to search for prices of products, search for jobs, look for potential buyers of products, get ready for weather and natural disasters, as well as remain connected with friends and family (Aker and Mbiti, 2010). Furthermore, it has been argued that such technologies enable a country to leapfrog development stages by being able to decouple information from other factors that were previously embedded together, which allows information to be immediately transmitted and shared by several agents without the actual physical movement of information or individuals (Chong, 2011; Evans and Wurster, 1997). This use of information may produce large content-related externalities. Thus, unlike typical technological innovations in the past information technologies can also increase the knowledge content of products and services and can bring about previously unknown products, jobs and livelihoods (Torero and von Braun, 2006). As a result of these network externalities, information technologies allow for the creation of new industries and open additional labor possibilities many that were unavailable before. Finally, they play a role in the development of public policies by augmenting the range of possibilities and the manner in which policies can be implemented, for instance in terms of being gender-specific or group-specific (Chong, 2011).

1.2 Good Research Design Is Important and Feasible

Despite the global, regional and internal digital divide, information and communication technologies have expanded dramatically in the region. During the last two decades, mobile phones have penetrated more quickly in our region than in developed ones at a rate that is nothing short of remarkable. Similarly, the per capita growth rates of users of the Internet have been higher in developing countries than in developed ones (Chong, 2011; Kenny, 2006). The really fast diffusion of these newer technologies, such as mobile telephony, broadband and the Internet has opened up big opportunities for using these technologies in the delivery of information in businesses and social service providers in Latin America and the Caribbean (Chong, 2011).

In this context, this set of chapters attempts to contribute to the limited empirical evidence that exists for Latin America by providing the findings of randomized and quasi-experimental studies for different information technologies applications, which range from traditional ones, such as DVDs and radios, to mobile phone applications, to traceability information systems and several others. In evaluating the impact of these technologies, a critical concern has been the lack of reliable data that may allow the specific role of a particular tool to be isolated. While some advances in data collection have been made in recent years this central issue persists. In fact, projects with information technologies components have been widely funded by multilateral organizations, bilateral aid agencies and nongovernmental organizations, but to this day they tend to lack rigorous evaluations of their impacts. This is particularly true in the case of Latin America (Chong, 2011).

One of the most reliable ways to evaluate the impact of any intervention is through randomized experiments, which allow creating statistically equivalent groups at the baseline, reduce the plausibility of threats to internal validity and allow estimating the treatment effect with minimal statistical assumptions. The majority of the studies presented in this special issue use this design to evaluate the impact of information technologies on development outcomes. As it will be described in some more detail below, the projects studied in this volume range from the use of short text messages to try to improve health promotion and management or job expectations to the use of radio and video to improve financial education in rural populations. The adequacy of randomized experiments to measure the impact of an intervention, estimating causation not correlation, relies on their implementation. Sometimes, randomization at the level of individual participants, even successfully implemented, may lead to inappropriate conclusions (McCall and Green, 2004). Some of the randomized experiments presented deal with some of these implementation issues. In particular, we place particular focus to compliance issues, an issue that is little studied in information technologies interventions, but that is critical in order to achieve results. For instance, the audio and video interventions in rural communities mentioned above faced an extreme problem of low compliance rates. Similarly, an intervention in this set of chapters that deals with internally displaced households had to deal with high attrition rates and selection concerns. These problems resulted in difficulties to assess the success of the interventions, although they did not diminish the quality of the research nor potential policy lessons that were learned from the research process. In this context, an important objective is to test one of the frustrating benefits of randomized controlled trials, namely, their ability to show that a program does not work when in fact it does not as in fact, important policy lessons can be gained from failed field experiments.

In our view, the value of this volume is to bring together a group of studies that are relevant in and of itself and that provide a number of innovative and well thought through research designs and guides researchers in design and hypothesis formation. Furthermore, we believe that the findings of this set of chapters can gain more relevance by presenting them as a collective piece of evidence as it provides a body of rigorous-based evidence on the role of information and communication technologies in Latin America. In this regard, we hope that the whole that emerges from reading them together will be greater than the sum of the parts given by the complementarities between the chapters. In addition, it is a topic that is directly relevant since future investments in areas such as agricultural extension, public safety net programs, market deepening, financial education and the like are likely to be increasingly driven through information technology platforms. This collection of essays aims to provide valuable insight on both the promise and the pitfalls of trying to replace conventional, high-cost outreach with technological alternatives. Thus, the collection of chapters may be relevant both to researchers working in the area of information technologies as well as to practitioners who are pondering how to leverage technology to improve outreach and to reach clients in innovative ways.

Thus, this special issue also attempts to improve future efforts in assessing the impact of information technologies in Latin America through the inclusion of different evaluation design methods and strategies to solve potential measurement issues. As we describe below, we provide interventions in which the adoption of information technologies can boost development by reducing asymmetric and imperfect information in markets by helping with tasks related to search and coordination, thus potentially resulting in a more efficient allocation of resources in the market. In some of our interventions, individuals and firms employ information technologies in order to search for prices of products, look for jobs, find potential buyers of products and learn about personal finance or health. Another characteristic of some of the interventions considered in this collection of chapters is the aim at searching for ways to increase knowledge content and thus potentially creating either new products or jobs, or both. Furthermore, another common characteristic of the interventions considered is the explicit consideration of public policy components as part of its implementation. For instance, one of the interventions considered in this special issue deals with the improvement in social policies targeting for the most vulnerable groups. Finally, in addition to the implementation difficulties in randomized experiments, and given its unique contribution, we also considered one exercise based on a quasi-experimental design as an alternative strategy to measure the impact of the intervention, which deals with a traceability information system on several farms' outcomes and employs matching procedures to create a control group

As seen above, information and communication technologies help address market failures caused by problems of coordination and asymmetric information. The great risk of these tools is, perhaps, expecting too much of them. This collection of chapters focuses on basic areas, which are particularly important for the region or in which applications using information technologies have been commonly applied. Furthermore, this collection of chapters tries to avoid the potential bias toward finding positive results (Ravallion, 2009). In fact, two of the studies considered conclude that their corresponding intervention under analysis does not yield any statistical significant impact. The sections below describe the interventions considered in more detail.

1.3 Interventions Considered

Many families in some Latin American countries highly depend on farming and cattle rising. The use of agricultural technology can help them to improve their quality of life through direct and indirect effects (De Janvry and Sadoulet, 2002). Direct effects are gains for the adopters, while indirect effects are gains derived from adoption by others leading to lower food prices, employment creation and growth linkage effects. The chapter by Jaitman finds that the implementation of a traceability system to electronically identify and track the production cycle of cowherds in small and medium rural farms in Argentina have those direct and indirect effects. Using a quasi-experimental design, the author finds that beneficiaries adopting this technology experienced an increase in their livestock and doubled the number of skilled workers. Farms using the traceability system also received a higher price for their high quality beef as they complied with strict standards that enabled them to export to the European Union and other regions. Treated farmers also reported improvements in efficiency, profits and risk managements.

The rapid expansion of some information technologies, such as Internet and the use of personal computers in Latin America also applies to the business sector. In this context, it results relevant to study if high information technologies skills matter for businesses demanding labor. In their research, Lopez-Boo and Blanco analyze whether people that self-reported in their resume an advanced level of knowledge of different software packages are more likely to be contacted in Bogota and Buenos Aires, two middle-income Latin-American cities. They sent approximately eleven thousand fictitious resumes for real job vacancies in both cities. These fake applications in each city were similar in all except having low or high electronic information and communication technology (ICT) skills, which is the characteristic being randomized. They find that people with high knowledge of ICT receive around 11 percent more callbacks than people with low knowledge of ICT. Their results also suggest that firms looking to fill vacancies pay special attention to ICT skills regardless of the fact that those skills are actually being used on the job. Moreover, the magnitude of the effect varies across occupations and cities under study.

In the last decades, mobile phones have become the most rapidly adopted technology in developing countries. Given the low costs of text messages associated to this technology, it seems relevant to analyze whether its use in government interventions produces major benefits for society. In their research, Dammert, Galdo and Galdo carried out a randomized experiment evaluating whether information about job-market opportunities sent to jobseekers via short text messages influences subjective expectations. Their design included a multiple treatments experiment as part of the Peruvian public intermediation system, which provides three months of subsidized job search assistance matching individuals' labor profiles with available job vacancies. Searchers that signed up to receive public labor-market intermediation were randomly assigned to four treatment groups according to two information channels (i.e., digital and non-digital intermediation) and the scope of information they received (i.e., short (public) and enhanced (public/private) information sets). The results show that jobseekers subject to digital labor-market intermediation based on a large set of information show a positive and statistically significant change in their job gain expectations three months after signing up for public labor-market intermediation. Then, it is not the technology itself that causes a statistically significant positive effect on job expectations, but rather it is an enhanced set of information about labor-market opportunities transmitted through digital means, which explains those results and their subsequent impact on work status.

For the government, and society in general, it is important to have horizontally adequate programs that reach their target population (Dolgoff and Feldstein 2009). In Colombia, one of the most vulnerable groups is formed by those families that have been forced to migrate as a result of the internal conflict with guerrillas and paramilitary forces. The majority of these displaced households live below the poverty line and face unemployment rates much higher than the rest of the population. According to government estimates, approximately 70 percent of households in the registry of displaced population are unaware of their ability to receive social benefits. To reach this specific target population, in their chapter, Blanco and Vargas carried out a randomized experiment in Bogota to assess whether the use of text message technology effectively informed the refuges of their eligibility to receive social benefits. The study finds that such an inexpensive intervention for the internally displaced people increases awareness of their entitlement to a variety of social benefits related to housing, supplies, medical care and food assistance.

1.4 Information May Not Be Enough

The results presented in this collection of chapters suggest that to obtain benefits from information and communication technologies, complementary characteristics may be important. The quality of institutions and regulations, the content available on networks, the skills of the population and the physical infrastructure are all crucial to the success of information technologies interventions. For instance, Lopez-Boo and Blanco find that these technologies are valuable in the labor market, but the returns vary across occupations and countries. In the study carried out by Dammert, Galdo and Galdo, they find evidence suggesting that it is not technology itself that causes a statistically significant positive effect on job expectations, but rather it is an enhanced set of information about labor-market opportunities transmitted through digital means, which explains those results and their subsequent impact on work status.

Another example of the need of having complementarity components is the intervention by Chong, Karlan and Valdivia. Despite of the benefits of establishing links with the financial system, very few households in the developing world use such links. On average, only 35 percent of Latin American and Caribbean households have a bank account—a low percentage compared to advanced economies, where no less than 90 percent of the population has this type of link with the financial system (Chong, 2011). Expanding access to financial services in places where the population is scant or where geographic or security conditions are difficult can be so costly that the benefit of including new people in the business of the institution is outweighed by its cost. In this context, ICTs can play a crucial role. They can allow many households to exploit the benefits of online banking through the Internet. ICTs can also be a useful tool to provide information to help people make better financial decisions. While many of the recent information technologies are used by the majority of the population in the developed world, this is not the case in developing countries. For the most part, outside of large cities, consumers in developing countries have very little exposure to computers and even less exposure to the Internet.

In this regard, Chong et al. analyze the initial impact of a financial literacy education model with ICTs that are popular and accessible in rural areas, such as radio and video. The intervention was carried out as part of a financial program, delivering financial literacy education by credit officers in monthly session with the support of video and radio material. The program was implemented as a randomized experiment with clients of 665 communal banks in 13 provinces from southern Peru. The program evaluated consists of nine monthly 45 minutes training sessions with a seven-minute video, nine 25-minutes radio programs and nine homework assignments. The results in this study suggest no impact of the financial literacy education module on the clients' saving, repayment and retention rates. However, due to partial completion and partial compliance, these results cannot be concluding. Besides, low compliance levels with the DVD and video components suggest that the low cost delivery methods chosen were not adequate for this context. Higher investments would need to be made in the delivery of the information technologies components in order to raise compliance levels to the point that would allow a future reevaluation to draw useful conclusions.

Understanding the cultural environment while using information technologies can provide low cost and effective alternatives to implement policies. An example of this, also related to financial education, lies in a large-scale program named "Strengthening Women Entrepreneurship in Peru (SWEP)" which provided short-term training to female micro entrepreneurs in Peru. The general objective of the project was to improve the contribution of women-headed micro and small enterprises to family incomes and the economy of Peru, by providing assistance aimed at broadening access to business training using a soap-opera format. This soap opera depicts the struggles of the owner of a cash-strapped grocery shop who decides to open a catering business when her husband gets fired from his job. The basic idea is that trainees could relate to the main character's problems while illustrating the advantages of timely cash flows, setting a fixed salary for the owners and keeping records. Nakasone and Torero present the results of a randomized experiment that reproduces SWEP at a small scale using a soap opera and practical exercises about a struggling micro entrepreneur. Their results show the program positively affects the adoption of business practices taught by the program. In particular, those who received the training were more likely to assign themselves a fixed salary rather than taking cash from their businesses based on personal needs, and more likely to keep better records of potential business contacts. They also find some positive impacts on the adoption of bookkeeping practices, though this result is not significant across all of our specifications. The authors, however, do not find any impact on average business performance, household expenditures or women empowerment in the household. This is explained as changes in adoption rates were small in absolute terms despite being large when compared to baseline levels. Variations in the design of this experiment could, at a relatively low cost, inform policy makers on potential improvements for further iterations of SWEP or similar policies in other latitudes where soap operas are of major influence.

Another example in which information technologies may not be enough is the case of the application of such tools in the area of health care, also referred to as e-health. While the theoretical potential to improve health care provision, cost-effectiveness and health outcomes in the region is high, it is still unclear whether e-health interventions in developing regions, such as Latin America, are effective and cost-effective. Balsa and Gandelman present the results of a randomized experiment that evaluates the impact of an Internet and text-message based information intervention on the health promotion and disease management of diabetic patients (type 2) treated in health care centers in Montevideo, Uruguay. The intervention consisted of the dissemination of information and materials related to type 2 diabetes through the Internet. In addition, patients in this group received periodic reminders about new topics through email and text messages. Balsa and Gandelman find that the intervention did not affect the distribution of the beliefs about diabetes, the level of patients trust in the physician–patient relationship, the quality of clinical communication, patterns of food consumption and health outcomes, such as blood pressure or blood glucose level. In contrast to previous results for developed countries, these findings present a less optimistic picture of the potential benefits of web platforms for the empowerment of patients with chronic diseases in developing countries. This may be associated to the fact that both Internet and health care systems in Latin America are less developed. Also, the intervention may have produced some effects beyond the six-month follow-up period used in this evaluation. Furthermore, participants may have not been interested ex ante in the information technology-based intervention, which may have affected their use of the technology. In fact, the authors find that women, younger patients and those who completed high school appeared to have a greater appreciation of the value of the information technology tool. Then, successful e-health interventions in Latin American should consider those factors in order to approximate how familiar with the Internet their target population is.

Also related to health care, adolescents' widespread adoption of new information technologies creates important opportunities for engaging youths in preventive services via e-Health. ICT technologies such as mobile phone SMS constitute cost effective vehicles to access youth in a widespread manner, however, raising awareness might not be enough to effectively affect health-risk behaviors of this group. An illustration of this point is presented by Balsa, Gandelman and Porzecanski who conducted a randomized control trial to estimate the impact of an Internet and SMS-based intervention on adolescents' information about substances and rates of consumption. The intervention, which lasted three months, had several components designed to take advantage of the wide range of ICTs used regularly by adolescents. The first component consisted in the posting of adolescent-friendly information and materials related to drug consumption and abuse on a website. In addition, intervention participants were reached through e-mails, announcing the disclosure of new materials and commenting different issues raised by students during their participation in the website. Second, a series of text messages were sent periodically to participants' cell phones. The authors find that the three-month intervention implemented was able to improve awareness on what substances constitute drugs but induced no change in conducts. Evidence also points to no differences among those that logged in to the web platform and those that only received e-mails and SMS, suggesting the web platform was probably cost inefficient. Balsa et al. advocate that changing students' behavior needs approaches that are not only informative but also involve students in more encompassing activities.

1.5 What Is the Common Thread?

The problem with randomized controlled trials is that they help us see the trees but not the forest. Information technologies have tremendous promise to push information out to low-income populations primarily because it can be done at a very low unit cost. There is thus a lot of excitement about how these technologies can change delivery of health and government services, financial information, training and education, and even to deepen markets by improving the flow of information. However, the hype needs to be backed up by solid empirical evidence. Information technology interventions happen to be an area that is very amenable to randomized trials, and so this collection of chapters aims at holding the bar high in this regard. Furthermore, along with the theme of complementarities, there is a deeper common thread that runs through practically all the studies presented in this volume, which is the issue of compliance. In fact, the paradox of old and new informations and communication technologies is that while it is very economical to do things like sending text messages and ask people to watch videos, it is also not very effective in that each individual contact has a very low probability of being noticed, let alone change behavior. Hence, while costs are low, cost effectiveness also appears to be low because a program with very low compliance is very unlikely to be effective.

The two extreme and opposite cases that illustrate this issue are the piece by Blanco and Vargas and the one by Chong, Karlan and Valdivia. In the former, they provide a rigorous and straight information and communication technology randomized controlled trial that finds big effects on final outcomes, which fits well into the overall narrative in that this exercise is providing information related to benefits that are given for free, and as such, while compliance is low, the benefits to participants from complying are very large and hence detectable in the intention-to-treat. On the other hand, Chong, Karlan and Valdivia show that they are unable to find any detectable impact in the intention-to-treat because while compliance is low, the benefits to participants are much more costly, either because individuals have to physically approach a training center or because the time commitment that is required from them is high in terms of their opportunity cost. Interestingly, these opposite results are analogous to the overall development experimental literature that is consistently finding large randomized controlled trials impacts of cash transfer programs but providing much more mixed evidence on interventions such as microfinance or extension services. In this regard, most chapters make explicit reference to the issue of compliance, which greatly improves the coherence of this special issue. Some researchers provide basic information on take up rates, and others provide more formal exercises that try to disentangle some of the key determinants of compliance, that is, directly as an outcome variable. Further, in order to complement the randomized controlled trial analysis, some of the studies explore possible heterogeneity of impacts using a somewhat broad of covariates. Whereas this is particularly clear in Chong, et al, where the authors find that gender is an important determinant factor of compliance and, in particular, they show that women tend to be more compliant than men, we were unable to uncover systematic patterns across chapters that would provide a common picture on the specific role of gender, geographical status, education and others. Future research may aim at further studying this issue as they could provide important meta-evidence on the populations that are likely to comply when offered information technologies interventions, and on the groups in which we may expect impacts to be larger. In short, while information and communication technologies hold great potential benefit on the cost and outreach side, the issue of compliance is the key one that may be taken into account for any program hoping to bring large benefits in an intention-to-treat sense through information and communications technologies.

1.6 Conclusions

In recent decades, information and communication technologies have become more and more common in Latin America. Experience shows that the impact of these technologies in the coming years will be greater. They are a potentially effective mean for development. They can close information gaps in the labor market, improve the efficiency in farms and targeting accuracy for social programs. Nevertheless, these new technologies depend on factors related to differences in access. Newer digital tools cannot be accessed in small towns and rural areas of the region. Poor and less educated families tend to have less access to Internet and computers, and are, consequently, less familiarized with them. This reduces the potential benefits for development of information and communication technologies, especially for the most vulnerable population. They may be not beneficial in all scenarios. Furthermore, their gains on welfare and efficiency may not only depend on the number of devices installed but also on the quantity, quality and the effective use of the digitized information and communications in the system (ECLAC, 2010). Aside from its reliance on technology, information and communication technologies for development also require an understanding of institutional framework, community development, poverty, health care and basic education.

In this volume we present a broad range of studies mostly based on randomized controlled trials that range from the use of short text messages to try to improve health promotion and management or job expectations, to the use of radio and video to improve financial education in rural populations. We find that there are several commonalities among the chapters presented, which are especially related to complementarity and compliance. We argue that the latter appears to be a particularly relevant issue, one that should also be taken into account in future studies related to information and communication technologies. In short, this summary chapter provides the lead-in to this special issue and attempts to summarize the landscape of information and communications technologies in Latin America, the research design and compliance issues pertinent for the study of information technologies and to provide an overview of the studies that make up the collection of chapters.

References

Aker, J., and I. Mbiti (2010). "Mobile Phones and Economic Development in Africa." *Journal of Economic Perspectives*, 24(3): 207–32.

Chong, A. (2011). *Development Connections: Unveiling the Impact of New Information Technologies.* Development in the Americas. New York: Palgrave Macmillan.

De Janvry, A., and E. Sadoulet (2002). "World Poverty and the Role of Agricultural Technology: Direct and Indirect Effects." *Journal of Development Studies*, 38(4): 1–26.

Dolgoff, R., and D. Feldstein (2009). "Examining a Social Welfare Program within the Context of Social Justice: Structural Components, Alternative Program Characteristics, and Evaluation." Chapter 7 in *Understanding Social Welfare: A Search for Social Justice*, 8th edition. Boston, MA: Allyn & Bacon.

Evans, Philip B., and Thomas S. Wurster (1997). "Strategy and the New Economics of Information." *Harvard Business Review* (September–October): 71–82.

Fafchamps M., and Bart Minten (2012). "Impact of SMS-Based Agricultural Information on Indian Farmers." *World Bank Economic Review*, 26(3): 383–414.

Kenny, Charles (2006). *Overselling the Web? Development and the Internet.* Boulder: Lynne Rienner.

McCall, R. B., and B. L. Green (2004). "Beyond the Methodological Gold Standards of Behavioral Research: Considerations for Practice and Policy." *SRCD Social Policy Report*, 18(2): 3–19.

Ravallion, M. (2009). "Evaluation in the Practice of Development." *World Bank Research Observer*, 24(1): 29–53.

Torero, M., and J. von Braun (2006). Impacts of ICT on Low-Income Rural Households. In: *Information and Communication Technologies for Development and Poverty Reduction. The Potential of Telecommunications*, edited by M. Torero and J. von Braun. Baltimore, MD: Johns Hopkins University Press, 234–39.

Webster, Frank (2006). *Theories of the Information Society*, 3rd edition. Routledge: New York.

Chapter 2

THE IMPACT OF ICT IN HEALTH PROMOTION: A RANDOMIZED EXPERIMENT WITH DIABETIC PATIENTS

Ana Balsa and Néstor Gandelman

2.1 Introduction

The World Health Organization defines e-health as the combined use of electronic information and communication technology (ICT) in the health sector. According to a systematic review of evaluations of e-health implementations by Blaya et al. (2010), the greatest potential for e-health may lie in systems that improve communication between health-care institutions, support medication ordering and management, and help monitor and improve patient compliance with care regimens. Evaluations of personal digital assistants and mobile devices may also indicate the level of effectiveness in improving data collection time and quality. Despite this potential, there is a severe need for more rigorous evaluation of the effectiveness and cost-effectiveness of these systems in less-developed countries (Blaya et al., 2010; Kahn et al., 2010).

In this study, we used a randomized controlled trial to evaluate the impact of an Internet and SMS-based information intervention on the health promotion and disease management of diabetic patients treated in health-care centers in Montevideo, Uruguay. The intervention granted access to information and materials related to type 2 diabetes through a private website called Diabetes 2.0. The intervention group had unlimited access to the site and could download all available materials at no charge. Materials included articles or brief presentations, videos and images, news, and links to other related websites. Patients in this group received periodic reminders about new topics through email and SMS. In addition, the intervention group had access to a social network through the site, aimed at facilitating the exchange of personal experiences, questions and knowledge between patients that shared the same condition.

Diabetes is one of the most expensive diseases for the health-care system. A recent study in the United States (Dall et al., 2010) shows that the average annual cost per case is $2,864 for undiagnosed diabetes, $9,975 for diagnosed diabetes ($9,677 for type 2 and $14,856 for type 1) and $443 for prediabetes (medical costs only). This amounts to approximately $700 annually for every American, regardless of diabetes status. The prevalence of diabetes in Uruguay is 8.2 percent, with 90 percent of these have type 2 diabetes (Ferrero and García 2005). Patients with diabetes require constant follow-up from the head physician and significant support to achieve self-control. An Internet-based intervention can empower diabetic patients by providing them with information and supportive tools that can help them improve their health-related decision-making and ultimately increase their quality of life and well-being. Better disease management by the patient can also result in lower health-care costs. These expected effects on health-care utilization, together with the relative low cost and massive scope of Internet-based programs, suggest that e-health interventions have the potential for substantial cost effectiveness.

Despite the promises of e-interventions, our study showed no significant impact on the knowledge, behaviors or health outcomes of diabetic patients. We found participation to be a main challenge for the success of the program. In particular, we found that prior lack of Internet literacy among the intervened patients, and the decision to offer the program to a general sample of patients, regardless of prior expressed interest, played against a satisfactory uptake rate. Our results suggest that barriers to participation should be taken into careful consideration when designing online interventions.

2.2 Background

The widespread use of the Internet and mobile phones is currently challenging the way patients are educated, supported and followed up. A number of US surveys show that between 40 and 50 percent of American adults use the Internet to look for advice or information about health or health care (Baker et al., 2003; Diaz et al., 2002; Dickerson et al., 2004; Fox, 2007). Through the Internet, patients can access wide-ranging, up-to-date information about their disease, available medical treatments, costs and preventive health practices on a 24/7 basis. Interactivity and anonymity provide patients with new communication options, the potential for accessing information tailored to their needs and new sources of support (Anderson and Klemm, 2008; Cline and Haynes, 2001). The information and support available through the Internet make it a promising cost-effective vehicle for empowering patients by improving their control over their health conditions and promoting better decision-making.

There are still a number of pitfalls associated with the use of the Internet as a health education, management and supportive tool. The quality of the information on the Internet is not uniform and is often inaccurate, which increases the vulnerability of the patient (Eysenbach et al., 2002). Patients face security and privacy issues (Hong et al., 2008). And access is usually unequal. In the United States, whites, more educated patients and individuals of higher socioeconomic status are more likely than others to access the Internet for health information reasons (Diaz et al., 2002; Dickerson et al., 2004). Age can also be a source of disparity when it comes to successfully accessing relevant health information (Ybarra and Suman, 2008).

While there is some skepticism about the value of the Internet for patients' health-related decisions (Baker et al., 2003), the literature shows very few reported cases of harm associated with the use of poor quality health information on the Internet (Crocco et al., 2002). On the other hand, a growing number of studies are showing positive effects of Internet-based interactive and informative tools on health, health-related decision-making and well-being, although most of them occur in developed countries. In a survey of patients with chronic conditions and disabilities (Fox, 2007), three out of four patients who used the Internet (e-patients) reported that their online searches had positively affected treatment decisions, their ability to cope with their condition and their dieting and fitness regimes. Kalichman et al. (2003) found an association between using the Internet for health-related information and health benefits among people living with HIV/AIDS. Fogel et al. (2002) found that Internet use for breast health issues was associated with greater social support and less loneliness than Internet use for other purposes or nonuse among breast cancer patients. Broom (2005) investigated how access to information and online support affected prostate cancer patients' experiences of disease and their relationships with their physicians. They found that online access had a profound effect on men's experience of prostate cancer, helping them gain control over their disease and limiting inhibitions in face-to-face encounters with the physician. Gustafson et al. (1999) used a randomized controlled trial to analyze the effects of a computerized system that provided HIV-positive patients with information, decision support and networking tools. They found that the system improved their quality of life and promoted a more efficient use of health care by these patients.

Several e-health interventions have been associated with the management of diabetes. Harno et at. (2006) conducted an evaluation of an e-health application with a diabetes management system and a home care link. They found significantly lower levels of HbA1c, blood pressure, cholesterol and fasting plasma glucose in the study group relative to the control individuals, and a lower number of visits by the study patients to doctors and nurses. Meigs et al. (2003) tested the effects of the Disease Management Application (DMA), a web-based decision support tool for diabetics developed to improve evidence-based management of type 2 diabetes. Patients in the intervention group increased the number of HbA1c tests, cholesterol tests and foot examinations within a year. They also experienced stronger decreases in levels of HbA1c and cholesterol than patients in the control group. McKay et al. (2001) evaluated the short-term benefits of an Internet-based supplement to usual care that focused on providing support for sedentary patients with type 2 diabetes to increase their physical activity levels. The study showed no difference in physical activity between patients that were randomized to the Diabetes Network (D-Net) Active Lives Physical Activity Intervention and patients assigned to an Internet Information-only condition.

One recurring problem with Internet-based interventions has been patient participation over time. Fell et al. (2000) found that younger diabetic patients showed increased interest in interactive Internet interventions, but older patients increased participation only when barriers to access were addressed. Glasgow et al. (2003) evaluated participation and effects of the "Diabetes Network (D-Net)" Internet-based self-management project, a randomized trial evaluating the incremental effects of adding tailored self-management training or peer support components to a basic Internet-based, information-focused comparison intervention. The study encountered a strong decrease in participation over time. Additions of tailored self-management and peer support components generally did not significantly improve results.

The use of the Internet by patients is also challenging the basis of the patient–physician relationship. There are studies suggesting that some physicians may react negatively to the demands of patients that use the Internet as a source of information and education (Broom, 2005). Research shows that the majority of the patients that use the Internet for health information do not discuss this information with their doctors (Diaz et al., 2002). And those who take information sought on the web to the physician want the physician's opinion rather than a specific intervention (Murray et al., 2003). In Murray's study, the effect of taking information to the physician on the physician–patient relationship was likely to be positive as long as the physician had adequate communication skills and did not appear challenged by the patient bringing in information.

While research on e-health interventions is growing exponentially in developed countries, less is known about the impacts of similar programs in less developed nations. A number of experiences using mobile phone technology are showing great promise in some Latin American countries. In Chile, a nurse-based telephone-care service linked with key clinical events and outpatient visits resulted in improved glycemic levels, blood pressure, perception of health and healthier eating. Another public health disease management program in Nicaragua based on SMS contributed to increased compliance of patients taking TB drugs (Anta, El-Wahab and Giuffrida, 2009). Blaya et al. (2010) and Kahn et al. (2010) highlight the need for more rigorous evaluations of the effectiveness and cost-effectiveness of e-health interventions in less developed countries. While e-health interventions are still relatively scarce in Uruguay, the country has shown a positive trend in the adoption of ICTs in recent years. In a 2008 ranking of 20 Latin American countries comparing the penetration rates of Internet, broadband Internet, personal computers (PCs), wireless subscribers and fixed telephone lines, Uruguay was rated Latin America's top technology country (LaRed21, 2009). According to data from the International Telecommunications Union, Uruguay's mobile penetration exceeded 100 percent in 2008, Internet penetration was 40 percent and broadband penetration was 9 percent in the same year. A study conducted in 2006 found significant socioeconomic and age-related inequities in access to ICTs. The gap in PC use between the poorest and richest income quintiles was only 2 among adolescents, but it increased to 20 when assessing the population age 50 and over (Pittaluga y Sienra, 2007). This generational gap is of particular concern when considering that many e-health interventions aim at reaching middle-aged or older individuals.

2.3 Methodology

2.3.1 Design overview

A randomized design was employed to evaluate the effects at six months following randomization of diabetic patients in primary care practices to an Internet-based education and networking intervention versus the distribution of a brief educational brochure. The aim of the study was to analyze the effectiveness and cost-effectiveness of the ICT intervention in terms of achieving higher overall patient well-being (self-reported and quality-of-life-adjusted years), treatment compliance, use of health care, patient's sense of control of the disease, information about the disease and its treatment, a better patient–physician relationship and technology-related skills. The study design was reviewed by an ethics committee at the University ORT Uruguay in July 2009.

2.3.2 Recruitment and participants

Our target population was defined as adult patients suffering from type 2 diabetes that had Internet access at home (i.e., had a PC and Internet connection at home) or reported navigating the Internet at least once a week and were currently being treated in one of three HMOs in Montevideo. Pregnant women, patients taking insulin, patients under dialysis treatment or patients with other complications (such as severe eye disease, cancer or celiac disease) were excluded from the study. Patients that had participated as leaders in diabetes education groups were also excluded from the study.

To recruit the participants, we contacted patients in the waiting rooms of internists treating diabetic patients or endocrinologists at three HMOs in Montevideo: a large HMO with 236,085 enrollees, and two smaller HMOs, one with 46,612 enrollees and the other with 43,427 enrollees.[1] Interviewers were assigned to the waiting rooms at different times of the day between April and July 2009. After ensuring that they qualified for the study, patients were asked to sign an informed consent form that described the study and the implications of their participation.

At baseline, most patients were interviewed while waiting for their appointment or right after the appointment. The survey consisted of two questionnaires. The first questionnaire was administered by the interviewer and inquired about sociodemographics, perceived health status, morbidity, severity of diabetes, diabetes-related care, disease management and compliance with treatment, health-care utilization in general, and knowledge about diabetes. A second self-administered questionnaire inquired about depression, the patient–physician relationship, the patient's sense of empowerment regarding the disease, use of alcohol and other substances, physical activity, and diet. All participants were given a brochure developed by experts in diabetes, which explained the fundamental aspects of type 2 diabetes treatment. Subjects completing the baseline interview were randomly assigned to the control group and the intervention group. We ended up with a sample of 388 individuals that qualified for the study. Patients were randomized to the e-health intervention or a no-intervention setting. Our final sample consisted of 195 individuals in the intervention group and 193 in the control group.

A follow-up interview was conducted six months after the initiation of the distance phase of the intervention, between January 26 and May 6, 2010. This second survey consisted of a subset of questions that had already been asked in the first questionnaire and that reflected attitudes or behaviors that could potentially be affected by the intervention and a small set of new questions referring to some of the topics covered in the e-health intervention. The surveys were completely administered by the interviewer, and the time and place of the interview were coordinated beforehand between the interviewer

1   Data from the October 2008 Health Census.

and the participant. We were able to complete 280 interviews in this way. Participants refusing to participate in the face-to-face interview (due to lack of time, lack of interest or unwillingness to let a stranger come into their homes or fear of a scam) were offered the option of answering the survey over the phone. Sixty additional surveys were completed using this modality. Final sample attrition was 48 observations (12 percent of the original sample): 3 patients died between the baseline and the follow-up survey, 4 could not be located and 41 refused to participate at follow-up.

The inclusion and exclusion restrictions that defined the study made recruitment difficult. Even though the survey took place in the diabetes departments of the above-mentioned HMOs, many individuals did not qualify for the project. By eliminating type 1 diabetics, we cut out the younger segment of the diabetic population. The remaining population had a greater chance of suffering any of the medical conditions that would exclude them from the project (except pregnancy). Furthermore, only 17 percent of Uruguayans over 50 use the Internet at least sporadically, according to a recent survey.[2] A great majority of those contacted in the waiting rooms were over 50 years old.

2.3.3 The intervention

The intervention had two aims: providing information and offering a platform to build peer-to-peer support. Before the *online* phase, patients in the intervention group were invited to participate in a short workshop that instructed them on how to search for information on the Internet and on the use of social network platforms (wikis, chat, forums). An expert in search and documentation coordinated each of these workshops, which lasted around two hours. The workshops included an organized set of practical activities using a PC (one participant per PC) and took into account the knowledge of participants regarding their "computer skills". The workshops took place at the facilities of the Universidad ORT Uruguay between July 20 and July 30, 2009. Out of the 195 participants in the intervention group, only 57 agreed to attend the workshop. The main reasons for non-attendance were: current illnesses, difficulty to travel due to lack of mobility, lack of available time to participate, lack of interest in the subject and particularly the risks of the Influenza A virus at the time (the workshops took place in winter). Eight workshops were originally scheduled, with an average of 20 participants each expected to attend. The first 10 minutes of the workshop were used for introductions and a brief presentation of the topics to be discussed in the session; in the

2   *"El perfil del internauta Uruguayo"* 2008—Grupo Radar.

next 30 minutes, the documentation specialist in charge of the workshops gave a tutorial of how to perform good and efficient searches on the Internet. After that, the participants were given 20–30 minutes to search the Internet with personalized assistance from the workshop coordinators. The remaining 50–60 minutes were devoted to introducing the diabetes platform created by EviMed[3] specifically for this project, with special attention to the forum, chat and wiki, which the participants were less familiar with. After the workshop, the instructions for logging on to the website were mailed and e-mailed to every participant whether they participated in the workshop or not. A week later, everyone received a phone call to check if they had received the information and to offer assistance with logging in. The intervention was active through January 2010.

The intervention facilitated the dissemination of information and materials related to type 2 diabetes through the Internet. These contents were published on a website (DIABETES 2.0) specially designed for the study and updated weekly. The intervention group had unlimited access to the site and could download all of the available materials at no charge. Materials included articles or brief presentations, videos and images, schedules, news, and links to other related websites. In addition, patients in this group received periodic reminders about new topics through e-mail and SMS. The messages and educational materials were developed and chosen by specialists and edited by EviMed's interdisciplinary team (documentation specialist, internist and communicators) using sources such as Medline Plus, eviDoctor and others. Besides providing access to information, one of the main advantages of the Internet in empowering individuals is its anonymity. The Internet allows individuals to ask questions they may be ashamed to ask in face-to-face encounters. For instance, sexual dysfunction may be associated with the evolution of diabetes. The anonymity of the Internet also allows patients to share their personal experiences and learn from each other. The intervention group had access to a social network through the site, aimed at facilitating the exchange of personal experiences, questions and knowledge between patients that shared the same condition. The network was facilitated through an electronic platform, where patients could meet in forums, chats and wikis to discuss ideas or ask about the materials or other aspects of their life as chronic patients. An example of a forum topic is "What physical workout do we usually do?" and a wiki topic is "Healthy recipes with spinach." An "animator" (nonmedical) organized and stimulated network participation. Periodically, a physician specializing in diabetes

---

3   EviMed is a private firm that develops information and educational products and services for physicians throughout Latin America. http://www.evimed.net/.

participated in the network by commenting on the patients' comments, clarifying points and answering some questions.[4]

2.3.4 Program evaluation

The evaluation of the effects of ICT programs is challenged by selection problems. Individuals that decide to participate in the program are in general subtly different from those that do not participate. These differences (e.g., motivation, laziness) may have an impact on the evolution of the disease, the satisfaction of the patient with treatment and other dimensions of disease management. The randomized controlled trial framework minimizes this endogeneity problem but does not completely eliminate it. In this scenario, there is still one concern that needs to be addressed: nonparticipation. Although each individual invited to participate in the intervention could have benefitted from the workshop and the online phase of the study, some of them chose not to participate. This nonparticipation may be associated with individual or contextual characteristics that may also affect the variables under study.

In order to avoid this situation, it is important to implement the treatment with an "intention to treat" variable, defined as all those that were invited to participate in the intervention whether they took part in it or not. Once the exogeneity of the treatment is established, the identification of the causal effects of ICT technologies follows from simple econometric techniques. Given a certain indicator that we would like to measure, Y, the effect of the intervention is given by a difference-in-difference procedure. We implement the difference-in-difference framework (Card, 1992; Gruber, 1994) by pooling observations in both surveys and estimating a regression of the form:

$$Y_{it} = \beta_o + \beta_1 ITT_i + \beta_2 Wave_{2t} + \beta_3 ITT_i * Wave_{2t} + \varepsilon_{it} \qquad \text{(Eq. 2.1)}$$

where ITT_i and $Wave_{2t}$ are dummies. Y_{it} is the outcome variable under study, ITT_i represents the "intention to treat" group and takes the value 1 if the ith patient was invited to participate in the Internet based intervention and 0 otherwise. $Wave_{2t}$ takes the value of 1 when the answer refers to the second survey. The coefficient multiplying ITT_i (β_1) reflects baseline differences between the intention to treat and control groups. The coefficient of $Wave_{2t}$ (β_2)

---

4   Our study shows some similarities with the Comprehensive Health Enhancement Support System (CHESS) aimed at facilitating patients with access to support groups and information about medical decisions. CHESS has been associated with positive outcomes for women with breast cancer and AIDS patients who used computers (Baker et al., 2011; Gustafson et al., 1999).

reflects time trends in outcomes that are common to the intervention and control groups. The effect of the intervention is captured by the coefficient multiplying the interaction term (β_3). When the dependent variable is discrete this same approach can be used in a probit or ordered probit regression.

2.4 Results

2.4.1 Participation in the Diabetes 2.0 intervention

According to the information automatically collected by the website Diabetes 2.0, 86 participants (44 percent of the *ITT*) logged on at least once during the experiment. Among this subgroup, 39 participants (45 percent) logged on one day, 14 (16 percent) did so two days and the remaining 38 percent did so three days or more. On average, those who logged on did so 4.3 times. Forty-seven participants (24 percent of the *ITT*) engaged in a variety of activities, such as forums, chats, wikis or online surveys.

There is some discrepancy between the participation records stemming from the web logs and levels of participation as reported by the participants in the second survey. Of the original 195 *ITT* participants, 162 took the second survey and answered the question: "How often did you enter the Diabetes 2.0 website?" Twenty-four participants (15 percent of respondents to the second survey) who had logged on at least once according to automatic registers did not remember having visited the site when asked about their participation in the follow-up survey. And 22 participants (14 percent) who did not log on according to our records reported having visited Diabetes 2.0. Some of the participants who attended the workshop were provided with a username and password during the workshop and had a chance to navigate the Diabetes 2.0 website that same day. Other participants that also attended the workshops were sent an email with the username and password later on. To avoid biases, we did not take into consideration that first login during the workshop as evidence of participation in the program. Considering this correction in total there were 77 participants (39 percent). This may partially explain the difference between our records and self-reports of participation. Another reason for the discrepancies between web registers and self-reports may be the lack of experience in the use of the Internet among some of the participants, which may have led to confusion regarding whether they actually entered the website or not.

Table 2.1 presents summary information on participation in the website Diabetes 2.0 and in the previously held workshop. Overall, females' participation rate was above males' participation rate for the website, 42 percent and 36 percent respectively. On the other hand, males (in percentage terms)

Table 2.1 Summary Statistics of Participation

		Participation in the website diabetes 2.0			Participation in the workshop		
		Female (%)	Male (%)	Full sample (%)	Female (%)	Male (%)	Full sample (%)
Age up to 55	Mean (%)	46	29	38	32	17	25
	Std dev (%)	51	46	49	48	38	44
	N	28	24	52	28	24	52
Age 55–64	Mean (%)	40	48	43	47	43	45
	Std dev (%)	50	51	50	51	51	50
	N	30	21	51	30	21	51
Age 65–69	Mean (%)	47	33	41	37	33	35
	Std dev (%)	51	49	50	50	49	49
	N	19	15	34	19	15	34
Ages 70 & more	Mean (%)	37	35	36	17	43	28
	Std dev (%)	49	49	48	38	51	45
	N	35	23	58	35	23	58
Total	Mean (%)	42	36	39	32	34	33
	Std dev (%)	50	48	49	47	48	47
	N	112	83	195	112	83	195

Source: Authors' own data.

tended to participate more in the workshop than females. Although we break participation by age categories, we do not observe any clear pattern.

In the second survey, we asked all participants who reported never logging on the reasons for not doing so. Participants were offered several alternatives and could select as many choices as they wanted. Eight percent declared that they did not log on because they were not interested in the topic, 12 percent reported that they preferred using other channels of information on diabetes, 54 percent reported that they were not frequent Internet users and 14 percent claimed to already have all the diabetes-related information they needed.

Although more than half of the participants never visited Diabetes 2.0, most members in the "intention to treat" group were reached by the experiment via e-mail messages and/or SMS messages. Around 65 percent of participants reported having received text messages related to the project and 57 percent reported having received e-mails from the project staff. Overall, 75 percent of the participants reported having received text messages or emails from the staff (again, some participants may have gotten e-mails or text messages but did not remember or simply considered it as spam). Combining this information with the web registers, only 30 participants never logged on to Diabetes 2.0 or do not recall receiving emails or text messages. However, the data indicate that 132 participants were reached by the project's information and communication technologies in one way or another.

In order to investigate the possible determinants of participation in the web based intervention, we estimated a probit model, with a dichotomous indicator of participation in the Diabetes 2.0 website (according to electronic records) as the dependent variable. The explanatory variables were gender, age, marital status, any children in the household, education, employment status, self-reported health status, time elapsed since the patient was first diagnosed with diabetes, self-reported knowledge about diabetes, Internet access at home, previous use of an e-mail account, previous use of the Internet for health related information and participant's HMO.

The first column in Table 2.2 shows the marginal effects of the participation regression for a selected set of explanatory variables. Women were 18 percentage points more likely to enter the Diabetes 2.0 website than men. Having Internet at home was not significantly related to participation in the website. One of the exclusion restrictions for recruitment into this study was that participants should have Internet access at home or access to the Internet at least once a week. The nonsignificance of the Internet dummy reflects that there are no differences between those that have Internet at home and those that browse the Internet from somewhere else. Having a previous e-mail account was not a significant determinant of the participation decision. Having previously searched for health-related topics on the Internet, on the

Table 2.2 Determinants of Participation in the Website Diabetes 2.0

Marginal effects of probit regression

	Includes workshop participation	Doesn't include workshop participation
Male	−0.18	−0.18
	(0.079)**	(0.080)**
Reports good health	0.03	0.04
	(0.078)	(0.079)
Diabetes diagnosed five years ago or less	0.10	0.09
	(0.085)	(0.086)
Reports high knowledge about diabetes	−0.07	−0.05
	(0.149)	(0.151)
Has Internet access at home	0.06	0.05
	(0.098)	(0.100)
Has an e-mail account	0.08	0.05
	(0.094)	(0.098)
Searched health related information on the Internet in the last 6 months	0.24	0.27
	(0.092)**	(0.089)***
Age 55–65	0.03	−0.02
	(0.108)	(0.108)
Age 65–70	0.10	0.09
	(0.129)	(0.135)
Age 70+	0.15	0.15
	(0.131)	(0.133)
Lives with a couple	0.23	0.20
	(0.081)***	(0.084)**
Lives with sons/daughters	−0.17	−0.13
	(0.077)**	(0.078)*
Interviewed in CASMU	−0.29	−0.27
	(0.177)	(0.182)
Completed high school or equivalent	0.17	0.18
	(0.096)*	(0.098)*
Completed college or equivalent	0.29	0.31
	(0.126)**	(0.127)**
Employed	−0.06	−0.04
	(0.093)	(0.095)
Participated in the workshop		0.21
		(0.082)***
Observations	195	195

Source: Authors' own data.

Notes

1. Standard errors in parentheses.

2. * Significant at 10%; ** significant at 5%; *** significant at 1%.

other hand, increased the likelihood of participation by 24 percentage points. This suggests that the source of access to the Internet and the frequency of use are not sufficient conditions for participation in these types of programs. Those who did participate in the program were inherently more interested in using the Internet as a source of health-related information.

In this aged population, age was not a significant determinant of the participation decision, but living with a partner was positively associated with navigating the diabetes website. In addition to encouraging the diabetic patient to take better care of him or herself, a partner might provide helpful insights to the infrequent Internet user. On the other hand, participation was negatively associated with the presence of children at home. Time constraints associated with taking care of children or the fact that kids monopolize the use of computers at home could explain this result. Finally, education was also significantly related to participation. Being a high school or a college graduate increased the likelihood of entering the Diabetes 2.0 website by 17 and 29 percentage points respectively relative to individuals with less than a high school education. In a second regression (second column of Table 2.2), we added an indicator for workshop participation to the set of controls. Participation in the workshop was positively associated with use of the Diabetes 2.0 website. While this effect could capture some unobservable characteristics of the patient, such as motivation, none of the previously significant variables lost statistical significance or changed magnitude significantly when accounting for this factor. This suggests that participation in a workshop could enhance participation in these types of programs.

2.4.2 Evaluation of the impact of Diabetes 2.0

The aim of the Diabetes 2.0 intervention was to improve diabetic patients' control over their health and promote better decision-making by providing patients with relevant up-to-date information as well as social support. First, we expected the intervention to improve patients' knowledge and beliefs about their disease and its management. Empowered by this information, patients might change their health-related behaviors and make more effective healthcare decisions. Health outcomes could improve as a result. Following this knowledge–behavior–outcomes paradigm, we proceed to evaluate the results in each of these three steps.

2.4.2.1 Impact on knowledge

In the baseline and follow-up survey, patients were asked several questions about what they knew or thought they knew about diabetes. Table 2.3 reports

Table 2.3 How Much Do You Know about …?

Baseline survey

	Nothing (%)	A little (%)	Enough (%)	A lot (%)	All (%)	Cases
1 the effect of being sick (e.g., flu) on diabetes?	36	16	42	6	100	340
2 maintaining an appropriate weight?	6	7	55	32	100	340
3 what happens when the level of glucose in blood is too low?	12	14	53	21	100	339
4 why medication is needed in treating diabetes?	8	12	53	28	100	339
5 the long-term impact of diabetes in health?	7	9	53	31	100	338
6 the impact of cholesterol on diabetes?	20	14	45	20	100	339
7 eye care and control?	14	9	50	27	100	340
8 foot care and control?	6	9	53	32	100	339
9 the impact of alcohol on diabetes?	16	10	50	24	100	340
10 the impact of smoking on diabetes?	16	9	49	26	100	340
11 the impact of stress on diabetes?	13	10	50	27	100	340
12 the impact of fatigue on diabetes?	16	11	49	24	100	339
13 diet plans to control diabetes?	5	5	54	36	100	340

Source: Authors' own data.

patients' perceptions of their knowledge in many relevant dimensions, including medical questions (need for medication), most common complications (eyes and feet problems and long-run effects of diabetes) and consumption habits (alcohol, smoking) among others. In all cases but one, the majority of patients considered their knowledge level to be good. The effect of being sick (e.g., having the flu) on their diabetes was the only dimension where the majority of patients considered that they lacked adequate knowledge. On the other hand, more than a quarter of respondents considered they had insufficient knowledge about the impact of cholesterol, alcohol and smoking on diabetes and what happens when their blood sugar level is too low.

In Table 2.4, we report the results of implementing the difference-in-difference framework in an ordered probit regression. The dependent variables, capturing knowledge about diabetes, take the following values: 1 for nothing, 2 for a little, 3 for enough and 4 for a lot. The interaction between the intention to treat and second wave dummies is not significant for any of the 13 knowledge questions. This means that the distribution of the beliefs about diabetes was not affected in any way by the intervention.[5]

2.4.2.2 Impact on empowerment and behavior

Table 2.5 reports the baseline values for several variables measuring physician–patient relationship and health-related behavior patterns. One of the ways in which the intervention can improve health-care decisions is by empowering the patient in the physician–patient relationship. We assessed patient trust and doctor–patient communication by implementing a scale developed for the Primary Care Assessment Survey (PCAS). The PCAS is a validated, patient-completed questionnaire designed to operationalize formal definitions of primary care. Extensive psychometric testing and evaluation have been conducted on the PCAS scales. All scales exceed established standards for excellent instrumentation and perform consistently well across population subgroups (Murray and Safran, 2000). The trust and communication scales range from 0 to 100 points, with higher scores indicating better outcomes. According to the baseline survey, the level of patient trust and the quality of clinical communication were very good. To facilitate interpretation of the magnitudes for someone not familiar with the PCAS, we also report a direct question on trust. Patients were asked to rank on a scale from 0 to 10 how much they trusted their medical doctors. The average answer was almost 9.

---

5   There was a significant effect of time on knowledge: both treatment and control patients gain knowledge about the disease over time.

Table 2.4 The Impact of the Intervention on Knowledge

Difference-in-difference estimation using an ordered probit model

	Question 1	Question 2	Question 3	Question 4	Question 5	Question 6	Question 7
ITT	0.078	0.063	0.082	0.014	0.080	0.083	0.071
	(0.119)	(0.127)	(0.121)	(0.121)	(0.124)	(0.119)	(0.122)
Wave2	−0.207	0.521	0.303	0.426	0.396	0.035	0.277
	(0.118)*	(0.125)***	(0.119)**	(0.121)***	(0.122)***	(0.117)	(0.120)**
ITTxWave2	0.011	−0.030	−0.044	0.153	0.234	0.068	0.016
	(0.170)	(0.178)	(0.171)	(0.172)	(0.176)	(0.168)	(0.173)
Observations	680	680	678	678	676	678	680

	Question 8	Question 9	Question 10	Question 11	Question 12	Question 13
ITT	0.059	0.059	0.020	−0.051	−0.023	−0.033
	(0.124)	(0.119)	(0.119)	(0.120)	(0.120)	(0.130)
Wave2	0.545	0.204	0.261	0.331	0.161	0.651
	(0.124)***	(0.118)*	(0.118)**	(0.119)***	(0.118)	(0.129)***
ITTxWave2	0.016	0.150	0.198	0.102	0.287	−0.037
	(0.176)	(0.170)	(0.169)	(0.171)	(0.170)*	(0.182)
Observations	678	680	680	680	678	680

Source: Authors' own data.

Notes

1. Standard errors in parentheses.

2. * Significant at 10%; ** significant at 5%; *** significant at 1%.

3. Dependent variable takes the following values: 1 for nothing, 2 for a little, 3 for enough and 4 for a lot.

Table 2.5 Trust, Communication and Consumption Patterns

Baseline survey

		Mean	**Standard deviation**	**Cases**
Trust (1–10)		8.8	1.5	318
Trust (PCAS)		88.7	11.7	329
Communication with M.D. (PCAS)		85.7	14.1	325
During the last week, on how many days did you consume …	Fruits	6.4	1.5	340
	Vegetables	5.6	2.0	340
	Ready-to-eat meals	0.6	1.1	340
	French fries	0.7	1.1	340
	Cookies and other pastry	1.4	2.0	340
	Regular soda and juices with sugar	0.4	1.2	339
	Fish	1.1	1.1	340
	Cold cuts and sausages	1.4	1.8	340

Source: Authors' own data.

We also collected information on food consumption in the past week, including things that diabetics should avoid (French fries, ready-to-eat meals) and foods that should be encouraged (fruits, vegetables). On average, the consumption pattern seemed reasonable at baseline: patients reported consuming fruits and vegetables almost daily, while the average frequency of intake of less healthy food was once a week or less.

The econometric results of Table 2.6 show that the intervention had no effect on any of the variables considered.

2.4.2.3 Impact on outcomes

Finally, in this subsection we address the effect of the intervention on health outcomes. Table 2.7 reports the baseline values for self-perceived health status, several medical tests and complications of diabetes. The majority of respondents reported that they were in good health. Only a minority considered themselves to be in very good or excellent health, and a sizeable share of respondents ranked their health at the bottom two levels of the distribution (fair or bad). Blood pressure is the pressure exerted by circulating blood upon the walls of blood vessels. During each heartbeat, blood pressure varies between a maximum (systolic) and a minimum (diastolic) pressure. According to Appel et al. (2006), the risk of cardiovascular disease increases progressively

Difference-in-difference estimation. OLS

	Trust (1–10)	Trust (PCAS)	Communication (PCAS)
ITT	−0.080	−0.838	−0.347
	(0.150)	(1.222)	(1.471)
Wave2	−0.251	1.612	−0.789
	(0.146)*	(1.198)	(1.442)
ITTxWave2	−0.166	−2.226	−1.723
	(0.212)	(1.728)	(2.081)
Constant	9.180	88.519	87.508
	(0.103)***	(0.847)***	(1.019)***
Observations	636	658	650

Consumption in the past week of:

	Fruits	Vegetables	Ready-to-it meals	French fries	Cookies and similar	Regular soda	Fish	Cold cuts and sausages
ITT	−0.230	0.124	−0.040	0.001	0.076	−0.094	0.036	0.021
	(0.173)	(0.216)	(0.129)	(0.112)	(0.225)	(0.135)	(0.116)	(0.207)
Wave2	0.040	0.040	−0.153	−0.080	0.028	−0.011	−0.080	−0.148
	(0.170)	(0.212)	(0.127)	(0.110)	(0.221)	(0.133)	(0.114)	(0.203)
ITTxWave2	0.180	−0.211	0.202	0.110	−0.187	0.011	−0.042	0.075
	(0.245)	(0.305)	(0.182)	(0.159)	(0.319)	(0.191)	(0.164)	(0.293)
Constant	6.358	5.608	0.705	0.676	1.449	0.411	1.165	1.534
	(0.120)***	(0.150)***	(0.089)***	(0.078)***	(0.157)***	(0.094)***	(0.080)***	(0.144)***
Observations	680	680	680	680	680	678	680	680

Source: Authors' own data.

Notes

1. Standard errors in parentheses.

2. * Significant at 10%; ** significant at 5%; *** significant at 1%.

Table 2.7 Outcomes: Descriptive Statistics

Baseline survey

	Bad	Fair	Good	Very good	Excellent	Cases
Self-perceived health (%)	4	36	53	7	1	340

		Mean	s.d.	Cases
Last measure	Systolic blood pressure	129	15	312
	Diastolic blood pressure	76	10	309
	Fasting blood glucose level	121	35	173
	After eating (2 hours) blood glucose level	136	40	66
In the last 6 months	% that had to stay a night in hospital	10	30	340
	% that had to go to the emergency room	29	45	340
	% with foot injuries	8	27	340
	% with eye problems	14	35	339
	% with kidney problems	6	24	337

Source: Authors' own data.

above 115/75 mmHg (millimeters of mercury), but for diabetic patients, higher levels are considered acceptable (below 130/80 mmHg). The average patient in this study is just below this limit. This suggests that a sizeable fraction of the patients in our sample have problems associated with hypertension. The blood glucose level is the amount of glucose (sugar) present in the blood. This level fluctuates throughout the day. In the morning, before the first meal of the day (termed "the fasting level"), glucose levels are the lowest and rise after meals for an hour or two. A healthy individual's blood sugar level is in a range of about 82–110 mg/dL (milligrams/deciliter). After eating, the blood glucose level may rise up to 140mg/dL for nondiabetics. The American Diabetes Association recommends a post-meal glucose level of less than 180 mg/dl and a premeal plasma glucose of 90–130 mg/dL. The mean glucose level for the patients in this study is considered acceptable for people with diabetes. From the baseline survey it is also clear that the population under study has a significant probability of suffering from diabetes-related incidents. Over the past six months, about 10 percent had to stay at least one night in a hospital, and about one-third made a visit to the emergency room. Of the sample, 8 percent, 14 percent and 6 percent had foot, eye and kidney problems, respectively.

Given the lack of significant results in the knowledge, assessment of quality of health care, and health behavior sections, the absence of significant

Table 2.8 The Impact of the Intervention on Health Outcomes

Difference-in-difference estimation

		Last measure of				
	Health evaluation	Systolic blood pressure	Diastolic blood pressure	Fasting blood glucose level	After eating (2 hours) blood glucose level	
ITT	−0.004	−1.999	−0.701	0.504	17.511	
	(0.121)	(1.704)	(1.160)	(5.753)	(9.280)*	
Wave2	0.070	0.203	0.236	−5.898	5.389	
	(0.119)	(1.693)	(1.150)	(5.703)	(8.849)	
ITT × Wave2	0.101	−0.917	−0.301	0.062	−5.422	
	(0.171)	(2.409)	(1.640)	(8.136)	(13.124)	
Constant		130.051	76.293	126.602	124.889	
		(1.197)***	(0.813)***	(4.033)***	(6.257)***	
Observations	680	624	618	346	132	
		0.01	0.00	0.01	0.04	

			In the last 6 months			
	Night stay in hospital	Emergency room	Foot injuries	Eye problems	Kidney problems	
ITT	0.010	0.095	0.154	−0.261	−0.335	
	(0.181)	(0.143)	(0.235)	(0.208)	(0.290)	
Wave2	0.030	0.066	0.345	0.289	0.346	
	(0.177)	(0.141)	(0.220)	(0.176)	(0.220)	

(continued)

Table 2.8 (*Cont.*)

	Night stay in hospital	Emergency room	Foot injuries	Eye problems	Kidney problems
				In the last 6 months	
ITT × Wave2	−0.212	−0.227	−0.198	0.175	0.025
	(0.262)	(0.203)	(0.309)	(0.269)	(0.365)
Constant	−1.237	−0.571	−1.753	−1.335	−1.751
	(0.126)***	(0.100)***	(0.172)***	(0.132)***	(0.172)***
Observations	680	680	680	678	674

Source: Author's own data.

Notes

1. Standard errors in parentheses.

2. * Significant at 10%; ** significant at 5%; *** significant at 1%.

econometric results among the outcome variables is not surprising. Table 2.8 reports these results. The regressions in the upper panel are OLS and in the lower panel are probits.

2.5 Conclusions

The evaluation of the intervention showed no significant impact of information technologies on knowledge, perception of health-care quality, health-related behaviors or health outcomes on the participating diabetic patients. Our results present a less optimistic picture of the potential benefits of web platforms for the empowerment of patients with chronic diseases than some of the previous literature (Harno et al., 2006; McKay et al., 2001; Meigs et al., 2003). There are several possible explanations for this discrepancy. First, the success of these types of programs may be different in developed and less developed countries where both the Internet development and the health-care system are at different stages of progress. Even among patients that had initially reported having Internet access at home or using the Internet at least once a week, a majority mentioned that they did not access the Diabetes 2.0 website because they were not frequent Internet users. Second, participants in our study were not necessarily interested ex ante in an IT-based intervention. Recruitment and the baseline survey were conducted in the waiting room of the HMO, and the randomization was conducted over the full set of respondents to this baseline survey. The majority of the patients selected for the intervention never logged on to the website and were only reached by email or SMS. In other studies, the randomization is conducted on a sample of individuals that have volunteered to participate in the research. Thus, a priori interest in these types of interventions may be a prerequisite for their success.

This conjecture is reinforced by our finding that prior use of the Internet as a source of health information significantly increased participation in the website. We found, in addition, that participation in the website is correlated with variables like gender, marital status and education. Women, patients living with a partner and those who completed high school appeared to have a greater appreciation of the value of the IT tool. One last reason for the lack of significant effects of the intervention could be related to timing. It may take some time for patients not used to checking the Internet as a source of information to adopt this new tool as an everyday aid to their disease management. Moreover, the effects of empowerment derived from the new information tool might appear with some lag. The positive perception of the intervention among those that ended up participating in the website partially supports this argument. Those that reported visiting the Diabetes 2.0 website gave it an average grade of 8.5 out of 10, and most of those who reported receiving e-mails from the program staff said they had read the emails. Thus, we cannot discount the fact that the intervention may have produced some effects beyond the six-month follow-up period, or that it could have been more effective had it been active for a longer period.

References

American Diabetes Association (2006). "Standards of Medical Care-Table 6 and Table 7, Correlation between A1C level and Mean Plasma Glucose Levels on Multiple Testing over 2–3 Months." *Diabetes Care*, 29 (Supplement 1): 51–580.

Anderson, A. S., and P. Klemm (2008). "The Internet: Friend or Foe When Providing Patient Education?" *Clinical Journal of Oncology Nursing*, 12(1): 55–63.

Anta, R., S. El-Wahab and A. Giuffrida (2009). "Mobile Health: The Potential of Mobile Telephony to Bring Health Care to the Majority." *Inter-American Development Bank*. Innovation Note. https://publications.iadb.org/en/mobile-health-potential-mobile-telephony-bring-health-care-majority.

Appel, L. J., M. W. Brands, S. R. Daniels, N. Karanja, P. J. Elmer and F. M. Sacks (2006). "Dietary Approaches to Prevent and Treat Hypertension: A Scientific Statement from the American Heart Association." *Hypertension*, 47(2): 296–308.

Baker, L., et al. (2003). "Use of the Internet and E-mail for Health Care Information: Results from a National Survey." *JAMA*, 289: 2400–06.

Baker, T. B., R. Hawkins, S. Pingree, L. J. Roberts, H. E. McDowell, B. R. Shaw … and D. H. Gustafson (2011). Optimizing eHealth Breast Cancer Interventions: Which Types of eHealth Services Are Effective?. Translational Behavioral Medicine, 1(1): 134–45.

Blaya, J., H. Fraser and B. Holt (2010). "E-Health Technologies Show Promise in Developing Countries." *Health Affairs*, 29(2): 244–51.

Blonde L., and C. G. Parkin (2006). "Internet Resources to Improve Health Care for Patients with Diabetes." *Endocrine Practice*, 12 (Supplement 1): 131–37.

Bonina C., and M. Rivero Illa (2008). "Telefonía móvil y pobreza digital en América Latina. ¿Puede la expansión de los teléfonos celulares reducir la pobreza en América Latina?" *DIRSI* (Serie Concurso de Jóvenes Investigadores, 2), Lima. 38 p.il. http://dirsi.net/sites/default/files/dirsi_07_CJ2_es_0.pdf.

Broom, A. (2005). "Virtually Healthy: The Impact of Internet Use on Disease Experience and the Doctor-Patient Relationship." *Qualitative Health Research*, 15(3): 325–45.

Bull S. S., et al. (2005). "Harnessing the Potential of the Internet to Promote Chronic Illness Self-management: Diabetes as an Example of How Well We Are Doing." *Chronic Illness*, 1(2): 143–55.

Card, D. (1992). "Do Minimum Wages Reduce Employment? A Case Study of California, 1987–89." *Industrial and Labor Relations Review*, 46: 38–54.

Cline, R. J. W., and K. M. Haynes (2001). "Consumer Health Education Seeking on the Internet: The State of the Art." *Health Education Research*, 16(6): 671–92.

Crocco, A. G., et al. (2002). "Analysis of Cases of Harm Associated with Use of Health Information on the Internet." *JAMA* 287: 2869–71.

Dall, T., et al. (2010). "The Economic Burden of Diabetes." *Health Affairs*, 29(2): 297–303.

Diaz J. A., et al. (2002). "Patients' Use of the Internet for Medical Information." *Journal of General Internal Medicine*, 17(3): 180–85.

Dickerson S., et al. (2004). "Patient Internet Use for Health Information at Three Urban Primary Care Clinics." *Journal of American Medical Informatics Association*, 11(6): 499–504.

Drummond, M. F., et al. (2005). *Methods for the Economic Evaluation of Health Care Programmes*. London: Oxford University Press.

Eysenbah, G., et al. (2002). "Empirical Studies Assessing the Quality of Health Information for Consumers on the World Wide Web: A Systematic Review." *JAMA*, 287: 2691–700.

Faridi, Z., L. Liberti, K. Shuval, V. Northrup, Al. Ali and D. L. Katz (2008). "Evaluating the Impact of Mobile Telephone Technology on Type 2 Diabetic Patients' Self-management: The NICHE Pilot Study." *Journal of Evaluation in Clinical Practice*, 14(3): 465–59.

Fell, E. G., R. E. Glasgow, S. Boles, and H. G. McKay (2000). "Who Participates in Internet-Based Self-Management Programs? A Study among Novice Computer Users in a Primary Care Setting." *The Diabetes Educator*, 26(5): 806–11.

Ferrero, R., and V. García (2005). "Encuesta de Prevalencia de la Diabetes en Uruguay." *Archivos de Medicina Interna*, 27(1): 7–12.

Fogel, J., et al. (2002). "Internet Use and Social Support in Women with Breast Cancer." *Health Psychology*, 21(4): 398–404.

Fox, Susannah. (2007). *E-patients with a Disability or Chronic Disease*. Washington, DC: Pew Internet and American Life Project.

Glasgow, R. E., et al. (2003). "The D-Net Diabetes Self-Management Program: Long-Term Implementation, Outcome, and Generalization Results." *Preventive Medicine*, 36(4): 410–19.

Gruber, J. (1994). "The Incidence of Mandated Maternity Benefits." *American Economic Review*, 84(3): 622–41.

Gustafson, D. H., R. Hawkins, E. Boberg, S. Pingree, R. E. Serlin, F. Graziano and C. L. Chan (1999). Impact of a Patient-Centered, Computer-Based Health Information/Support System. *American Journal of Preventive Medicine*, 16(1): 1–9.

Harno, K., R. Kauppinen/Makelin and J. Syryalainen (2006). "Managing Diabetes Care using an Integrated Regional e-Health Approach." *Journal of Telemedicine and Telecare*, 12 (1):13–5.

Hong, Y., T. B. Patrick and R. Gillis (2008). "Protection of Patient's Privacy and Data Security in E-Health." *BMEI*, 1: 643–47.

Kahn, J., J. Yang and J. Kahn (2010). "'Mobile' Health Needs and Opportunities in Developing Countries." *Health Affairs* 29(2): 252–58.

Kalichman, S. C., E. G. Benotsch, L.Weinhardt, J. Austin, W. Luke, C. Cherry (2003). "Health-Related Internet Use, Coping, Social Support, and Health Indicators in People Living with HIV/AIDS: Preliminary Results From a Community Survey." *Health Psychology*, 22(1): 111–16.

LaRed21 (2009). http://www.lr21.com.uy/economia/371909-uruguay-es-n-1-de-america-latina-en-nivel-tecnologico.

McKay, H. G., D. King and E. G. Eakin (2001). "The Diabetes Network Internet-Based Physical Activity Intervention. A Randomized Pilot Study." *Diabetes Care*, 24(8): 1328–34.

Meigs, J. B., et al. (2003). "A Controlled Trial of Web Based Diabetes Disease Management. The MGH Diabetes Primary Care Improvement Project." *Diabetes Care*, 26(3): 750–57.

Murray, E., et al. (2003). "The Impact of Health Information on the Internet on the Physician Patient Relationship." *Archives of Internal Medicine* 163(14): 1727–34.

Murray A., and D. G. Safran (2000). "The Primary Care Assessment Survey: A Tool for Measuring, Monitoring and Improving Primary Care." In: *Handbook of Psychological*

Assessment in Primary Care Settings, edited by Mark E. Maruish, 623–51. Mahwah, NJ: Lawrence Erlbaum Associates.

Pittaluga, L., and M. Sienra (2007). "Utilización de las Teconologías de la Información y las Comunicaciones en el Uruguay. Encuesta Nacional de Hogares Ampliada." *Módulo TIC 2do trimestre de 2006*. Montivideo, Uruguay: Instituto Nacional de Estadística.

Rivero Illa, M. (2007). *Enhancing the Livelihoods of the Rural Poor. The Role of Information and Communication Technologies*. Montevideo, Uruguay: ICP-Universidad de la República.

Ybarra, M., and M. Suman (2008). "Reasons, Assessments and Actions Taken: Sex and Age Differences in Uses of Internet Health Information." *Health Education Research*, 23(3): 512–21.

Wangberg, S. C. (2008). "An Internet-Based Diabetes Self-Care Intervention Tailored to Self-Efficacy." *Health Education Research*, 23(1):170–79.

Chapter 3

THE IMPACT OF ICT ON ADOLESCENTS' PERCEPTIONS AND CONSUMPTION OF SUBSTANCES: EVIDENCE FROM A RANDOMIZED TRIAL IN URUGUAY

Ana Balsa, Néstor Gandelman and Rafael Porzecanski

3.1 Introduction

Due to biological and psychosocial factors, adolescence is a stage during which individuals are particularly vulnerable to the risks of substance use and abuse (Steinberg, 2007). In Uruguay, the rates of adolescent substance use are high when compared to those in other countries (CICAD/OEA 2006). A 2007 survey of Uruguayan students enrolled in Secondary Education showed that 70 percent had experimented with alcohol by the age of 13 and almost all students had consumed alcohol at least once by the age of 17. The rate of alcohol use in the past 30 days was 33 percent for students in the second grade of secondary school, 61 percent for students in the 4th year and 75 percent for those in the 6th year. Around half of these students reported drinking to intoxication or binge drinking in the past 30 days. With respect to other drugs, 25 percent reported using tobacco and 6 percent reported using marihuana in the past 30 days and 9 percent reported consuming marijuana in the past year (Junta Nacional de Drogas, 2008).

Adolescents' fast and early adoption of new information technologies creates important opportunities for engaging youths in preventive services via e-health. The Internet and other ICT technologies, such as mobile phone SMS, constitute cost effective vehicles to access youth in a widespread manner and create opportunities for the use of interactive technologies that can increase students' skills and information assimilation (Marsch, Bickel and Badger, 2006). A number of preventive substances use interventions have been introduced in developed countries through the Internet with rela-tive success (Bosworth et al., 1994; Marsch et al., 2006; Pahwa and Schoech, 2008). While there is little evidence of success of similar programs in less developed countries (Kaplan, 2006), the potential of e-health preventive efforts in Uruguay acquires a special dimension when considering the recent introduction of a national education plan aimed at providing each student in the country with a laptop computer with Internet access (Plan Ceibal, "One Laptop per Child"). By the end of 2010 all students in Uruguay's elementary public schools as well as all students enrolled in the first year of secondary public schools are expected to have a laptop. Considering the potential of ICT based interventions for youth, in this chapter we use a randomized con-trolled trial to assess the impact of an Internet and SMS based intervention on adolescents' substance use behavior and perceptions about drugs. Participants include adolescents enrolled in third and fourth grades at 10 private secondary schools in Montevideo, Uruguay.

3.2 Background

A number of studies for developed countries have explored adolescents' perceptions and experiences of using the Internet to find information about health and medicines (Borzekowski and Rickert, 2001a, 2001b; Gray et al., 2005; Skinner et al., 2003). These studies show that the Internet is the primary general information source for adolescents, regardless of their socioeconomic and ethnic backgrounds, and that most health information is accessed through search engines with a high success rate. In terms of topics investigated, Skinner et al. (2003) found that Canadian adolescents used information technology for school-related reasons in the first place, followed by interactions with friends, social concerns, specific medical conditions, body image and nutrition, vio-lence and personal safety, and sexual health. Another study by Borzekowski and Rickert (2001b) reported that sexually transmitted diseases, diet, fitness, and exercise and sexual behaviors were the health-related topics most sought by adolescents on the Internet.

There are critical challenges associated with adolescents' search for infor-mation on the Internet. A number of authors indicate that adolescents lack the ability to discern the relevance of information retrieved by search engines and do not know which sites to trust (Gray et al., 2005; Hansen et al., 2003; Skinner et al., 2003). Adolescents do not consider the source of the content when searching for health information and scan web pages randomly rather than systematically. Other challenges involve adolescents' ability to apply the identified health information to their own personal health concerns and the need of privacy in accessing information technology. Inequality in access has also been identified as a serious barrier to the success of e-health programs. Koivusilta et al. (2007) reported that computer use was most frequent among adolescents whose parents had higher education or socioeconomic status, who came from nuclear families and who continued studies after compulsory education. In addition to disparities in access to ICTs at home, access issues are deepened if there are insufficient school computers or computers that are unable to cope with increasing website sophistication. Software on school-based machines preventing exposure to material that is deemed to be unsuitable may also prohibit access to educational sites about sexual health and drug misuse (Gray et al., 2002).

Several programs suggest that a computer-based system may be a powerful tool for the reduction of risk-taking behavior by adolescents. Bosworth et al. (1994) evaluated the effects of BARN (Body Awareness Resource Network), a computer-based health promotion/behavior change system that provided students (grades six–twelve) with information and skill-building activities on AIDS, substance use, body management, sexuality and stress management. During the two years that BARN use was studied, it was used heavily by both middle school and high school students, and particularly attracted adolescents who had already experimented with risk-taking behaviors. Those teens at higher risk for escalating problems selected the relevant BARN topics. Overall, users of BARN were more likely to remain free of risk-taking behaviors than nonusers. BARN use was also associated with improvements in risk-relevant behaviors such as contraceptive use, stress reduction, cessation of smoking by light smokers, reduction of alcohol use and reduction of problems associated with alcohol use. No relationship was found between BARN use and initiation of sexual activity, stress prevention or onset of either alcohol use or smoking. Nooijer et al. (2008) assessed the opinions of adolescents regarding an Internet-based health monitoring instrument and its individually tailored electronic feedback at a number of Netherlands' schools. While the majority of students appreciated the Internet-based monitoring questionnaire and the individually tailored feedback, one out of three respondents claimed that the information was not new to them and 40 percent indicated that the information failed to provide them with additional insight into their behavior. Recommendations for future interventions included (1) embedding monitoring and feedback in school curriculum, (2) providing immediate feedback and (3) adapting tailored messages to educational levels and age.

Using a randomized controlled trial, Croom et al. (2009) assessed the short-term effectiveness of a web-based alcohol education program on entering freshmen. The intervention consisted of an online course prior to arrival to campus. At six-week follow-up, the intervention group showed significantly higher alcohol-related post-course knowledge compared to the control group.

However, protective behavior, risk-related behavior, high-risk drinking and alcohol-related harm did not favor the intervention group, with the sole exception of playing drinking games. Pahwa and Schoech (2008) evaluated an interactive multimedia anger management exercise that was part of a teen substance abuse prevention website. They found that a 30-minute exposure to a web-guided prevention exercise could increase teens' prevention knowledge and that completing the online exercise as supplemental homework reinforced the classroom experience. However, positive changes in other measures of behavior change were not supported. Marsch et al. (2006) report findings of a controlled evaluation of "Head On: Substance Abuse Prevention for Grades 6–8TM." This program was designed to deliver drug abuse prevention tools to youth via computer-based educational technologies (fluency-building computer-assisted instruction and simulation-based technology) that promote learning of information and drug refusal skills, self-efficacy and social competency. Results demonstrated that the Head On program promoted significantly higher levels of accuracy in objective knowledge about drug abuse prevention relative to other effective programs. Participants in the Head On also achieved positive outcomes in self-reported rates of substance use, intentions to use substances, attitudes toward substances, beliefs about prevalence of substance use among both their peers and adults, and likelihood of refusing a drug offer. The Head On program offers the potential of providing comprehensive substance abuse prevention science that is more cost-effective than other efficacious but labor-intensive prevention interventions.

Participation is quite a challenge in programs targeted at preventing adolescent substance use. Some of the programs described above were implemented mandatorily, ensuring high rates of participation from adolescents. The modules in Head On were delivered as part of the school curriculum (Marsch et al., 2006). The Web-based alcohol online education program described in Croom et al. (2009) had to be completed mandatorily by all entering freshmen prior to arrival to campus. Other programs such as BARN (Bosworth et al., 1994) were voluntary but were available at participating schools' computers for quite a long period (two years), and included games and simulations that helped attract teens to the system. During the period of the study, 67 percent of students in experimental schools interacted with BARN at least once and BARN users came back an average of almost 18 times during the 14 months it was available. Other programs, such as the health monitoring instrument with tailored feedback implemented in the Netherlands could not assess the extent to which the feedback had reached the students because only 3 percent of these students returned a follow-up assessment of the feedback system. Balsa et al. (2011) derive lessons to enhance participation in this type of preventive ICT interventions. Apart from the Internet, another vehicle with the potential for delivering successful health behavior interventions is mobile telephone SMS. This service has wide population reach, can be individually tailored and allows instant delivery with asynchronous receipt. In a review of the literature Fjeldsoe et al. (2009) found four studies targeted at preventive health behaviors and ten focused on clinical care that used SMS to deliver text messages. Positive behavior change outcomes were observed in 13 out of the 14 reviewed studies. For example, Riley et al. (2008) conducted a smoking cessation program using mobile phone text messaging to provide tailored and stage-specific messages to college smokers. The intervention reduced smoking rates and dependence, indicating that mobile phone text messaging is a potentially efficacious and easily disseminated method for providing cessation interventions for young adult smokers. Another study used mobile phone messages to send tailored information to obese adolescents enrolled in a multidisciplinary weight management program. Most adolescents found the messages relevant to them personally and reported that the messages helped them to keep focused (Woolford and Clark, 2009).

3.3 Methods

A randomized controlled trial was conducted to evaluate an Internet and SMS-based intervention that provided adolescents with information about the risks and consequences of substance use. The object of the study was to analyze the effectiveness of the ICT intervention in terms of knowledge acquired by the participants about drugs and its consequences, actual substance use and related behavioral outcomes such as violence and crime, sexual behavior, academic achievement and health-care utilization. The study underwent review by an Ethics committee of Universidad ORT Uruguay in July 2009. The target population was composed of teenagers who were in their third or fourth year of secondary school. The majority of these students were between 14 and 16 years of age. We chose to work only with students attending a selection of private schools in Montevideo because interventions in public schools usually require much longer and complicated bureaucratic processes.[1] Compared to the average Uruguayan teenager, students who attend private secondary schools have a significantly higher socioeconomic status. This could indicate higher access to PCs and Internet connections for our sample, although the One Laptop per Child initiative, currently being implemented in Uruguay, is likely to universalize use of PCs and Internet in secondary public education in the near future. Before initiating the study, all

---

1   Interventions such as this one in public schools cannot be authorized directly by the school authority but need to be approved by the National Administration of Public Education.

parents were sent informative letters by school authorities and were asked to provide their written consent regarding their children's participation. Students were repeatedly told that their participation in the survey and in the intervention, if selected, was completely voluntary and that they were free to abandon the project at any stage.

A total of 10 schools agreed to participate in the project. A set of students was randomly selected to participate in the study and the rest remained in a control group. Ideally, individuals in the control group should have in average the same characteristics as those in the treatment group but should not be affected by the intervention. We were concerned that if the randomization was performed at the individual level there could be contagion between treatment and control classmates. Therefore, participants were randomized to intervention and control groups not individually but by class within each grade and school. In general, school authorities confirmed that assignment of students to each class was random. We collected data on 1,044 students corresponding to 47 classes and selected 17 out of the 47 classes (359 students) for the intervention. We refer to these students as the group intended to be treated (ITT). Each student was asked to complete two surveys, one at baseline and the other after the project culmination, at 3 months follow-up. In these surveys, a variety of information was collected on drug consumption, knowledge about drugs, sexual activity, violence, leisure activities and sociodemographic topics. The first survey was the first contact and the second survey was the last contact that the project staff had with students. The surveys were self-administered by students at schools with the supervision and help of the research staff of Universidad ORT and took around one hour to complete. During the second survey, around 206 interviews had to be conducted by phone due to scheduling problems. In the second survey 48 students refused to participate.

3.3.1 *The intervention*

The intervention, which lasted three months (from September through November 2009), had several components designed to take advantage of the wide arrange of ICTs used regularly by adolescents. The first component consisted in the posting of adolescent-friendly information and materials related to drug consumption and abuse on a website named "COLOKT." The website, which was based on the widely popular Moodle platform, was specially designed and administered by EviMed for this study. Information on the website was updated weekly. EviMed is a private firm that develops information and educational products and services for physicians throughout Latin American. COLOKT offered valuable information on a variety of topics such as the relationship between adolescence and substance use, the risks and problems associated with this use and the particular characteristics of the most popular drugs among Uruguayan adolescents. All participants in the intervention group with a valid e-mail address (the majority of students) were given a unique nickname and password that gave them anonymous access to the website. These students were able to access the site unrestrictedly and could download all available material in the web.

Besides the educational material posted in COLOKT, the site offered the opportunity to meet in forums and chats, to complete short surveys on the topics and to discuss ideas or ask about the materials or other topics related to substance use. This internet-based social network component was aimed at generating discussion, questions and knowledge exchange among participants. In order to stimulate and organize participation, an educator, who was either a psychologist or a family physician with expertise on adolescents' substance use, mediated the exchanges. Periodically, one of the educators commented on the issues discussed to clarify concepts or specific information misconceptions. These comments were posted on the site and sent to all participants by e-mail.

Before being granted access to COLOKT, adolescents in the intervention group attended a workshop of about two hours long. At the workshop, a brainstorming activity was proposed in which students posed questions and raised concerns about the use of substances. The object of this activity was to get a closer sense of adolescents' expectations and needs regarding this topic, but no answers or content were addressed in this instance. The workshop also provided a brief introduction to the project site COLOKT as well as instructions on how to log in and use the different resources available at the site. The workshops were offered at all schools participating in the study, although some students did not participate in them for reasons such as lack of parental authorization or scheduling problems.

In addition to the site COLOKT, intervention participants were reached through two other channels. First, all students received a series of e-mails from the project staff, announcing the disclosure of new materials at COLOKT or commenting different issues raised by students during their participation in the website. Second, a series of text messages were sent periodically to participants' cell phones. These text messages also announced forthcoming activities at COLOKT and provided basic information about substance use and risks. During the three months of the intervention the project staff sent eight e-mails and seven SMS.

3.3.2 Levels of participation

According to the information automatically collected by COLOKT, 74 students (21 percent of the ITT) logged in at least once during the experiment. Among this subgroup, 41 students (55 percent) logged in one day (18 percent),

13 did it two days and the remaining 27 percent did it three days or more. Most visitors simply took a look at the site and/or read posts or materials uploaded. Around 25 students (7 percent of the ITT) showed a strong interest in the site and engaged in a variety of activities, such as forums, chats or online surveys. There is some disagreement between the participation records stemming from the web logs and levels of participation as reported by the students in the second survey. Twenty-one students (6 percent) who had logged in at least once according to automatic registers did not remember having visited the site when asked about their participation in the follow-up survey. And 45 students (12 percent) who did not log in according to our records reported having visited COLOKT. It is possible that some students visited the site's page for a few minutes and do not remember the visit. The other inconsistency may be due to some students having visited the website with other classmates without using their nickname. This would explain the failure to identify these visitors among the site records. Despite this disagreement between our records and self-reports of participation, the data show that only a minority of those in the intervention group visited the project's website. Although this relatively low level of participation merits further research, we believe that the lack of interest in the topic, together with the unstructured and non-mandatory character of the intervention, were the main reasons for nonparticipation. In the second survey we asked all students who reported never logging in the reasons for not doing so. Students were offered several alternatives and could select as many choices as they wanted. In this survey, 64 percent declared that they did not log in because they were not interested in the topic, 12 percent reported that they preferred using other channels of information on drugs, 2 percent was not sure that their anonymity was guaranteed, 10 percent reported they were not frequent Internet users and 2 percent argued that the site was not recommended by other classmates.

Although most students never visited COLOKT, most members in the "intention to treat" group were reached by the experiment via e-mail messages and/or text messages. Around 75 percent of students reported having received text messages related to the project and another 68 percent reported having received e-mails from the project staff (again, it might be possible that some students got e-mails or text messages but did not remember this or simply considered it as spam). Combining this information, 52 students (15 percent) never logged-in at COLOKT and never received e-mails or text messages according to their self-reports. On the other hand, the data indicate that 307 students (85 percent of the target population) were reached by the project's information and communication technologies in one way or another. In sum, out of the 359 students originally selected to participate in the intervention (the randomized group of students we intended to treat), only 74 logged in to the COLOKT website according to the automated records in COLOKT. We refer to this group as the "Web + SMS Intervention" group. The rest of the a priori participants (N = 285) did not access the web, but should have received SMS and e-mails. We refer to this other group as the "SMS only Intervention."

3.4 Results

3.4.1 What is a drug?

The most basic piece of information is whether a particular substance is a drug or not. According to the World Health Organization (1969), a drug is any substance that when absorbed into the body of a living organism alters its normal bodily function. We analyze drugs that are considered recreational because their use pursues the creation or enhancement of recreational experiences through the manipulation of the central nervous system. Not all drugs necessarily cause addiction and habituation. We gave the participants a list of 10 substances and asked them to assess which of these constituted drugs. The "correct" answer was that all 10 of them were drugs. As seen in Table 3.1, some substances were clearly perceived as drugs before the intervention. More than 9 out of 10 students considered cocaine, ecstasy, "pasta base" (a variation of crack) and marijuana to be drugs. Around 60 percent of participants rated anxiolytics, antidepressants, LSD and tobacco as drugs. But less than 50 percent of participants considered that alcohol (either in low or high graduation) was a drug. The perceptions were similar for individuals in the control group and those a priori selected to participate in the intervention. The following summary statistics are disaggregated between control students, intervention students that logged in to COLOKT (Web + SMS) and the rest of the selected participants that could only be reached by SMS or e-mail (SMS only).

The intervention provided information that altered the perceptions of what is a drug. Table 3.2 reports changes in responses to this question between the pre- and post-intervention surveys. Most of the individuals in the control and "Intention to Treat" groups gave the same answer in both surveys but a sizeable proportion changed their answer. In the "right-wrong" row we report the percentages of participants that in the first survey considered the substance to be a drug but in the second survey asserted it was not a drug. The "wrong-right" row shows the opposite direction of change. For most drugs (except cocaine, marijuana and pasta base), the fraction of adolescents in the "wrong-right" row is higher than the percentage in the "right-wrong" row. This is observed both for adolescents in the intervention and in the control groups. The general better perception of what constitutes a drug might be

Table 3.1 Is It a Drug? Percentage of Students That Asserted That Each of the Following Substances Is a Drug

Baseline survey

	Anxiolytics	Antidepressants	Beer/Wine	Cocaine	Ecstasy
Control (%)	59.7	65.1	43.6	98.4	93.5
SMS only (%)	58.9	66.1	45.2	99.6	91.9
Web + SMS (%)	69.0	73.2	41.4	100.0	91.4
Total (%)	60.1	65.9	43.9	98.9	92.9
N	976	975	975	986	980

	Whisky/ron	LSD	Marijuana	Pasta base	Tobacco
Control (%)	46.4	75.5	95.4	98.6	74.9
SMS only (%)	50.0	79.2	93.3	99.0	70.9
Web + SMS (%)	47.1	63.4	95.8	98.6	77.5
Total (%)	47.5	75.7	94.8	98.7	73.9
Cases	977	978	987	990	978

Source: Author's own data.

Table 3.2 Is It a Drug? Changes in Answers between the First and Second Surveys

	Anxiolytics				Antidepressants			
	Control	SMS only	Web + SMS	Total	Control	SMS only	Web + SMS	Total
Right-Wrong (%)	12	12	8	12	10	12	10	10
Same answer (%)	73	71	79	73	76	71	75	75
Wrong-Right (%)	14	17	13	15	14	16	15	15
Cases	625	280	71	976	624	280	71	975

	Beer or wine				Cocaine			
	Control	SMS only	Web+SMS	Total	Control	SMS only	Web + SMS	Total
Right-Wrong (%)	10	10	7	10	2	1	0	2
Same answer (%)	73	70	69	72	96	99	100	97
Wrong-Right (%)	17	20	24	18	1	0	0	1
Cases	624	281	70	975	631	284	71	986

	Ecstasy				Whisky/ron			
	Control	SMS only	Web + SMS	Total	Control	SMS only	Web + SMS	Total
Right-Wrong (%)	4	2	3	3	9	11	7	9
Same answer (%)	91	93	93	92	72	70	73	72
Wrong-Right (%)	5	6	6	5	19	19	20	19
Cases	627	283	70	980	627	280	70	977

(continued)

Table 3.2 (*Cont.*)

	LSD				Marijuana			
	Control	SMS only	Web + SMS	Total	Control	SMS only	Web + SMS	Total
Right-Wrong (%)	6	3	3	5	5	2	4	4
Same answer (%)	77	81	69	78	92	94	94	93
Wrong-Right (%)	17	16	28	18	3	5	1	3
Cases	624	283	71	978	632	284	71	987

	Pasta base				Tobacco			
	Control	SMS only	Web + SMS	Total	Control	SMS only	Web + SMS	Total
Right-Wrong (%)	2	1	0	2	12	9	4	10
Same answer (%)	97	98	99	97	76	75	82	76
Wrong-Right (%)	1	1	1	1	13	17%	14	14
Cases	633	286	71	990	625	282	71	978

Source: Author's own data.

the result of other formal or informal transfers of information (e.g., school workshops). Alternatively, these changes may be due to "seasonal" awareness. The first wave of the survey was conducted at the end of the winter in the middle of the school year while the second wave was conducted at the end of spring in the last weeks of school. The participation in parties and the exposure to substance consumption are very likely to be different between these two moments in time and may affect the perception of what is a drug. Another explanation is that the control group may have been contaminated by the ITT students. We do not have evidence of this contamination but we cannot rule it out either. If the intervention produced a real effect in the perception of what constitutes a drug, the difference between the "right-wrong" and "wrong-right" rows should be lower in the control than in the intention to treat group. This is the case for anxiolytics, low graduation alcohol like beer or wine, ecstasy, LSD, tobacco and marijuana.

In order to provide a more rigorous estimation we use the "difference-in-difference" framework (Card, 1992), This involves a simple comparison of changes in perceptions about drugs before and after the intervention between the control and the ITT groups. Note that our main indicator of exposure to the intervention is not the real ex post exposure (as captured by the Web + SMS or SMS only groupings) but the a priori ITT group. This variable is completely exogenous due to randomization and by using it we ensure that our results are not biased by selection in participation. Estimation is implemented by pooling observations in both surveys and estimating a probit regression of the form:

$$\Pr(Y_i = 1) = f(\beta_0 + \beta_1 ITT_i + \beta_2 Wave_{2i} + \beta_3 ITT_i * Wave_{2i} + \varepsilon_i \qquad \text{(Eq. 2.2)}$$

where Y_i, ITT_i and $Wave_{2i}$ are dummies. Y_i takes the value 1 if the i-student asserted that a certain substance was a drug, ITT_i takes the value 1 if the i-student was in the ITT group (i.e., he was in a class that was selected to participate in the intervention) and $Wave_{2i}$ takes the value of 1 when the answer refers to the second survey. The coefficient multiplying, ITT_i (β_1) reflects baseline differences between the intention to treat and control groups. The coefficient of $Wave_{2i}$ (β_2) reflects changes in answers due to the passing of time. The effect of the intervention is captured by the interaction term.

In Table 3.3 we report the estimation of the difference-in-difference model where we cluster standard errors at the school level. This is to relax the usual assumption that observations are independent. Instead, we assume that observations are independent across schools (clusters) but not necessarily within schools. According to our results, the intervention improved students' perceptions of what constitutes a drug in four cases (ecstasy, LSD, marijuana

Table 3.3 The Impact of the Intervention in Adequately Perceiving Substances as Drugs

The difference-in-difference model

	Anxiolytics	Antidepressants	Beer/Wine	Cocaine	Ecstasy
ITT	0.033	0.067	0.022	0.620	-0.120
	(0.092)	(0.138)	(0.098)	(0.388)	(0.074)
Wave2	0.058	0.134	0.181	-0.194	0.094
	(0.075)	(0.050)***	(0.077)**	(0.107)*	(0.116)
ITT × Wave2	0.071	-0.003	0.098	-0.040	0.238
	(0.110)	(0.095)	(0.137)	(0.454)	(0.129)*
Constant	0.245	0.387	-0.161	2.148	1.511
	(0.060)***	(0.063)***	(0.122)	(0.109)***	(0.149)***
Observations	1952	1950	1950	1972	1960

	Whisky/ron	LSD	Marijuana	Pasta base	Tobacco
ITT	0.076	0.016	-0.148	0.092	-0.081
	(0.062)	(0.111)	(0.088)*	(0.223)	(0.105)
Wave2	0.253	0.430	-0.171	-0.148	0.036
	(0.057)***	(0.134)***	(0.078)**	(0.201)	(0.075)
ITT × Wave2	-0.036	0.256	0.327	0.148	0.243
	(0.078)	(0.083)***	(0.117)***	(0.318)	(0.114)**
Constant	-0.090	0.690	1.686	2.191	0.671
	(0.120)	(0.172)***	(0.124)***	(0.166)***	(0.094)***
Observations	1954	1956	1974	1980	1956

Source: Author's own data.

Notes

1. Clustered standard errors in parentheses.

2. Significance at *** p<0.01, ** p<0.05, * p<0.1.

and tobacco) and had no significant effect in the other six. In the case of Pasta base and Cocaine, the perceptions were already high. However, the intervention did not change perceptions about alcohol as a drug or anxiolytics and antidepressants. The unconditional probability that a participant in the study asserts that ecstasy, LSD, marijuana and tobacco are drugs is 94.0 percent, 83.1 percent, 94.6 percent and 75.9 percent respectively. In some cases the unconditional probability is close to 100 percent and, therefore, the room for improvement is small. The marginal effects of the intervention on drug perception (the changes in the probability of perceiving the substance as a drug) were 2.5 percent, 6.0 percent, 3 percent and 7.1 percent respectively for ecstasy, LSD, marijuana and tobacco. It is interesting to note from Table 3.2 that the individuals in the ITT who did not participate in the web-platform actually performed better than those who participated in the web-platform with respect to the two drugs where we find the larger effects: tobacco and marijuana. If we had to evaluate the intervention in terms of this single question only, an SMS intervention would probably be more cost effectively than a web based intervention.

3.4.2 Consumption

The pre and post intervention surveys had a detailed module on substance use. Table 3.4 presents the percentage of individuals who smoked or drank alcohol in the past 30 days and the percentage of individuals who consumed marijuana or cocaine. Rates of consumption for our sample are similar to those derived from a nationally representative survey of students in public and private secondary schools in 2007 (Junta Nacional de Drogas, 2008). Findings from this survey show a prevalence of current alcohol use (past 30 days) of 32.5 percent for students in the second grade of secondary school and of 61.3 percent for students in the fourth grade. Our estimates, corresponding to students enrolled in third and fourth grades, are in between (55 percent in Wave 1 and 50 percent in Wave 2), The national sample also showed rates of consumption of tobacco of 14 percent and 31 percent for students in the second and fourth grades of secondary school, respectively, right around our estimate of 20 percent for students in third and fourth grades. We did not find statistically significant differences in rates of consumption between Waves 1 and 2 as a result of the intervention. We observed a decrease in the consumption of alcohol that could be associated with the end of year finals. On the other hand, we found an increase in the 3-month prevalence of marijuana and cocaine. These changes are present in the control and treatment groups. Table 3.5 reports the estimation of a difference-in-difference model

Table 3.4 Percentage of Participants that Consumed the Following Substances

	Cigarettes (last 30 days)		Alcohol (last 30 days)		Marijuana (last 3 months)		Cocaine (last 3 months)	
	Wave 1	Wave 2	Wave 1	Wave 2	Wave 1	Wave 2	Wave 1	Wave 2
Control (%)	18.0	18.8	54.1	48.6	10.0	15.0	0.3	6.4
SMS only (%)	22.0	22.3	56.2	53.3	14.3	17.0	1.7	5.7
Web + SMS (%)	20.3	17.6	51.4	51.4	12.2	18.9	1.4	4.1
Total (%)	19.3	19.7	54.5	50.1	11.4	15.9	0.8	6.0
Cases	1046	1045	1044	1045	1046	1046	1046	1046

Source: Author's own data.

Table 3.5 Probability of Consuming Substances

The impact of the interventio

	Cigarettes (last 30 days)	Alcohol (last 30 days)	Marijuana (last 3 months)	Cocaine (last 3 months)
ITT	0.136	0.026	0.133	0.197
	(0.153)	(0.149)	(0.155)	(0.253)
Wave2	0.034	−0.142	−0.000	0.317
	(0.048)	(0.072)**	(0.055)	(0.249)
ITTxWave2	−0.043	0.082	0.014	−0.317
	(0.069)	(0.077)	(0.136)	(0.198)
Constant	−0.920	0.105	−1.285	−2.731
	(0.146)***	(0.117)	(0.153)***	(0.252)***
Observations	2090	2086	1974	1978

Source: Author's own data.

Notes

1. Clustered standard errors in parentheses.

2. ** significant at 5%; *** significant at 1%.

that confirms that the intervention had no statistically significant effects on substance use.

3.5 Conclusions

We found that the three-month intervention implemented was able to improve the information about drugs but induced no change in conducts. We found an increased awareness that ecstasy, LSD, marijuana and tobacco constitute drugs. The evidence also suggests no differences among those that logged in to the web-platform and those that only received e-mails and SMS. Therefore, in this intervention, the web platform was probably cost inefficient. We are not particularly surprised about the fact that the intervention had null effects on the actual behavior of the ITT students regarding substance use. The primary purpose of the intervention was to provide students with basic information on substance use and not to produce a significant change in their behavior. Also, we should recall that most students did not visit the project site but simply read a few e-mails or SMS. In sum, we think that changing students' behavior needs a different approach that is not only informative but also involves students in more encompassing activities.

The fact that only a fifth of students visited the project's site also merits some comments. First, based on the students own reports, we think that the main reason that explains such low level of participation is the lack of interest in the topic. Therefore, to ensure higher levels of participation in future experiments, there are two possibilities. One option is to implement mandatory interventions in which students need to log in a certain number of days per week, complete online surveys and participate in chats with the project educators. In this case, the intervention would be more like a school course where the student participation could even be graded. Naturally, this type of intervention would require school authorities to participate much more actively in the intervention. The other option would be to create a website that combines informative activities on drugs (like those offered by COLOKT) with leisure activities especially suited for the adolescent population such as the opportunity to video-chat with local music or TV stars, play online games or download music or TV series. Applications using state-of-the-art programming, such as video gaming or simulations would probably help to get hold of this population.

References

Balsa, A., N. Gandelman and D. Lamé (2011). "Lessons from Participation in a Web-Based Substance Use Preventive Pogram in Uruguay." Unpublished manuscript.

Borzekowski, D. L. G., and V. I. Rickert (2001a). "Adolescents, the Internet, and health: Issues of Access and Content." *Journal of Applied Developmental Psychology*, 22 (1): 49–59(11).

Borzekowski, D. L., and V. I. Rickert (2001b). "Adolescent Cyber Surfing for Health Information: A New Resource that Crosses Barriers." *Archives Pediatrics & Adolescent Medicine*, 155(7): 813–17.

Bosworth, K., D. H. Gustafson and R. P. Hawkins (1994). "The BARN System: Use and Impact of Adolescent Health Promotion via Computer." *Computers in Human Behavior*, 10(4): 467–82.

Card, D. (1992). "Using Regional Variation in Wages to Measure the Effects of the Federal Minimum Wage." *ILR Review*, 46(1): 22–37.

CICAD/OEA (2006). Jovenes y Drogas en Paises Sudamericanos: Un desafio para las Politicas Publicas. Primer estudio comparativo sobre uso de drogas en población escolar secundaria de Argentina, Bolivia, Brasil, Colombia, Chile, Ecuador, Paraguay, Perú y Uruguay Oficina de las Naciones Unidas contra la Droga y el Delito (ONUDD), la Comisión Interamericana para el Control del Abuso de Drogas (CICAD/OEA) Lima, Perú

Croom K., D. Lewis, T. Marchell, M. L. Lesser, V. F. Reyna, L. Kubicki-Bedford, M. Feffer and L. Staiano-Coico (2009). "Impact of an Online Alcohol Education Course on Behaviour and Harm for Incoming First Year College Students: Short Term Evaluation of a Randomized Trial." *Journal of American College Health*, 57(4): 445–54.

de Nooijer, J., M. L. Veling, H. Ton and N. K. de Vries (2008). "Electronic Monitoring and Health Promotion: An Evaluation of the E-MOVO Web Site by Adolescents." *Health Education Research*, 23(3): 382–91.

Fjeldsoe, B. S., A. L., Marshall and Y. D. Miller (2009). "Behavior Change Interventions Delivered by Mobile Telephone Short-Message Service." *American Journal of Preventive Medicine*, 36(2): 165–73.

Gray, N. J., J. D. Klein, J. A. Cantrill and P. R. Noyce (2002). "Adolescent Girls' Use of the Internet for Health Information: Issues beyond Access." *Journal of Medical Systems*, 26(6): 545–53.

Gray, N. J., J. D. Klein, P. R. Noyce, T. S. Sesselberg and J. A. Cantrill (2005). "Health Information-Seeking Behaviour in Adolescence: The Place of the Internet." *Social Science & Medicine*, 60(7): 1467–78.

Gray, N. J., J. D. Klein, P. R. Noyce, T. S. Sesselberg and J. A. Cantrill (2005). The Internet: A Window on Adolescent Health Literacy." *Journal of Adolescent Health*, 37(3): 243.

Hansen, D. L., H. A. Derry, P. J. Resnick and C. R. Richardson (2003). "Adolescents Searching for Health Information on the Internet: An Observational Study." *Journal of Medical Internet Research*, 5(4): e25.

Junta Nacional de Drogas (2008). III Encuesta Nacional Sobre Consumo de Drogas en Estudiantes de la Enseñanza Media. Montevideo, Uruguay: Presidencia de la República.

Kaplan, W. A. (2006). "Can the Ubiquitous Power of Mobile Phones Be Used to Improve Health Outcomes in Developing Countries?" *Globalization and Health*, 2(1): 9.

Koivusilta, L. K., T. P. Lintonen and A. H. Rimpelä (2007). "Orientations in Adolescent Use of Information and Communication Technology: A Digital Divide by Sociodemographic Background, Educational Career, and Health." *Scandinavian Journal of Public Health*, 35(1): 95–103.

Marsch, Lisa A., Warren K. Bickel and Garry J. Badger (2006). "Applying Computer Technology to Substance Abuse Prevention Science: Results of a Preliminary Examination." *Journal of Child and Adolescent Substance Abuse*, 16(2): 69–94.

Michaud, P. A., and P. Colom (2003). "Implementation and Evaluation of an Internet Health Site for Adolescents in Switzerland." *Journal of Adolescent Health*, 33(4):287–90.

Moreno, M. A., J. D. Ralston and D. C. Grossman (2009). "Adolescent Access to Online Health Services: Perils and Promise." *Journal of Adolescent Health*, 44(3):244–51.

Pahwa and Schoech (2008). "Issues in the Evaluation of an Online Prevention Exercise." *Journal of Technology in Human Services*, 26: 259–81.

Punamäki, R. L., M. Wallenius, C. H. Nygår, L. Saarni and A. Rimpelä (2007). "Use of Information and Communication Technology (ICT) and Perceived Health in Adolescence: The Role of Sleeping Habits and Waking-Time Tiredness." *Journal of Adolescence*, 30(4): 569–85.

Riley, Obermayer, Jean-Mary (2008). "Internet and Mobile Phone Text Messaging Intervention for College Smokers." *Journal of American College Health*, 57(2): 245–448.

Skinner, H., S. Biscope, MHSc, B. Poland and A. Goldberg (2003). "How Adolescents Use Technology for Health Information: Implications for Health Professionals from Focus Group Studies." *Journal Medical Internet Research*, 5(4): e32.

Steinberg, L. (2007). "Risk Taking in Adolescence: New Perspectives from Brain and Behavioral Science." *Current Directions in Psychological Science*, 16: 55–59.

Woolford, S. J., and S. J. Clark (2009). "Tailored Mobile Phone Text Messages as an Adjunct to Obesity Intervention for Adolescents." *Journal of Adolescent Health*, 44(2) (Supplement 1): S2–S3.

World Health Organization (1969). *WHO Expert Committee on Drug Dependence. Sixteenth Rreport*. Technical report series. No. 407. Geneva: World Health Organization.

Chapter 4

TEXT MESSAGES AS SOCIAL POLICY INSTRUMENT: EVIDENCE FROM A RANDOMIZED CONTROLLED TRIAL WITH INTERNAL REFUGEES IN COLOMBIA

Mariana Blanco and Juan F. Vargas

4.1 Introduction

Like other Latin American countries, Colombia witnessed the rise of guerrilla movements in the 1960s and 1970s. However, unlike the rest of the region, armed opposition is still active to date and it is largely represented by the Revolutionary Armed Forces of Colombia (hereafter FARC from its acronym in Spanish). In addition to the guerillas the conflict features another illegal armed group since the early 1980s—the paramilitary forces. These right-wing militias were originally formed by local elites, landowners and drug lords to counteract guerrilla extortion and ransom tactics of the guerrillas. The Colombian conflict has been especially harmful for the civilian population. Both guerrillas and paramilitaries have specialized in victimizing civilians which includes the forced displacement of a large share of the population (Vargas, 2016). In fact, violence-driven internal migration has become the most dramatic social consequence of the conflict, affecting up to 90 percent of the country's municipalities.[1] Many municipalities that receive internally displaced people (IDP) lack the capacity to handle the inflow of refugees. Moreover, 98 percent of displaced households live below the poverty line

---

1 Ibáñez (2009) and Ibáñez and Velásquez (2009) report a list of displacement episodes that have caused the majority of a town's population to flee. For instance, 95 percent of inhabitants left Bojayá, in the department of Chocó. Cocorná, in Antioquia, saw 94 percent of its inhabitants flee, and in El Tarra and Peque 82 percent and 78 percent of the population, respectively, were forcibly displaced.

and face unemployment rates much higher than the rest of the population (Ibáñez and Moya, 2010). IDP are among the most vulnerable populations in Colombia. For this reason, the United Nations classified this situation as "the biggest humanitarian crisis in Western Hemisphere" (UN, 2004).

According to *Acción Social*, Colombia's governmental agency in charge of social policy and humanitarian aid, by the end of 2009 approximately 3.5 million people had been forcibly displaced from their homes. This represents almost 9 percent of the nation's total population and roughly 8 percent of all IDP worldwide. According to statistics from the UN High Commissioner for Refugees (UNHCR, 2009), Colombia is one of the countries with the highest numbers of IDP worldwide, together with Iraq and Sudan.

Land disputes are the main driver of forced displacement: up to 4 million acres of land have been abandoned by the original owners. Colombia has today the most unequal land distribution of Latin America (Ibáñez, 2009). The illegal expropriation of large amounts of acreage is also attributed to the need for arable land for the cultivation of coca, the main element used in the production of cocaine. Estimates show that Colombia exports approximately 70 percent of the world's supply (Mejía and Restrepo, 2010). Other key causes of displacement are the extortion of businesses, landowners and farmers by armed groups; the forced recruitment of soldiers, especially child soldiers and the intimidation of social and community leaders, which greatly hinders civil resistance and the ability to engage in collective action (Ibáñez, 2009).

The costs of forced displacement are pervasive, as evidenced by the extensive loss of assets and dissolution of family and community networks: 80 percent of IDP never return to their households (NVS-II, 2008). IDP are further put at risk by limited access to formal and informal risk-sharing mechanisms, which consequently exposes them to more acute shocks to their personal income and consumption (Ibáñez and Moya, 2010).

According to NVS-II (2008), 43 percent of displaced households are female-led (this is 50 percent more than the national average), and one-fifth of household heads are illiterate. In addition, children and adolescents are at greater risk through a displacement than adults. This group makes up approximately two-thirds of IDP, and they are heavily economically dependent upon their parents and child labor practices for survival.

In recent years the Colombian Constitutional Court has specifically targeted the needs of IDP. In decree T-025 of 2004, the Court established that IDP are more vulnerable than the rest of the population and that their basic rights are "largely and systematically violated" and thus require special care and benefits from the government. Despite the government's attempts to comply with the Court's mandate by targeting benefits, by the end of 2007 the Court had ruled that the rights of IDP still had not yet fully been reinstated.

In this chapter we identify a particular mechanism through which a relatively low-cost intervention may boost the efficiency of public policies directed at IDP: the use of SMS technology.

Law 387 of 1997 created the Unique Registry of Displaced Population (hereafter RUPD from its acronym in Spanish). The RUPD, managed by *Acción Social*, constitutes the official account of displaced households nationally and its mission is to assist the government in identifying the recipients of welfare benefits. This legislation established that a displaced household has the right to apply for its inclusion in the RUPD. Most applications are submitted upon IDP's arrival at their new destination. The application requires a detailed account of the facts that precipitated the IDP's flight, and this information thus enables *Acción Social* to assess whether the household can be included in the RUPD. Inclusion in the Registry entitles the IDP household to access a wide range of government benefits.[2]

Nonetheless, this system has several major limitations. First, in order to receive updates about their status in the inclusion process an applicant must visit a designated office created for aiding IDP known as Attention and Orientation Units (hereafter UAO from its Spanish acronym). Second, the procedures involved are very costly, including transportation costs, long waiting lines and the implicit loss of income due to consecutive appointments because of information delays. This loss is significant for this population, whose income depends upon labor in the informal sector. Another contributing factor to the low benefit demands of displaced households is the lack of readily available information about what benefits can be claimed.[3]

---

2   These benefits are demand-driven, and often households have to fulfill additional requirements. For instance, public schools are mandated to offer a place to school-aged children from displaced households. However, this does not always guarantee that the child is actually enrolled in school. Sometimes this is because of a family choice (perhaps a working child is more useful for the household) or because the household does not have enough resources to buy books or a uniform.

3   During the survey stage of our intervention we collected direct accounts of the experiences of our subjects going to the UAO to obtain information about their status and benefits. One commonality that surfaced was that, in order to be able to obtain the tickets authorizing attention at the UAO customer service windows, IDP have to arrive the night before and maintain their place in line overnight. Some IDP cannot afford transportation costs to UAOs (of which there are only five in Bogota). Yet another group cannot leave their job to go to the UAO or have no one who can take care of their children in the meanwhile. Among those who can make it to the UAO, once they finally reach the service window they are often told to come back some other day because their information is not yet loaded into the system. Sometimes personnel at UAOs simply are not aware of the information requested on how to access certain benefit—or are simply unwilling to provide it.

Acción Social estimates that approximately 70 percent of households included in the RUPD are unaware of their ability to receive benefits. To address this problem we carried out a randomized-controlled trial to assess whether a government's communication strategy involving the use of SMS technology could raise awareness about the IDP's RUPD inclusion, along with the knowledge of what benefits are people entitled to. Hence, the objective of this experiment was to corroborate the hypothesis that information and communication technologies (ICTs), such as SMS, could empower Colombia's IDP population to better emerge from their precarious situation.

4.2 Experimental Design

The experiment was composed of the transmission of simple text messages directed to the registered cell phones of a random half the displaced households upon inclusion by *Acción Social* to the RUPD.[4] The SMS sent to treated households was the following: *ACCIÓN SOCIAL informs that you have been included in the RUPD. Please go to the closest UAO for more information.*[5]

IDP households assigned to the control group had to follow the regular procedure (i.e., arrive at UAO center and wait to be assisted) in order to be informed of the status of their application. Finally, a post-intervention survey, described in Section 4.2.1, was conducted in order to evaluate the impact of the SMS strategy on IDP households' awareness of their inclusion in the RUPD and their entitlement to benefits.

4.2.1 Implementation

The entire intervention was executed during six months in coordination with *Acción Social*. It occurred between September 2009 and February 2010, and a survey was subsequently carried out between March and May 2010. *Acción Social's involvement in this experiment* was twofold and took place both at the beginning and the end of the implementation phase. First, the agency provided

---

4   It is estimated that over 98 percent of displaced households have cell phones (NVS-II, 2008). This is because penetration of mobile telecommunications is very large in developing countries, especially in the case of our target population because they move around often because of their displaced condition.

5   A second SMS reminder that RUPD inclusion entitled them to official benefits was also sent to half of those receiving the baseline treatment. However, due to the reduced sample of subjects taking part in the follow-up survey who actually received this second message, we have no power to analyze the impact of this additional piece of information. Section 4.2.2 discusses the issues of selection and attrition and assesses whether these are likely to generate any bias.

us with the data on the newly included IDP in the RUPD. These data were then used to allocate households randomly into treatment and control groups. Second, after we assigned households into treatment and control groups, the agency transmitted the SMS to the treated subjects. Because we found no reliable or comprehensive official information system with which to monitor awareness and subsequent appropriation of social benefits by included IDP, we conducted our own follow-up survey to identify whether the use of SMS to communicate inclusion in the RUPD had a significant impact on benefit awareness and knowledge. We executed a survey pilot run on March 12 and 13, 2010, which allowed us to adjust the original questionnaire and assess the length of the interview. Then the fieldwork took place between April 7 and May 19, 2010. In order to measure the impact of the SMS intervention on the awareness of benefits our survey includes questions regarding: (1) whether households knew they were included in the RUPD,[6] and (2) whether they knew some or any of the benefits to which they were entitled. In addition, we included a complete set of questions that allowed us to build a demographic profile of the displaced household, which we use as controls in our empirical analysis (Section 4.3).

4.2.2 Sample issues and threats to inference

4.2.2.1 Selection

Given IDP's vulnerable status and the fact that they have been victimized by armed groups, the office of the Colombia's General Prosecutor mandated that any person or institution wishing to contact displaced individuals by cell phone or any other means must first have their written consent. As a result, we staged a pre-intervention phase whereby we provided every office receiving RUPD-inclusion applications in Bogotá with a package of consent forms.[7] The consent form (which is provided in the online appendix) was to be attached to the displacement declaration form and returned to *Acción Social*, which in turn would forward it to our research team in order to select from the RUPD only those who had consented. On the other hand, we were not permitted to contact by SMS the households that did not consent. Of course,

---

6   For reasons that we will explain in Section 4.2.2, we cannot guarantee that text messages sent to the registered cell phones of treated households will actually be received and read by the target party. Thus with the answer to this question we are able to measure *compliance* and then apply instrumental variable methods to compute the *causal effect* of being assigned to treatment on awareness and take-up of benefits.

7   To ensure that every IDP was given the choice to sign one such form, the number of forms provided was based on estimated flow of IDP to each office.

the households that did not consent were not part of the control group either, because we eventually needed to interact with all participating households during the survey stage and for this we needed consent. Thus the mandate of the General Prosecutor and the subsequent pre-intervention consent stage was made so that there is substantial self-selection of IDP into the experiment. Out of the entire population of IDP households that arrive to Bogotá during our intervention (1,433 households) only 43 percent (607) signed the consent form.[8]

This could potentially constitute a threat to our results. If the households that agree to be contacted by phone happen to be systematically different than those who did not sign the form according to characteristics that may be correlated with the awareness of the social benefits then our estimates would be biased. For instance, if signing the consent form is correlated with households' own assessment of how likely it is to reach them via cell phone, then by excluding those who did not consent we are filtering out several potential noncompliers, which in turn would lead us to overestimate the intention to treat effect. In general, if self-selection into the intervention is correlated with either treatment compliance or the potential outcomes, then by relying on a nonrandom share of the population of IDP, our results would be biased.

4.2.2.2 Attrition

Moreover, the attrition rate was rather high compared to other randomized experiments. In the survey stage of the experiment, in spite of the great effort by the enumerators, only 36 percent of the 607 households that signed the consent for were found. A high attrition rate was expected due to two reasons. First, IDP households migrate at a higher rate than other populations, which makes them difficult for survey teams to locate. For example, IDP tend to declare their status in the first location they reach following displacement. This can be misleading, however, as many IDP do not stay long-term at this first location: The spontaneous nature of forced displacement usually causes this population to flee to the nearest safe area (usually urban centers), which is not necessarily that where the household will settle on a permanent basis. Second, the communication medium used during the experiment, cell phones, increased the likelihood of observing a high attrition rate. When trying to locate households through their registered cell phone to arrange a meeting for

---

8   The complex logistics involved in the distribution of consent forms throughout the city and the training of officials receiving declarations factored into this low rate. Indeed, officials taking the statement of the newly arrived IDP were not obliged to hand them the consent form and many of them actually saw this extra step in the process as a burden to avoid.

the survey to take place, we found that the IDP's cell phones were often shared among family and neighbors, and often lost or stolen. During the survey stage we collected qualitative evidence in the forms of narratives. These illustrate the most common reasons for attrition as follows:

1. *Outdated contact details included in the consent form.* In several instances the registered cell phone was not in service or calls were forwarded automatically to the mailbox, or the cell phone was registered under an unrelated name. Upon visiting registered addresses, the enumerators often discovered that the sample subjects either had left or had never resided there.
2. *Mobility of IDP.* Due to budget constraints and the narrow scope of the trial in Bogotá the enumerators were not able to track subjects that had moved to other locations.
3. *Appointment defectors.* The enumerators encountered numerous IDP who reneged on their interview appointments. The two contributing factors were IDP's inability to leave work and the provision of false addresses. The former is a direct result of IDP's employment instability and the informal job sectors in which they work. The latter stems from distrust and their suspicion based on their prior victimization.

As with selection, the attrition problem is also likely to generate bias estimates if there are systematic differences, according to characteristics that are associated with the awareness of benefits, between households actually surveyed and those who were not found.

We now test whether the problems of selection and attrition, inherent to our experiment because of the target population and the institutional constraints, are likely to bias the results relative to the treatment effect that we would get if we were to scale the intervention to the entire IDP population. The reason we can run such test is because we have data, albeit on only few observable characteristics, on the 1,433 IDP's households that constitute our universe of interest. These data were obtained from *Acción Social* and include information on the *gender* of the household head (or the representative that signs the RUPD application on behalf of the entire household), the *number of beneficiaries* or household members attached to a single declaration,[9] the *cause of the displacement* and the *region of origin*. From the 1,433 households we can identify those that signed the consent form and, moreover, conditional of having signed it, we can identify those that were surveyed. This information allows us

---

9   Every declarant includes in his or her declaration a certain number of beneficiaries comprised of the number of household members who fled together and for whom the facts reported in the declaration apply.

to test whether there are systematic differences across such samples and hence whether selection or attrition are likely to cause any bias to our estimates of the impact of the SMS reception on benefits' awareness.

In the case of potential differences between households that signed the consent form and those that did not, results from a t-test of mean differences are summarized in Table 4.1. For expositional reasons, in the main text we focus on the first two variables (*gender of the household head* in Panel A and *number of IDP beneficiaries claimed* in Panel B).[10] This tests whether self-selection into the experiment (by filling the consent forms) is correlated systematically with the available observable characteristics and thus is likely to cause any obvious bias. Mean differences are not significant for any of the observable characteristics (standard errors are in parentheses). This suggests that the sample of households that participated in the experiment is presumably not different from the sample that did not.

In terms of actual figures, Panel A of Table 4.1 shows that over half of the household representatives are women, which is consistent with the aforementioned fact that women largely head IDP households. The difference in the proportion of women between those who signed the consent form and those who did not is a non-significant 0.3 percentage points. In addition, households that signed the consent form include on average 0.1 additional beneficiaries relative to those who did not sign. This difference is not only small but also not statistically significant.

Importantly, within the sample of households who signed the form and thus participated in the experiment, comparing those that were eventually interviewed versus those affected by attrition does not yield statistically significant differences either. T-tests of mean differences for this are summarized in Table 4.2. According to Panel A, the difference in the proportion of households headed by a woman who participated in the follow-up survey and those who were not located for an interview is somewhat larger (6.7 percentage points), but it is not significant. Moreover, as in the case of selection, households who participated in the follow-up survey include on average 0.1 additional beneficiaries relative to those who were not found.

We then claim that neither selection nor attrition constitute big threats to our results. But we have only suggestive evidence to back such claims as unfortunately there are a limited number of observable characteristics available for the entire population and we ignore how the samples differ across other

10 Equivalent tables dealing with the *cause of displacement* and *the region of origin* are reported on the online appendix. These comparisons use a nonparametric chi-squared test instead of the "t," as there are multiple categories in each variable. In this case the null hypothesis is that the samples come from the same distribution of "causes" or "regions of origin."

Table 4.1 Assessment of Potential Bias Due to Self-Selection into Experimental Sample

Consent	No consent	Difference
Panel A: Sample differences in declarant's gender (=1 if female)		
0.563	0.559	0.003
(0.020)	(0.017)	(0.027)
Panel B: Sample differences in number of beneficiaries attached to declaration		
2.163	2.043	0.120
(0.088)	(0.099)	(0.132)

Table 4.2 Assessment of Potential Bias Due to Attrition

Interviewed	Not found	Difference
Panel A: Sample differences in declarant's gender (=1 if female)		
0.606	0.539	0.067
(0.033)	(0.025)	(0.042)
Panel B: Sample differences in number of beneficiaries attached to declaration		
2.235	2.123	0.111
(0.154)	(0.107)	(0.184)

dimensions. However, of the 218 households (902 people) surveyed, exactly half were treated and half belonged to the control group. Since we did not fix the number of survey respondents but rather this was determined by the high attrition rate, the fact that the originally assigned proportions of units treated and controlled (50/50) remained unchanged post attrition is a remarkable coincidence that further supports the idea that attrition rates are not systematically related to the treatment status. Therefore, we firmly assert that our results are not likely to be biased.

Nonetheless selection and attrition did hurt the experiment by reducing the expected sample importantly. But the fact that we do find significant results in spite of our large standard errors is again suggestive of the important role that SMS can play as social policy tools.

Table 4.3 Descriptive Statistics

	Treated (N = 109)	Control (N = 109)	Difference
Panel A: Cause of displacement			
Threats	0.798	0.734	0.064
Killings	0.092	0.11	−0.018
Attack to town	0.009	0.018	−0.009
Forced recruitment	0.083	0.083	0.000
Other	0.018	0.055	−0.018
Panel B: Perpetrator			
Paramilitaries	0.266	0.33	−0.064
Guerrillas	0.624	0.642	−0.037
Not Known	0.128	0.073	0.055
Panel C: Household characteristics			
Size at displacement	3.624	3.991	−0.367
Current size	4.165	4.110	0.055
No. displacement episodes	1.202	1.239	−0.037
Assets prior to disp.	0.633	0.679	−0.046
Ethnicity: Afro-Colombian	0.064	0.092	−0.028
Ethnicity: Indigenous	0.046	0.046	0.000
Ethnicity: Other	0.89	0.862	0.028
SMS literacy	0.881	0.872	0.018*
Panel D: Declarant's characteristics			
Sex (1 = woman)	0.633	0.606	0.028
Age	36.972	36.11	0.862
Education	2.358	2.367	−0.009
Sick last week	0.486	0.450	0.037**
Looked for job last week	0.459	0.468	0.009
Community network	0.037	0.055	−0.018

4.3 Results

The first substantive question is whether the randomization was successful in generating comparable households in the treatment and the control groups. Table 4.3 shows that this is the case as there are no significant differences between treated and controlled households in terms of a large set of variables. We divide these into four categories: (1) cause of displacement, (2) perpetrator, (3) household characteristics and (4) individual (declarant) characteristics. Since the *t-tests* reveal no significant difference between treated and control units in over 90 percent of the observable pretreatment characteristics (the only two exceptions are whether the declarant was sick the week before the survey or whether she knew how to *send* SMS), then the sample appears to be

Table 4.4 Awareness of Benefits—Intention to Treat

	Treated	**Control**	**Difference**
All benefits	0.336	0.314	0.023
	(0.014)	(0.013)	(0.019)
Housing	0.436	0.385	0.050
	(0.034)	(0.033)	(0.047)
Supplies	0.087	0.094	−0.007
	(0.014)	(0.014)	(0.019)
Med. Care	0.489	0.433	0.055*
	(0.024)	(0.024)	(0.034)
Food	0.523	0.569	−0.046
	(0.048)	(0.048)	(0.068)

Notes

* Significant at 10%, ** significant at 5%, *** significant at 1%.

largely balanced and hence we believe that the effect of the SMS treatment on the posttreatment outcome variables is likely to be *causal*.

Given that the randomization was successful, the next question is whether treated households benefited from the experiment. Table 4.4 reports the incidence of benefit awareness in the treatment and the control group (first two columns) and the mean difference (column 3). We first look at the aggregated set of benefits in the top row. Benefits are then disaggregated in subsequent rows as follows: (1) *Housing* aggregates temporary housing and rent subsidy; (2) *Supplies* aggregates kitchen and cleaning supplies, beds and mattresses and clothing; (3) *Medical care* aggregates the right to medical assessment, psychological assessment, emergency medical care and medicines; (iv) *Food* aggregates the right to receive food supplies.[11]

As it turns out, the only significant difference (at the 10 percent level) is that of *Medical Care*. Treated households are 6 percentage points more aware than the control of their right to request benefits related to medical care. We argue that the reason that the difference is not significant for the rest of benefit indicators may be due to noncompliance. Indeed, a non-negligible share of households that were assigned to treatment reported in the survey not to have received the text message. The reasons behind the noncompliance are closely related with the large attrition rate: many cell phones were not currently in use

11 Because our survey was carried out shortly after the treatment took place, we refrain from looking at its effect on benefits that are not usually claimed in the first few months of the displacement episode. In particular, we focus on the benefits that constitute the so-called Emergency Humanitarian Help (Decree 2569 of 2000).

or were uncharged, lost or stolen. Or the message was perhaps accidentally deleted.

The presence of non-compliers suggests that the SMS reception is likely to be endogenous because it may be correlated with characteristics that we are not controlling for and that may affect the benefits awareness. However, the actual treatment assignment, which was fully under our control, is random. This suggests that the most sensible empirical strategy to identify the causal effect of the SMS reception on the IDP-benefits awareness is an Instrumental Variables (IV) one, where the actual message reception is instrumented with the (exogenous) treatment status.

The IV estimate of the causal effect is in essence the ratio of the mean difference of the rate of benefit knowledge to the mean difference of SMS reception, with both differences computed across treatment status. This IV estimator is called the *Wald* estimator, and it holds in cases like ours, when the instrument is *binary*. The causal effect computed this way is called Local Average Treatment Effect (LATE), and it provides information only on the impact of the treatment on the IDP households affected by the instrument.

In order to be able to use this empirical strategy it must be the case that treatment status is a good instrument of SMS reception. That is, the coefficient from a regression of the SMS reception on the actual treatment assignment has to be significantly different from zero. We now show that this is the case. Table 4.5 reports the probit estimates of the impact the treatment had on (self-reported) SMS reception. While the estimate presented in column 1 includes no controls, columns 2 through 5 include all the controls described in Table 4.3 one extra category at a time: column 2 includes controls regarding the cause of displacement, while column 3 adds perpetrator dummies. Finally, columns four and five add household and individual characteristics, respectively. In all cases the estimate of the causal effect is positive and significant at the 1 percent level.

Table 4.6 reports the results for the five sets of benefits as defined above. All regressions include the full set of controls (as in the last column of Table 4.5) and report robust standard errors. Importantly, the treatment increases significantly (at the 5 percent level) the awareness of the aggregate of all benefits. This is, however, driven by the large and positive impact of the treatment of the awareness of *Medical care* benefits and by the impact on the awareness on the right of claiming housing-related benefits. The treatment does not increase awareness of the right to *Food* or *Supplies*.[12]

---

12 We do not analyze the effect of treatment on the *take-up* of the different benefits. The reason for this is the fact that while awareness can be influenced by an improvement on communication, the actual request of benefits is a choice of the IDP. Therefore, the relevant variable to observe is awareness.

Table 4.5 Effect of Treatment on Reported SMS Reception—Probit Regression

Dependent variable: SMS reception					
$T = 1$	1.064***	1.097***	1.124***	1.184***	1.249***
	(0.028)	(0.029)	(0.032)	(0.000)	(0.000)
Controls					
Cause of displacement		✓	✓	✓	✓
Perpetrator			✓	✓	✓
Household character				✓	✓
Declarant					✓

Notes

1. * Significant at 10%, ** significant at 5%, *** significant at 1%.

2. Robust standard errors in parentheses.

Table 4.6 Effects of SMS on Benefit Awareness—Wald Estimator

Awareness of benefits					
	All benefits	**Medical care**	**Housing**	**Supplies**	**Food**
SMS^	0.075**	0.148**	0.150*	−0.014	−0.014
	(0.037)	(0.063)	(0.090)	(0.037)	(0.116)
All controls	✓	✓	✓	✓	✓

Notes

1. * Significant at 10%, ** significant at 5%, *** significant at 1%.

2. Robust standard errors in parentheses.

4.3.1 Heterogeneous effects

We now explore potential heterogeneity in treatment effects. To that end we repeat the analysis of Table 4.6 but split the sample according to characteristics of the household representative in charge of applying for benefits on behalf of all household members. We focus on the aggregate measure of awareness of all benefits.

Recall that, when looking at the entire sample, SMS reception— instrumented with treatment assignment—increases the awareness that the household is entitled to receive benefits by 7.5 percentage points (see column 1 of Table 4.6). We first explore whether this average effect is differential according to the sex of the declarant. In the first two columns of the top panel of Table 4.7, we split the sample according to whether the household head

Table 4.7 Effect of SMS on Benefit Awareness (*All Benefits*)

Heterogeneous Effects

Applicant characteristics	Sex		Age		Education	
Subsample	Woman	Man	>36 yr	≤36 yr	>Primary	≤Primary
$\widehat{SMS}$	0.115**	0.0117	0.0690	0.137***	0.00329	0.110**
	(0.0532)	(0.0631)	(0.0758)	(0.0466)	(0.0564)	(0.0531)

Applicant characteristics	H/hold member		Sick		Works	
Subsample	>4	≤4	Yes	No	Yes	No
$\widehat{SMS}$	0.165**	0.0632	0.153***	−0.0230	0.0179	0.0945
	(0.0702)	(0.0441)	(0.0580)	(0.0593)	(0.0477)	(0.0595)
All controls	✓	✓	✓	✓	✓	✓

Notes

1. * Significant at 10%, ** significant at 5%, *** significant at 1%.

2. Robust standard errors in parentheses.

is a woman or a man. We find that the average effect, reported on Table 4.6, is entirely driven by women, while in the subsample of men the effect is very small (1 percentage point increase in awareness of benefits eligibility after SMS reception) and not significant, in the subsample of women it is large and significant at the 5 percent level. For households with women in charge of the displacement declaration process, receiving the SMS increases awareness in 12 percentage points. This heterogeneity is important to note as it suggests that the types of communication strategies like the one analyzed here are likely to be more successful in terms of achieving the policy objective if they target women rather than men.

It is also worth looking at potential heterogeneous effects according to other observable characteristics of the applicants. For instance using information and communication technologies for social policy purposes is likely to be more effective if targeted individuals are relatively younger. This is because younger adults use such technologies more than older ones. This hypothesis is confirmed in columns 3 and 4 of the top panel of Table 4.7. There, we split the sample according to the mean age of the applicant (36 years old), and note that while the effect of SMS reception on the awareness of benefits of the relatively older is not significant, that on the relatively younger is large and significant at the 1 percent level. Receiving the SMS increases the awareness of this subpopulation in 14 percentage points.

Table 4.8 Determinants of Benefit Awareness (*All Benefits*)

Sample of non-treated

Dependent variable	Benefits awareness
Characteristic of declarant	
Sex (=1 if woman)	−0.008
	(0.082)
Age	−0.001
	(0.003)
Education level	0.010
	(0.030)
H/hold members	0.045***
	(0.016)
Sick last month	0.163**
	(0.077)
Worked last week	0.046
	(0.078)

Notes

1. * Significant at 10%, ** significant at 5%, ***
   significant at 1%.

2. Robust standard errors in parentheses.

Contrary to what one would expect the effect if larger for relatively less educated individuals. After dividing the sample according to the mean score of the education level indicator (equivalent to having up to primary education), we find that the effect of the SMS reception is not significant for households whose representative has an education level beyond elementary school (last two columns of the top panel of Table 4.7). In the bottom panel of the table we show that the effect is higher for bigger households (that have over 4 members) and for households that have had a sick member in the last month. This is not surprising as, as suggested by Table 4.6, results are driven by health care-related benefits and households that have sick members are more likely to pay attention to opportunities to obtain medical assistance. Finally we find no differential effect according to whether the household head works or not, as evident from the last two columns of the bottom panel of Table 4.7.

In a final exercise we look at the characteristics that make the control group more likely to know about their eligibility. Indeed, it is important to know what are the factors that make displaced household knowledgeable of their rights in the absence of an expedite communication strategy like the one we analyze here. To explore this issue we regress the dummy that indicates that the household is aware of its entitlement to benefits from the government on the same characteristics used to investigate the heterogeneous effects in Table 4.7. We focus, however, on the subsample of control households, dropping the treated from the sample. Consistent with the findings reported in the previous table, Table 4.8 shows that both bigger households as well as households with a member experiencing sickness during the previous month are more likely to know of its eligibility. Both factors increase the demand for social services within the household, which may explain why household heads are pushed to find out what type of help they can receive from the government.

4.4 Conclusion

We presented evidence from a randomized-controlled trial that the use of SMS as a channel to improve the communication between the government and beneficiaries of social programs can empower vulnerable populations and substantially increase their welfare. In this respect, we conclude that SMS represents a potentially effective instrument for social policy. Our findings are specific to the Colombia context, a country that has experienced internal conflict for 40 years and has the world's largest IDP population.

We demonstrate that an inexpensive intervention such as SMS directed to vulnerable households increases awareness of their entitlement to social benefits. The significance of our results, coupled with the low intervention costs, provides a strong argument for the inclusion of this research in policymaking under Colombia's new administration. The present is an opportune time for more experimental pilots to be replicated nationwide. The purpose of this strategic approach would ensure the increase of social benefits available to IDP. Undoubtedly, this issue would be high on the government's social policy agenda.

References

Angrist, J., and J. Psichke (2008). *Mostly Harmless Econometrics*. Princeton, NJ: Princeton University Press.

Ibáñez, A. M. (2009). "Forced Displacement in Colombia: Magnitude and Causes." *Economics of Peace and Security*, 4(1): 47–54.

Ibáñez, A. M., and A. Moya (2010). "Vulnerability of Victims of Civil Conflicts: Empirical Evidence for the Displaced Population in Colombia." *World Development*, 38(4): 647–63.

Ibáñez, A. M., and A. Velásquez (2009). "Identifying Victims of Civil Conflicts: An Evaluation of Forced Displaced Households in Colombia." *Journal of Peace Research*, 46(3): 431–51.

Mejía, D., and P. Restrepo (2010). "The War on Illegal Drug Production and Trafficking: An Economic Evaluation of Plan Colombia." *Documento CEDE*, Universidad de los Andes, Bogota, Colombia.

NVS-II (2008). "Second National Verification Survey on Forced Displacement." Bogota, Colombia: *Comisión de Seguimiento de la Política Pública sobre Desplazamiento Forzado* and *Centro de Investigaciones para el Desarrollo* (CID).

Rubin, D. (1974). "Estimating Causal Effects of Treatments in Randomized and Nonrandomized Studies." *Journal of Educational Psychology*, 66(5): 688–701.

United Nations (2004). "Colombia has Biggest Humanitarian Crisis in Western Hemisphere." United Nations News Service. May 10, 2004.

UNHCR (2009). *Statistical Yearbook 2008*. Available at: http://www.unhcr.org/4bcc5bb79.html (accessed April 30, 2010).

Vargas, J. F. (2016). "Strategic Atrocities: Civilians under Crossfire—Theory and Evidence from Colombia." In: *Economics Aspects of Genocides, Other Mass Atrocities, and Their Prevention*, edited by Charles Anderton and Jurgen Brauer. London: Oxford University Press, 425–51.

Chapter 5

RADIO AND VIDEO AS A MEANS FOR FINANCIAL EDUCATION IN RURAL HOUSEHOLDS IN PERU

Alberto Chong, Dean Karlan and Martin Valdivia

5.1 Introduction

This chapter analyzes the impact of a financial literacy training of a Peruvian microfinance institution, which is delivered by credit officers in monthly sessions with the support of video and radio materials. The program, conducted by Arariwa, a non-government organization, was implemented as a field experiment working with 49 credit officers across 665 communal banks in 13 provinces of the departments of Cusco and Puno, Peru. The objective of the study is to rigorously evaluate the effect of an ICT-based financial literacy education program that follows best practices on financial literacy and financial behaviors. We study the impact of a financial literacy education program using a randomized evaluation, which was designed to determine short-term effects and may be extended to determine long-term effects. Furthermore, we determine the effectiveness of using a radio and video supplemented credit with education financial educational program. The literature and experiences worldwide suggest that this methodology is likely to be the most cost-effective and we would like to quantify the benefit of this approach.

The field experiment included working with 49 credit officers across 666 communal banks in 13 provinces of the departments of Cusco and Puno during 2010. The program evaluated consists of (1) nine monthly 45 minute training sessions which involve the use of a 5- to 7-minute video, (2) nine 25-minute radio programs that reinforce the material in the training sessions and (3) nine homework assignments that encourage households to commit to behavioral changes. Credit officers were expected to deliver the training session with the video during the routine communal bank meetings and clients were expected to listen to the radio and do the homework assignment between bank meetings.

The low-cost strategy for implementation of the video and radio components led to low compliance rates with the video and radio components. According to credit officer's estimates, the median treatment bank received only one video session and only 7 percent of its clients listened to the radio program. Given this, we divide our analysis into four parts that allow us to determine the impact of the program. First, we determine the impact of the program on those that the program intended to treat. Second, we determine the impact of the program on those that completed a relatively high number of training sessions but with average ICT compliance. Third, we determine the impact of the program on those that completed a relatively high number of training sessions where the video was used. Finally, we determine the impact of the program on those that were in banks in which relatively high percentages of the clients listened to the radio program. Impact was measured in terms of savings rates and client retention. We find that the program has no impact on those that we intended to treat. This can be partially attributed to low completion levels. We also find that the program has no impact on those that were treated with training sessions, video supplemented training sessions or radio. We cannot draw any conclusions about the impact of the credit with education model on financial literacy financial behavioral outcomes. However, we can conclude that in order to evaluate the effectiveness of video supplements and radio programs in the context of the credit with financial education model, higher investments in the delivery of these components would have to be made.

5.2 Review of the Literature

Financial literacy education programs have not been prevalent as long in the developing world as in the developed world. Nonetheless in recent years there have been a number of initiatives across the globe. These education programs range from public campaigns to months of training sessions. Many of these programs are promising in nature, but there are few impact evaluations and, as with the research in the developed world, no rigorous impact evaluations of financial literacy programs that are designed according to best practices.

A few examples of often mentioned financial literacy education programs in the developing world include (1) SEWA bank's Project Tomorrow in India, which is a financial counseling service for poor self-employed women, (2) World Education's financial literacy program for women in Nepal, which uses new financial literacy tools that World Education and Pact have developed, (3) the FAO's Food Security and Nutrition project in Zambia, which includes a guide on money and (4) Freedom from Hunger's financial education modules that are used by microfinance institutions (MFIs) around the world to deliver education with credit (Sebstad and Cohen, 2003). There are two impact evaluations that add to the research conducted in the developed world. The first is a randomized impact evaluation of a business education module delivered by an MFI as credit with education. While this is not strictly a financial literacy training program, the subject matter is closely related and the method of delivery is very similar to the method that we are evaluating. The second is a randomized impact evaluation of a short financial literacy training session, which is directly relevant to the subject at hand.

Karlan and Valdivia (2011) evaluate the impact of a business education training module delivered by FINCA to its microfinance clients in Peru. The authors use a randomized control trial to measure the marginal impact of business training education. They find that the treatment improved business knowledge, practices and revenues, and also improved repayment and client retention rates for the microfinance institution. The authors also showed that the stronger effects in terms of repayment and improvements in business outcomes are for those clients who expressed the least interest in the training education. This rigorous evaluation demonstrates that the delivery method that MFIs use to educate their clients is effective in this case. This suggests that it is likely to be effective for related topics, such as financial literacy. Cole, Sampson and Zia (2009) use a randomized control trial to determine the impact of a two hour financial literacy education session on trainees' financial literacy and their subsequent demand for financial services in Indonesia. They measure financial literacy through a survey using the questions that Lusardi (2003) propose. In this trial there are two orthogonal treatments, the financial literacy training session and a small subsidy, both of which are intended to encourage consumers to open a bank account. They find that the financial literacy education program has no effect on the likelihood that the average client will open a bank account, but that the program seems to be effective for those that are least financially literate. The authors also find that the subsidies are effective in motivating the average client to open a bank account. In fact, price subsidies are a 2.5 times more cost effective way of encouraging poor people to open a bank account than financial literacy education. Despite these results, Cole, Sampson and Zia (2009) do not provide strong evidence against financial literacy programs. While the evaluation is methodologically sound, unlike the studies in the developed world, the program being evaluated is not particularly strong. The first deficiency with the training program is that it is only two hours long. Clancy, Weiss and Schreiner (2001), mentioned above, suggest that two hours may not be enough to have a significant impact. Another deficiency is that the program is not as cost effective as it could be. The program hired new trainers who earned above average salaries to work solely on this training. The "credit with education" model employed by FINCA and other MFIs is far more cost effective since the marginal cost of asking a credit officer to give educational session during regular bank meetings is minimal. A final short-coming of this study is the fact that the sample size used was quite small, 736, and that the metrics for financial literacy, while widely used, are in fact quite simplistic and poorly contextualized. These factors may combine to obscure any true effects of the financial literacy education program being evaluated.

5.3 Operational Model of Microfinance Institution: The Case of Arariwa

Arariwa is a Peruvian NGO that is based in the city of Cusco, Peru and serves the entire department of Cusco, three Northern provinces of the department of Puno and a few districts of the departments of Madre de Dios, Arequipa and Apurimac. Arariwa was founded in 1985 and has three branches: (1) Arariwa Promoción, which focuses on livelihoods, health and institutional strengthening, (2) Cenfopar, a technical education center for young adults and (3) the microfinance unit, which offers microfinance products and services.

Arariwa's productivity standards require each credit officer to manage 25 communal banks. Each communal bank is a self-selecting group of 10–30 clients that participate in group savings, loan and learning mechanisms. Each communal bank elects a board of directors from its members, among them a president, secretary, treasurer and the training leader. Arariwa's objective is to empower the board of directors so that they can manage most of the bank's activities with the credit officer's supervision. However, with new banks the credit officer cannot count on this support. Each of Arariwa's clients has as many as five accounts that can be classified into two broad categories: (1) internal accounts, where funds are provided by the members of the communal bank and managed by the communal bank with the credit officers assistance, and (2) external accounts, where funds are provided by Arariwa and managed directly by the credit officer with the bank members assistance. The system used by Arariwa initially seems similar to self-help-group-bank-linkage models (SHGBL) prevalent in South Asia; however, it is quite different. The SHGBL model facilitates the formation of groups of lenders who start activities with internal accounts and are then linked to a bank that provides an external account when they are prepared to do so. In contrast, Arariwa's clients must first open an external account in order to initiate internal account activity.

Peruvian financial regulations forbid Arariwa, as an NGO, from collecting clients' savings. Therefore, all of the external accounts that Arariwa offers are credit accounts. There are three types: (1) the main external account, (2) the complementary account and (3) the complementary extended account. Once a group of potential clients has agreed to apply to become a new communal bank, the credit officer evaluates each individual's credit worthiness. After this step, each approved individual is given a main external account. Each new client guarantees two other bank members' loans in the main external account. Although, if both guarantors are unable to pay, then all the members of the bank are responsible for the defaulters' loan. The amount that each client can borrow from the main external account increases in steps as clients go through loan cycles. Each step has a maximum amount that the credit officer is authorized to lend, but the amount lent to each individual is often less if the client does not want to borrow the full amount or if the credit officer's evaluation of credit worthiness established a lower limit. All of these accounts can be in Peruvian nuevos soles or in US dollars. In Peruvian nuevos soles the interest rate is 4 percent monthly declining balance; in US dollars the interest rate is 3 percent monthly declining balance.

Some clients that have proven to be reliable over several cycles engage in economic activities where the payback period on their loan is several months, which would make it impossible to start paying the loan back the month after the loan is disbursed. In order to retain these clients, Arariwa created the complementary and complementary extended accounts. The complementary account allows a small group of clients within a communal bank that have an established positive track record to borrow a larger amount for up to six months without paying monthly installments. The entire value of the loan is repaid at the end of the period agreed upon. The complementary extended account operates much like the complementary account except the loan term is extended to a maximum of 12 months. In these cases the members that are borrowing for extended periods form a solidarity group within the communal bank and guarantee each other's complementary or complementary extended loans.

There are two types of internal accounts that are dependent on each other: (1) the internal savings account and (2) the internal loan account. Although Arariwa is not allowed to hold client's savings, it obliges clients to save in the internal account. In order to borrow from the main external account, clients have to make an involuntary contribution of 5 percent of the capital of the loan in savings during the main loan cycle. Involuntary savings contributions become a part of the monthly installment (capital on external account, plus interest on external account, plus involuntary savings contribution). In addition to this involuntary contribution clients can contribute a voluntary amount towards their savings. While individual clients are free to contribute as much as they like and can vary this amount month to month, in practice, members of each communal bank tend to make commitments to save a fixed amount voluntarily each month for an entire cycle. They tend to reevaluate this amount every time a new loan is disbursed from the external account. Voluntary savings are not considered part of the monthly installment and are tracked as a separate quantity even though they are ultimately pooled together with involuntary savings. Arariwa encourages communal banks to open a savings account with a commercial bank where the communal bank can store collective savings. However, there are communal banks that choose to store their savings in far less reliable ways.

Part of the savings that each bank accumulates is lent to group members at a rate that the bank agrees upon (usually 3–4 percent monthly declining balance). The interest charged on the internal loan account translates to interest accumulated in the internal savings account. Even when little of the group savings is lent to group members, the equivalent interest on savings is higher than rates at commercial banks and the saving mechanism is generally considered to be safer than other high-return options such as saving in the form of animals.

There is no official limit on how much of the group savings can be used to fund the internal loan account. However, in practice it is in Arariwa's interest to use the savings in the internal savings account to cover the risk of default on the external loan accounts. Therefore, each credit officer recommends that a certain proportion of the internal savings should be kept in a non-Arariwa liquid savings account. The credit officer uses his or her judgment to determine how high this percentage should be; however, it is typically no larger than 50 percent since it is in the clients' interest to increase the amount that is cycled through the internal loan account in order to improve the return on their internal savings account.

There are three periodic concepts that govern each communal bank's progress through time: (1) the monthly meeting, (2) the loan cycle and (3) the savings cycle. The monthly meeting is the basic unit of time that is used to track the progress of each bank. All financial transactions and training sessions occur in these 1.5–2 hour meetings, to which all clients are required to attend. There are two types of loan cycles that apply to the external loans: (1) the main loan cycle, associated with the main external account and (2) the complementary loan cycle, associated with the complementary and complementary extended accounts. The main loan cycle consists of four or six monthly meetings. Each main loan cycle consists of a disbursal and four or six monthly installments. If outstanding debt has been cancelled by the last installment and if bank members what to borrow another amount, then the next cycle's disbursement occurs in the same month as the current cycle's last installment. The savings cycle consists of several loan cycles. The members of each communal bank decide how many loan cycles they would like to save for—the minimum is six loan cycles for a bank that operates on four-month loan cycles. Each of the complementary loan cycles lasts 6 months and the complementary extended loan cycle lasts 12 months. However, the amount is repaid in full at the end of that period and no monthly installments are required. The rhythm of the banks progression is set by the main loan cycle, as few clients have complementary accounts.

Internal loans also operate on the main loan cycle. However, there are two main differences in the way internal loans operate. The first difference is that internal loans can be disbursed on any month in the cycle, depending on availability of funds from the internal savings accounts. The second is that for the internal loans only the interest must be covered in monthly installments. The capital borrowed through one or many disbursements throughout a main loan cycle is returned in full on the last bank meeting of that cycle. Clients are free to return the full amount borrowed from the internal lending account prior to the last meeting. Access to savings is restricted until the last monthly meeting of the last main loan cycle of the savings cycle, which is referred to as the "graduation meeting." During the graduation meeting each member's savings plus any interest earned is returned and a new savings cycle begins during the next meeting.

Each communal bank meeting typically lasts between 1.5 and 2 hours. The standard meeting is divided into the following parts: (1) description of the Agenda and record of attendance and tardiness; (2) payment of each group member's monthly installment and any amount that each client would like to repay towards their internal loans and any amount that each client would like to contribute voluntarily to savings; (3) disbursement of internal loans to members that the bank determines to be worthy borrowers; (4) training session (45 minutes) given by credit officer.[1]

---

1   Arariwa' slogan is "Credit with Education." Prior to the implementation of the financial literacy module, Arariwa had three training modules: (1) Family wellbeing, (2) Health and (3) Business skills. The credit with education model allow Arariwa to optimize the efficiency of the delivery of educational services. There are four main mechanisms that make this educational delivery method more efficient than other potential methods: the institution has already incurred the cost of selecting a group of credit officers that are culturally and linguistically adept given the context, credit officers have already incurred the cost of travelling to the bank reunion place, credit officers have already incurred the cost of disciplining trainees into meeting at a particular location on a monthly basis and credit officers have already incurred the cost of getting to know each client, their personal strengths and weaknesses, which facilitates personal training. The trade-off is that credit officers have a lot of other responsibilities, which means that the financial literacy education is usually not their top priority. Also, teaching ability is only one of many criteria that the institution looks for when hiring a credit officer, which means that some credit officers may be strongest in areas other than those needed to effectively teach a group of clients.

5.4 Design

Arariwa adapted Freedom from Hunger's (FFH) modules on savings, budgeting and debt management, which are each seven–nine sessions long. The final product was one module that is nine sessions long and that covers the topics that were found to be most relevant for Arariwa's clients. Since the main loan cycle lasts four to six months, this financial literacy education module takes advantage of "teachable moments". Even in the most optimistic scenario, each bank will go through a minimum of one complete cycle during the nine-month training period. The end of each cycle is an opportunity for clients to decide how much they will borrow and save in the next cycle, which make the months preceding these decisions an ideal moment to teach about financial decisions. Each of the nine monthly sessions includes three components: a 45-minute training session during the monthly communal bank meeting, a 25-minute radio program that clients should listen to at least once between bank meetings and a homework assignment that clients should complete before each bank meeting. These components are described in more detail below:

1. *Training session during bank meeting:* The credit officer bases the 45-minute training sessions on a formal script that has been developed for each session. Most of the sessions also have a plastic poster that is used as a visual aid to go through decision making exercises. The training sessions were carefully designed based on the FFH training modules mentioned above, adapted to the local context and revised by Arariwa to focus more on commitments. There are four components to these training sessions: (1) introduction of the subject matter using interactive exercises intended to raise clients' awareness of their current financial decision making processes; (2) presentation of key theoretical concepts, reflecting upon the results of the interactive exercises; (3) use of a DVD to provide examples of Arariwa clients that have been successful because of following the advice given in the session; (4) A moment to commit to a behavioral change by thinking about key questions that are captured in a client training notebook.[2]

2. *Radio program:* Each 25-minute radio program is broadcast four times each month. The radio programs parallel the class training with stories, expert opinions and testimonies by Arariwa clients. The radio program is intended to reinforce the subject matter taught to clients in the training session and involve key decision makers in the client's household so that households are more likely to change their behavior.

---

2   While a few TVs and portable DVD players were purchased, credit officers were asked to borrow equipment from their clients in order to make the intervention more cost effective.

3. *Homework assignment:* Each client has a 40-page notebook that contains summaries of each session, tables to track their savings and loans and questions regarding their commitment and the radio program. Each client is supposed to sit down with her or his family to commit to a behavioral change by filling out the commitment questions. Each client is also supposed to answer some questions about the radio program to prove that he or she listened to the program. In order to incentivize clients to take these homework assignments seriously, a small prize is given to one member of each bank that has completed the commitment and radio questions at the beginning of each session. If multiple clients have answered the questions correctly, then the winner is determined through a simple lottery.[3]

Whereas the radio program was broadcast publicly, we included an encouragement design in order to help us define treatment and control groups. The clients were encouraged to listen to the program during the training sessions. Furthermore, the homework assignments included questions about the training and the radio program, and they were tied to lottery prizes. While true that the control group was not excluded, our expectation was that the announcements and incentives would generate significant differences in actual exposure.

Given Arariwa's communal bank methodology, we decided to use a clustered design in which the unit of randomization is the communal bank and the units of measurement are the clients within each bank. The sample was determined using a multistep process, which included: (1) power calculations, (2) application of exclusion criteria to reduce the sample to the required size and (3) randomization and division of the sample into an administrative sample and a survey sample. Power calculations were performed in order to design a clustered sample frame that would guarantee enough power to measure changes in key metrics that are considered relevant by the microfinance industry. Power calculations were not performed on every metric due to the lack of data. However, they were performed on four metrics for which data was available and which were considered to cover the spread in variation in the types of metrics in the data collection strategy. These metrics

---

3   The sessions focused on training related to balance of income, expenditures, investments and financial obligations, determination of personal, family and business goals and on how to plan financially to achieve these goals; determination of a saving plan to account for financial goals, necessary expenses and emergencies; determination of what to invest in, how much, how much will come from savings versus loan, how long to borrow for and whether or not borrowing will be profitable; how to calculate how much debt a client can afford based on income, expenditures and current debt, and characteristics of responsible borrowers.

Table 5.1 Stratification of Banks in Survey Sample

Banks in sample	Treatment	Control	Treatment-control
Average level of education	3.33	3.27	0.06
Average number months as clients	15.8	16	−0.02
Average loan outstanding (S/.)	1852	1816	36
Average number of clients in bank	15.8	15.4	0.4

Notes

1. Banks in treatment group: 172, banks in control group: 168.

2. Statistical significance in parenthesis.

were reliability in repaying external loans from Arariwa, tendency to save voluntarily in the internal account, amount borrowed from the external account in the current cycle and client's number of children.

The sample was selected and randomized through a multistep process. At each step the sample was balanced according to stratification criteria that were chosen partially because they were considered to be important factors to balance and partially because the data were readily available. For the bank selection process the following criteria were used: average level education of clients, average number of months that clients have been members of the bank, average amount of loan outstanding, and number of clients in the bank. For client selection processes within banks the following criteria were used: level of education, number of months as member of bank, amount of loan outstanding, and percentage of bank clientele that is female. Our random samples are displayed in Tables 5.1 and 5.2. Since the administrative sample had already been divided into treatment and control, the banks in the survey sample were already divided into treatment and control. Table 5.1 displays the treatment and control banks in the survey sample.[4]

5.5 Findings

This study was partially inspired by the rapid spread of the credit with education microfinance model, in which credit officers use preestablished communal bank meetings to train clients on a number of topics. The model has

---

4   We generated a list of all the clients in the survey sample by randomly picking seven clients from each bank to be eligible in order to allow for the fact that in some banks it might not be possible to locate two clients. Table 5.2 provides characteristics of clients eligible to be in the survey sample. We considered this possible attrition when making power calculations.

Table 5.2 Balance of Characteristics of Clients Eligible to Be in the Survey Sample

Clients eligible sample	Treatment	Control	Treatment-control
Number of clients	1204	1176	28
Level of education	3.3	3.3	0
Number months as client	15.8	16	−0.2
Loan outstanding (S/.)	1842	1791	51
% female	0.78	0.82	0.04

Notes

1. Treatment: 7 per bank; control: 7 per bank.
2. Statistical significance in parenthesis.

spread rapidly due to the low marginal cost with which it reaches rural clients. The main concern in the literature is whether the quality of such a low cost approach is likely to be so low as to render it ineffective from the perspective of a cost benefit analysis. In fact, our monitoring data progress through the financial literacy module was quite slow. Our initial assumption was that each communal bank that runs on a 4 month loan cycle should be able to complete nine sessions in 11 months, which would allow for two sessions to close and open cycles. However, in practice, in a series of 11 monthly meetings, only 1 percent of the communal banks in the treatment group were able to complete the nine sessions in the financial literacy module. The median bank was able to complete only three out of nine sessions and could be expected to take roughly three years to complete the module.

Our qualitative work suggests that there were three reasons for why many credit officers do not train on a regular basis. The first is due to attendance problems of bank members. In many banks several members come late and want to leave early. In others a large proportion of members don't come to the meeting at all and send their money with other members. In these circumstances credit officers often choose not to train in the hope that next session there will be more clients to train. This behavior by clients shows the limitation of imposing mandatory training sessions, which some clients do not value. In fact some of the banks in our treatment group explicitly asked the credit officer not to waste their time by training them.

The second reason is due to delinquency. If half way into a meeting a client has still not arrived and has not sent her money with another person, then the credit officer must track her down before his next bank meeting. Recovering the money becomes a much higher priority than giving a training session, especially if there are many clients that are delinquent or many clients that have become progressively later and later over the past few meetings. This is the sort of natural trade-off that clients must face when the institution is providing two services through one person who has conflicting priorities.

The third reason is that credit officers are often unwilling or unprepared to give the training sessions. Credit officers are not recruited for their ability as educators but rather for their ability to open new banks, their ability to recover loaned money and their familiarity with their work zone. While some of the credit officers are excellent teachers, this is not generally the case. Those that are not naturally inclined towards teaching are usually eager to avoid this part of their role whenever there is a plausible excuse to do so. Furthermore, given the limited amount of training that credit officers receive, lack of confidence in the training materials encourages credit officers to avoid their training tasks.

In fact on average only a third of the intended treatment package has been delivered. This fact lays the ground for our analytical approach, in which we seek to determine (1) the impact of the program on those that were intended to be treated in a reasonable timeframe and (2) the impact of the program on those that were actually treated in this timeframe. The first question is most relevant to the formulation of policy regarding financial literacy education, since it directly answers the question of whether this specific program is effective with the typical client in a communal bank. Since the treatment package has only been partially delivered at the time of this evaluation, the second question is also relevant to policy. The impact of the program on those that have made significant progress through the training model thus far is likely to be similar to the impact the program will have on those that will progress through the module in the next 15 to 20 months.

Prior to the implementation began, credit officers were asked if clients would be likely to own TVs and DVD players and whether they would be willing to lend their equipment for the sake of watching a video in the training session. The response was generally very positive. They were also optimistic about the possibility of sharing a few portable DVD players and stationary TV/DVD sets. In order to cover the geographical areas in the impact evaluation, 12 radio stations were contracted to broadcast the radio program. In order for this to be cost-effective nonpeak times were selected to broadcast the program.[5] Qualitative work suggests that there are three main reasons for the low video compliance levels. The first is that despite an attempt to eliminate banks from the sample that had no access to electricity, there were several banks that were inadequately classified as having access to electricity and others whose meeting place changed to a location with no electricity. Without

---

5   These strategies were not as effective as predicted. The median bank was trained with the DVD one time and only 7 percent of the clients in the median bank listened to the radio program.

electricity it is usually not possible for the bank to watch the DVD. The second reason is the fact that clients are not as willing to lend the credit officer their TVs and DVD players as credit officers had initially predicted. They are willing to lend their equipment once or twice, but after this it becomes an inconvenience. Sharing their equipment is an inconvenience because clients do not want to carry their equipment to the meeting place, they do not want to show their relative wealth to other bank members by showing their new equipment and they do not want to inconvenience other household members who would like to use the equipment. The third reason is that credit officers are not willing to put the effort into creating a schedule that will allow them to efficiently share the portable DVD players. The result is that only one credit officer uses them in some cases and in most cases nobody ends up using them.

Further qualitative work suggests that there are three main reasons for the low radio compliance levels. The first is that despite an attempt to eliminate banks that have no access to radio signal from the sample, there are several banks that cannot tune into the selected radio stations. It is logistically too complex and expensive to pay every local radio station in order for all banks that have access to radio signal to be able to listen to the program. In many cases local radio stations crowd out all other radio signals, preventing clients from accessing the radio stations that they would need to listen to in order to tune into the financial literacy program. The second reason is that many clients are working when the radio program is broadcast. It would be too expensive to ask radio stations to replace their prime-time programs (usually news programs) with the financial literacy radio program. The third reason is that women in rural areas often do not know how to change the radio station to tune into our program. This is an unforeseen technology adoption problem that Arariwa has not overcome.

The monitoring and qualitative data collected demonstrate that the low cost delivery mechanisms chosen for this intervention were not appropriate for this context. Therefore, the analytical approach described at the end of the previous section is unlikely to capture the effects of the components. The overall low DVD and radio compliance levels in the treatment group suggest that our estimates of the impact of the treatment on those that we intended to treat only weakly reflect the effect that the ICT components might have. This is also true for our estimates of the effect of the impact of the treatment on those that received training sessions.[6] In order to estimate impact, we extend

---

6   The percentage of clients consistently receiving a DVD supplement in their training session is not much greater than 20 percent regardless of how many sessions have been received. Similarly, the percentage of clients listening to the radio is not much higher than 15 percent regardless of how many sessions have been received.

our analysis to look at the impact of the treatment on those that were treated with (1) training sessions where the DVD was used and (2) the radio program.

We use the following main groups of indicators to assess the impact of the program on Arariwa's institutional well-being and on client's financial behavior: savings rates and retention rates. Savings rates are indicators that allow us to measure changes in financial behavior that benefit the client. Retention rates allow us to measure changes in behavior that benefit Arariwa as an institution. We use indicators to measure differences in savings behavior. The first, *total savings accumulated*, is the total amount in Peruvian Nuevos Soles (PEN) that each client had accumulated in savings in their internal savings account by the end of their last complete cycle as of May 2010. The second, *voluntary savings commitment* is the monthly amount in PEN that each client voluntarily decided to save during the last complete cycle as of May 2010. The end of the last complete cycle could fall anywhere between February 2009 and May 2010 for banks with a four-month loan cycle and December 2009 and May 2010 for banks with a six-month loan cycle. The data on savings come from notebooks that credit officers use to keep track of each client's financial activity in the internal and external accounts. We use one indicator to measure differences in retention rates. *Retention* indicates whether a client originally in the sample was still a client of Arariwa on June 30, 2010. These data come from Arariwa's MIS, which has a record of which clients are active for any given time period. Retention is reported in the savings regression tables in order to save space.

5.6 Impact of the Program on Those That the Program Intended to Treat

In order to estimate the impact of the intention to treat of the program we use an OLS regression with our key variables of interest as dependent variables. We ran these regressions in three progressions, each time with a different set of independent variables. The first set of regressions includes the assigned treatment dummy as an independent variable, only. The second group of regressions includes the treatment dummy and a series of dummy variables that are used to control for the fixed effect of the credit officers.[7] The third group of regressions includes the treatment dummy, the credit officer fixed effects dummies and cluster the standard errors by communal bank.

Table 5.3 shows that the impact on savings for those that we intended to treat is statistically indistinguishable from zero. However, for all three progressions of regressions the coefficients for both savings indicators are

---

7   In total, there were 42 credit officers.

Table 5.3 Impact of the Intention to Treat: Client Retention and Savings

	Retention [a/]	Savings [a/]	
	Retention at end of study (% in decimal form)	Total savings accumulated (PEN)	Voluntary savings commitment (PEN)
I) With credit officer fixed effects and clustering of standard errors [b/]			
Treatment	−0.0225	29.52	1.857
	(0.0189)	(75.31)	(3.592)
Number of observations	9,843	609	741
R-squared	0.157	0.123	0.250
II) With credit officer fixed effects, clustering of standard errors [b/] and covariates [c/]			
Treatment	−0.0201	27.83	1.719
	(0.0188)	(74.85)	(3.703)
Number of observations	9,843	609	741
R-squared	0.170	0.161	0.257

Notes

1. Each coefficient reported in the table is from a separate OLS regression.

2. *Coefficient is statistically significant at the 10% level; ** coefficient is statistically significant at the 5% level; *** coefficient is statistically significant at the 1% level; no asterisk means the coefficient is not different from zero with statistical significance.

3. Standard errors in parenthesis.

4. a/ Dependent variables are defined as follows: Retention at end of study: Dummy variable indicating whether individual was still an Arariwa client in June 2010. Total savings accumulated: Amount of internal savings at the end of the last complete cycle as of May 2010. Voluntary savings commitment: monthly amount client committed to save voluntarily during the last complete cycle as of May 2010.

5. b/ Standard errors are clustered by communal bank c/ Covariates for regressions III) include months as Arariwa client, gender and education level.

positive, which suggests that there may have been a positive effect on savings. The sample of savings data that we were able to collect was much smaller than the data for retention and repayment due to the inaccessible nature of the notebooks that contained it.[8] It is possible that a positive effect is masked

8   Given the extreme difficulty in retrieving data from the notebooks we ended up missing a very substantial share of the sample as there was no alternative institutional variable

in the standard errors typical of a sample that is too small. The table also shows that the impact on client retention for those that we intended to treat is generally indistinguishable from zero. While in the first set of regressions the coefficient is significant at the 5 percent level, once covariates, fixed effects and clustering are added the significance disappears.[9] We can conclude that at the time of evaluation, the program did not have an impact on those we intended to treat. This is consistent with our expectations given that meaningful amounts of the treatment have only been delivered to a small percentage of the treatment group.

5.7 Summary and Conclusions

Our evaluation does not allow us to draw any statistically significant conclusions about the effectiveness of financial literacy programs or about the value that the information and communication technologies considered in this chapter may add to the delivery of financial literacy training. Given that at the time of this evaluation the median bank had only progressed through one third of the training sessions. Low compliance levels with the DVD and video components suggest that the low cost delivery methods chosen were not adequate for this context. Higher investments would need to be made in the delivery of the ICT components in order to raise compliance levels to the point that would allow a future reevaluation to draw useful conclusions. A rural microfinance institution would have to buy personal portable DVD players for each of its credit officers in order for the use of the DVD to become viable. The radio program would have to be aired at peak times in order for clients to listen to radio supplements.

While the study does not allow us to determine the impact of the program, the results spark questions about the effects of financial literacy training programs on retention rates and repayment rates. Throughout all of the regressions in the results section the coefficients associated with retention rates are negative, which suggests that the program may have adverse effects on client retention. Due to the way that monitoring visits were carried out it is likely that clients in treatment banks received more training than clients in control banks, regardless of the subject matter. One possible interpretation

that was employable. Interestingly, the loss of information in notebooks was random enough as to not bias our remaining data, which is confirmed by balance tests to the key variables that yielded no statistically significant differences between attrited and remaining samples.

9   The impact on client repayment behavior for those that we intended to treat is also generally indistinguishable from zero.

is that clients would rather not be trained and that when mandatory training in bank meetings is intensified they would rather move to a different financial institution, which brings to the fore the issue of compliance in this kind of interventions, a somewhat rarely studied issue. Our data do not allow us to draw any strong conclusions of this sort, but this possibility could be further explored with future research.

References

Bayer, Patrick, B. Douglas Bernheim and John Karl Scholz (1996). *The Effects of Financial Education in the Workplace: Evidence from a Survey of Employers*. NBER Working Paper No.5655. Cambridge, MA: National Bureau of Economic Research. http://www.nber. org/papers/w5655.pdf (accessed September 2019).

Bernheim, Douglas (1995). "Do Households Appreciate Their Financial Vulnerabilities? An Analysis of Actions, Perceptions, and Public Policy." In *Tax Policy and Economic Growth: Proceedings of a Symposium*, pp. 1–30. Washington, DC: American Council for Capital Formation.

Bernheim, Douglas (1998). "Financial Illiteracy, Education and Retirement Saving." In: *Living with Defined Contribution Pensions*, edited by Olivia S. Mitchell and Sylvester Schieber, 38–68. Philadelphia: University of Pennsylvania Press.

Clancy, Margaret, Michal Ginstein-Weiss and Mark Schreiner (2001). *Financial Education and Savings Outcomes in Individual Development Accounts*. Working Paper 01–2, Center for Social Development, Washington University of St. Louis. http://129.3.20.41/eps/ hew /papers/0108/0108001.pdf (accessed September 2019).

Shawn, Cole, Thomas Sampson and Bilal Zia (2009). *Valuing Financial Literacy Training*. Manuscript, World Bank. http://siteresources.worldbank.org/INTFR/Resources/ Ziaetl030309.pdf (accessed September 2019).

Danes, Sharon M., Catherine Huddleston-Casas and Laurie Boyce. 1999. Financial Planning Curriculum for Teens: Impact Evaluation. *Financial Counseling and Planning*, 10 (1): 25–37.

De Mel, Suresh, David McKenzie and Christopher Woodruff (2014). "Business Training and Female Enterprise Start-Up, Growth, and Dynamics: Experimental Evidence from Sri Lanka." *Journal of Development Economics*, 106: 199–210.

Duflo, Esther, and Emmanuel Saez (2003). "The Role of Information and Social Interactions in Retirement Plan Decisions: Evidence from a Randomized Experiment." *Quarterly Journal of Economics*, 118: 815–42.

Elliehausen, Gregory, E. Christopher Lundquist and Michael E. Staten (2007). "The Impact of Credit Counseling on Subsequent Borrower Behavior." *Journal of Consumer Affairs*, 41 (Summer): 1.

Fox, J., S. Bartholomae and J. Lee (2005). "Building the Case for Financial Literacy." *Journal of Consumer Affairs*, 35(1) (Summer): 195–214.

Jacobs, Francine H (1988). "The Five-Tiered Approach to Evaluation: Context and Implementation." In: *Evaluating Family Programs*, edited by Heather B. Weiss and Francine H. Jacobs, 37–68. New York: Aldine DeGruyter.

Karlan, Dean, and Martin Veldivia (2011). "Teaching Entrepreneurship: Impact of Business Training on Microfinance Clients and Institutions." *Review of Economics and Statistics*, 93(2): 510–27.

Lusardi, Annamaria (2003). "Saving and the Effectiveness of Financial Education." *Pension Research Council Working Paper*, PRC WP 2003–14.

Mbabazi, I. (2007). "The Magic of Bringing Financial Education to the Rural Poor through Radio Talk shows." *Financial Education Update-Fall 2007—Global Financial Education Project.*

McKenzie, David, and Christopher Woodruff (2014). "What Are We Learning from Business Training and Entrepreneurship Evaluations Around the Developing World?" *World Bank Research Observer*, 29 (1): 48–82.

Muller, Leslie A. (2003). "Does Retirement Education Teach People to Save Pension Distributions?" *Social Security Bulletin*, 64 (4).

Organization for Economic Co-Operation and Development (2005). *Improving Financial Literacy: Analysis of Issues and Policies.*

Schreiner, Mark, Margaret Clancy and Michael Sherraden (2002). *Saving Performance in the American Dream Demonstration: A National Demonstration of Individual Development Accounts.* Research Report, Center for Social Development, Washington University.

Sebstad J., and M. Cohen (2003). "Financial Education for the Poor." *Financial Literacy Project Working Paper Number 1.*

Tennyson, S., and C. Nguyen (2001). "State Curriculum Mandates and Student Knowledge of Personal Finance." *Journal of Consumer Affairs*, 35(2) (Winter): 241–62.

Thaler, Richard H., and Schlome B. Bernatzi (2001). *Save More Tomorrow: Using Behavioral Economics to Increase Employee Savings.* Working Paper. University of California at Los Angeles.

Willis, L. (2008). "Evidence and Ideology in Assessing the Effectiveness of Financial Literacy Education." *Legal Studies Paper NO 2008–6*, Loyola Law School.

Chapter 6

DIGITAL LABOR-MARKET INTERMEDIATION AND SUBJECTIVE JOB EXPECTATIONS

Ana C. Dammert, Jose C. Galdo and Virgilio Galdo

6.1 Introduction

In the last decade, Information and Communication Technologies (ICT) have expanded at unprecedented rates in both developed and developing economies. In contrast to the Internet, mobile phones have become the most rapidly adopted technology in developing countries.

Due to the fact that the costs associated with the installation of mobile phone towers is relatively low (Jensen, 2010). Recent statistics for mobile phone penetration indicate that 8 of 10 people in the world had a subscription in 2011, up from 1 in 10 in 2000 (World Bank, 2012). Not surprisingly, a small but growing body of empirical literature has credited mobile phones with reductions in transaction costs and efficiency gains in agriculture (e.g., Aker, 2010; Goyal, 2010), health (e.g., Dammert et al., 2014; Pop-Eleches, 2011) and financial markets (e.g., Karlan et al., 2010). In the labor markets, the expansion of ICT technologies has invigorated research on a new array of labor market intermediaries, such as online job boards, social media sites, and e-recruiting firms (e.g., Bagues and Sylos, 2009; Nakamura et al., 2009; Stevenson, 2009), which has led to the reallocation of job search effort (Kuhn and Mansour 2014; Stevenson 2009), and more diversified search behavior (Cahuc and Fontaine, 2009; Kroft and Pope, 2010).

This chapter is partially based on two studies: "Digital Labor-Market Intermediation and Job Expectations: Evidence from a Field Experiment" (published in *Economics Letters* 2013, 120(1): 112–16), and "Integrating Mobile Phone Technologies into Labor-Market Intermediation: A Multi-Treatment Experimental Design." *IZA Journal of Labor and Development* 2015, 4(11).

Understanding the role of subjective expectations on economic behavior is central to economic modeling and policy design. While most progress in the literature pertains to the influence of subjective expectations on a number of economic outcomes including education, income, migration and productivity (see the surveys in Delavande et al., 2011; Manski, 2004), little is known about how individuals use the available information to formulate and update their subjective expectations. In fact, few studies have directly addressed the role of information on the formation of subjective expectations (e.g., Jensen, 2010; Luseno et al., 2003; Stinebrickner and Stinebrickner, 2012). In this study, we investigate how (digital) information about job-market opportunities sent to jobseekers via short text messages (SMS) influence subjective expectations about their job market prospects. By providing faster and cheaper access to information, mobile phone technologies might influence how individuals shape their expectations regarding future job prospects as searchers can access relevant, less costly and up-to-date information on job vacancies.

From a theoretical perspective, job decisions are forward looking and thus involve expectations. For instance, sequential search models that incorporate uncertainty about wage distribution are based on expectations that depend on information signals coming from the wage offers individuals observe during their search time (e.g., Diagne, 2010). As such, job search decisions and behaviors can be affected by expectations of wage offers and, therefore, have real consequences on preferences (employment decisions).

Given that expectations about future job prospects could be merely proxying for other unobserved characteristics, a distinctive feature of this study is its field experimental design with multiple treatments. We use data from the Public Labor Market Intermediation System (LMI) in Peru, a country that adopted an innovative e-government initiative in labor inter-mediation. We implement a social experiment with multiple treatments as part of regular (nonexperimental) public labor intermediation services. From June 22, 2009 to September 1, 2009, the experimental sample was selected at the initial registration filing for the normal inflow of applicants into Lima. Jobseekers who signed up to receive public labor-market intermediation were randomly assigned to four treatment groups according to two informa-tion channels (i.e., digital and non-digital intermediation) and the scope of information they received (i.e., restricted [public] and unrestricted [public/private] information sets). The restricted information set only considers SMS messages regarding job positions from firms that have registered with the public LMI system in Peru, while the unrestricted one considers SMS messages regarding job positions from firms inside and outside of the LMI system (e.g., firms advertising job positions in newspapers). For all participant groups, the treatment consisted of three months of subsidized job search assistance (labor-market information) after matching individuals' labor profiles with available job vacancies.

Measurement of subjective expectations is an ongoing topic in the literature, as different approaches have been adopted across different institutional settings. Indeed, non-probabilistic and probabilistic methods of the elicitation of subjective expectations have been implemented in the literature, the latter being considered the most sophisticated one, as it allows one to measure subjective probabilities that can be used to calculate the moments of the distribution of interest (Manski, 2004). In this study, we use an ordinal measure of subjective expectation that is based on a Likert scale from one (very pessimistic) to four (very optimistic) with respect to the likelihood of finding a job within the next three months following the information treatment.

Four main results emerge from this study. First, information matters for subjective expectations on future job prospects. Relative to a control group, individuals who receive tailored information about job opportunities show a positive and statistically significant change in their job expectations three months after signing up for public labor-market intermediation. Second, we do not find differential treatment effects between digital and non-digital treatment groups after conditioning in the same set of information (restricted set). Third, the scope and size of the information matters, as this study finds a positive and statistically significant change in the job expectations among individuals who received unrestricted SMS information relative to individuals who received restricted SMS information. Four, unrestricted SMS information not only causes changes in future subjective expectations but also increases employment in the first two months following the treatment intervention.

6.2 Background Discussion on the Public Intermediation System in Peru

Prior to 1996, the Peruvian Public Employment Services operated as a centralized intermediation office, hosted at the headquarters and regional branches of the Ministry of Labor and Social Promotion, with the aim of connecting workers to jobs. The employer–employee matching process was highly bureaucratic and done manually case-by-case without any regard for the automatization of the data collection and dissemination of the information. Not surprisingly, the job intermediation process was inefficient and costly. The average time it took for a worker to complete the registration process was four days after completing a battery of aptitude, knowledge and psychometric tests (MTPS, 1998). As a result, only 3 percent of active jobseekers used the public employment services in 1996, and in particular, they were those with chronic problems of employability (Chacaltana and Sulmont, 2004).

In 1996, the Peruvian government launched an ambitious e-government initiative aimed to modernize the role of the public employment agencies. With technical and financial support from the Swiss government and the European Union, a new National Information System (SIL) was put into place to support the adoption and design of e-government procedures, to lower the administrative burden and to improve the efficiency of the intermediation process. Bureaucratic processes were replaced by simpler and time-saving protocols, the compilation and dissemination of information changed from manual to automated matching algorithms, centralized labor-market institutions were replaced with decentralized offices through partnerships with not-for-profit institutions such as NGOs and vocational schools, and more caseworkers were hired and trained in labor-market intermediation (MTPS, 1998, 1999).

This active labor-market initiative started its operations in 1998 with the introduction of CIL-PROEMPLEO, an LMI institution that offers intermediation services. Bureaucratic practices were greatly simplified as participation only requires individuals and firms to register in-person at any labor mediation office by filling a simple application form and answering a short standard labor-market survey.[1] This information is subsequently uploaded to SILNET, a customized informatics system of job intermediation available only through an intranet. SILNET has simplified enormously the search costs in time and effort for both firms and workers. The registration process, for instance, went from four days prior to 1998 to less than an hour (MTPS, 1999). The computer software analyzes and matches workers' skills and experience with job openings. Once a suitable match is found, the jobseeker is contacted in person (or in some cases, by telephone or e-mail if available), in order to pick-up a letter of presentation from the Ministry of Labor with details about the job vacancy. It is worth noticing that job matches are based only on job opportunities generated from firms that have previously signed up on CIL-PROEMPLEO. Unlike other experiences, particularly in developed countries, participation in these services is voluntary given the absence of an unemployment insurance system in Peru.

Two years after the implementation of CIL-PROEMPLEO, the number of intermediated workers significantly increased. While in 1996, the total number of employee–employer intermediation was 10,275 at the national

---

1   The information collected from jobseekers includes standard demographic variables, schooling, training participation, computing knowledge, foreign-language knowledge, driver's license, labor market experience and current labor-market situation. Firms provide contact information (address, contact name, telephone, location etc.), detailed description of the job vacancy (work schedules, salary, location, main responsibilities and tasks) and job requirements (education, experience, computing and language knowledge, years of experience, driver's license).

level, it jumped to 22,764 in 1998. The corresponding numbers for metropolitan Lima, which represents more than 55 percent of the total intermediation, were 7,914 and 12,682, respectively (MTPS, 1999). All in all, the number of unemployed persons using the public intermediation system has increased significantly in the past decade from 3 percent in 1997 to 14 percent in 2007. Likewise, the number of job vacancies that has been offered through the public system has increased by five times from 12,707 in 1997 to 66,691 in 2007. According to administrative data, the average cost for each intermediated worker reaches US$ 25 dollars, which reflects a US$ 191 dollars per capita of social savings with respect to the cost of using private employment agencies (MTPS, 1998).[2]

Administrative data also shows that the effective rate of intermediation was quite steady over time. As a percentage of applicants, CIL-PROEMPLEO was able to intermediate one-out-of-four workers, with small variations over time. As a percentage of the number of job vacancies, there is more variability ranging from 60 to 80 percent between 1998 and 2007. One potential explanation for this flattened profile is the relatively small number of job vacancies that are still advertised via the public intermediation system. Indeed, only 15 percent of firms located in metropolitan Lima were registered with CIL-PROEMPLEO in 2004 (Vera, 2006).

A second wave of reforms in the operation of the Peruvian public intermediation system occurred in 2004 when the online version of CIL-PROEMPLEO started its operation in an effort to expand the adoption of information and communication technologies in the labor market.[3] In practice, this e-government innovation allows all registered jobseekers and firms online access to CIL-PROEMPLEO services, provided they have access to the Internet.[4]

The main attribute of this online service is that workers and firms can upload their information and exchange suitable matches without the intervention of any caseworker. In 2005, one year after the full operation of this electronic version, 59,137 people used the online version, along with more than 5,000 firms that offered 32,000 job vacancies (MTPS, 2006). There is no available data, however, on the rate of labor intermediation for this component as firms and workers exchange freely without the direct intervention of CIL-PROEMPLEO.

2   A common practice for private employment agencies in Peru is to charge each worker half of the monthly salary they would receive in the new job.
3   The service is free and accessible to anyone with a computer at http://www.empleosperu.gob.pe (accessed September 25, 2019).
4   It is estimated that 34 percent of registered jobseekers make use of this electronic version of the program (MTPS, 2006).

6.3 Experimental Design and Treatments

A primary concern in the literature of labor-market intermediation is the role of "selection on unobservables," which has plagued nonexperimental empirical studies (e.g., Kuhn and Skuterud, 2004; Meyer, 1995,). A distinctive feature of this study is its experimental design with multiple treatments that minimizes considerable empirical difficulties associated with both self-selection in labor intermediation and the endogenous placement of mobile phones. Early in 2009, we signed a formal agreement of cooperation with the Ministry of Labor and Social Promotion. This agreement allowed us access, in real time, to the SILNET intranet system. The field experiment was implemented as part of the regular (nonexperimental) public intermediation services, which affords us some advantages. The experimental sample is formed exclusively with new registered users of the public employment system, which greatly minimizes issues of selection on unobservables. Regardless of the treatment group assignment, all individuals in our sample were chosen randomly, and they did not self-select to be part of the experimental sample. On the other hand, due to institutional restrictions, we were only allowed to leave the control group individuals out of public intermediation for three months after registration in the LMI system, and thus, we were only able to measure the short-run treatment effects. Starting in the fourth month, all individuals, regardless of their treatment status, were subject to the standard non-digital labor market intermediation.

Random assignment was carried out on a daily basis (excluding weekends and holidays) from June 22, 2009 to September 1, 2009, among new registered users to CIL-PROEMPLEO. The experimental sample was selected at the initial registration filing for the normal inflow of applicants in Lima after excluding registered individuals who do not own mobile phones or hold occupations with very high turnover rates, that is, unskilled persons. Each day, among the set of new applicants, we randomly assigned jobseekers into three different groups: traditional treatment group, SMS treatment group and control group, following a random allocation of 30, 40 and 30 percent, respectively. Table 6.1 shows important features of this experimental design. The traditional treatment group was subject to the regular CIL-PROEMPLEO intermediation practices. The treatment consisted of three months of subsidized job search assistance in which individuals' labor profiles were matched with available job vacancies.[5] On the other hand, the SMS treatment group was exposed to technological innovation aimed to reduce job search costs. Jobseekers assigned to this group were informed about job-market

5   The matching algorithm was able to map specific job requirements (e.g., gender, age, schooling level, prior experience and skills) to individuals' profiles.

Table 6.1 Experimental Design

| | Traditional treatment (D^{T_1}) | Digital treatment | | Control (D^C) |
		Restricted-SMS treatment (D^{T_2})	Unrestricted- treatment (D^{T_3})	
Random allocation (%)	30	13	27	30
Treatment intervention	Three months of labor-market intermediation	Three months of labor-market intermediation	Three months of labor-market intermediation	None
Information channel	No digital	SMS	SMS	None
Information sets	Public sources	Public sources	Public and private sources	None
Sample size	345	188	303	354

Source: Author's own data.

opportunities that match their labor profile through digital services, that is, delivery of SMS messages to their mobile phones. The difference between traditional and SMS treatment groups is that the former is mainly contacted in person (or, by phone), while the latter is electronically contacted via text messages. There is no other salient difference between these two treatments, as the regular counselor-based and mobile phone-based intermediation services follow the same protocols.

Furthermore, a key feature of CIL-PROEMPLEO is that registered jobseekers can be intermediated only with job vacancies from firms that signed up through the public intermediation system. Therefore, to test whether it is the technology by itself or the set of information available to jobseekers that matters most, we implement a second set of randomizations that manipulates the size of the information sets available. Within the SMS treatment group, individuals were randomly assigned into two different groups—the restricted-SMS treatment group and the unrestricted-SMS treatment group—following an allocation ratio of 1:1.5. The former is matched only with job opportunities generated within the CIL-PROEMPLEO system (i.e., the public information set), while the latter is matched with both CIL-PROEMPLEO vacancies as well as job opportunities posted on alternative channels such as national newspapers ads and not-for-profit private employment agencies (i.e., public/private information sets). Otherwise, there is no difference in the content, wording and format of the SMS messages between both SMS treatment groups. Therefore, independent of whether individuals belong to the restricted- or unrestricted-SMS treatment groups, the framing of the information transmitted via SMS follows a standard structure and is limited to the description of the occupation and contact information as the following (fictional) example describes: "*PROEMPLEO. Hostess wanted Restaurant Amador. Av. La Mar #3453 Lince Tel 3038145. Contact: Elizabeth Bartra.*"

This multi-treatment experimental approach allows us to test some hypotheses with regard to the role of information on the change of subjective job expectations. First, we test whether information matters at all by comparing the (aggregated) treatment and control groups. From a theoretical standpoint, information does not automatically lead to the updating of subjective job expectations. If individuals update their expectations (or change their behavior) in response to new information they receive, then that information offers them value. Information theory states that the value of information is determined by three important factors—confidence, novelty and ability and willingness to act based on updated beliefs—all of which involve different forces and trade-offs (Hirshleifer and Riley, 1992).

Individuals process new information largely based on their prior beliefs. If job seekers, for instance, place strong confidence in their initial beliefs, more information is not necessarily more valuable, all else held constant. Evidence from behavioral economics, for instance, suggests that individuals who formulate their initial beliefs based on poor past experiences have difficulty interpreting subsequent new information, as initial expectations tend to anchor one's processing of information (Tversky and Kahneman, 1974), thus leading to the so-called cognitive "confirmation bias," a state in which people tend to ignore new information altogether or misread it (Griffin and Tversky, 1992). In this regard, it is noteworthy to recall that public labor market intermediation systems are populated with individuals with chronic problems of employability (Autor, 2001).[6] As such, they could have developed strong initial beliefs given their relatively poor experience in the marketplace, a genuine distrust of information coming from public sources, or both. If that is the case, they will not update mechanically their initial expectations in response to more information. On the other hand, if new information constitutes a novelty relative to the individual's initial expectations, then one would expect a strong updating effect.

Second, this multi-treatment assignment allows us to test the effectiveness on the delivery mechanism by comparing the traditional treatment group and the restricted-SMS treatment group while holding fixed the set of information. The only difference between these groups is that while the former is mainly contacted in person (or in some cases, over the phone), following the standard protocols from CIL-PROEMPLEO, the latter is electronically contacted via text messages. Indeed, the scope and size of the information sets are the same for both groups, so it is not clear whether the information channel per se could have the power to cause differential effects on subjective job expectations. Of course, there is a technology-driven novelty factor attached to the restricted-SMS treatment that might influence expectations about future job prospects. Yet, at the same time, the confidence or reliability posited to new SMS messages by jobseekers can be low, affecting any positive effects attached to the information channel. Moreover, digital literacy can counteract any potential updating effect of subjective expectations, as it can affect the effectiveness of SMS interventions due to the language barriers between the users of the digital technology and the technology itself (Chong, 2011).

Third, the multi-treatment design also allows us to assess the impact of expanding the set of information on subjective expectations by comparing the restricted- and unrestricted-SMS treatment groups while holding fixed the information channel. The scope of the information received by the unrestricted-SMS group (i.e., public and private information sets) involves a

---

6 The unemployment spells for users of the public intermediation system in Peru is two- to threefold higher than that for nonusers.

novelty factor, since historically, the restricted public intermediation system has operated only with information from a (low-quality) number of firms. Moreover, the frequency of information provided to the unrestricted-SMS treatment group is expected to be higher than that for the restricted-SMS treatment group, as more information (e.g., newspapers ads) are directly transmitted to the former group. Therefore, these two information qualities—scope and size—might indeed cause a strong updating effect on future job prospects. However, while more job information should be better, if there is "bad" information in the unrestricted information set that distracts attention away from the "good" information in the restricted information set then that could counteract any potential positive effect.

All in all, the effect of more information on subjective expectations is ultimately an empirical question and depends on the relative strengths and forces of different attributes of information.

6.4 Baseline Data

In total, 1,280 individuals were randomly assigned from June 22 to September 1, 2009, to four different groups, of which 354 corresponded to the control group (Dc), 344 to the traditional treatment group ($DT1$), 188 to the restricted-SMS group ($DT2$) and 303 to the unrestricted-SMS treatment group ($DT3$). The baseline dataset contains information for 1,189 individuals, which implies an attrition rate of 7 percent relative to the original sampling design. The low rate of attrition was similar in all treatment groups and it is not statistically related to any particular sociodemographic variable. All 1,189 individuals who provided information in the baseline period were also able to participate in the follow-up survey.

A critical step in the estimation of the causal treatment effects is to analyze the effectiveness of randomization in balancing the distribution of covariates across all treatment groups. Table 6.2 shows the mean baseline distribution for a large set of sociodemographic and labor-market variables across all treatment groups. Panel A shows that the average individual in our sample has completed high school education, is younger than 30 years of age and is single. There is a slight disproportion in the rate of enrollment by gender, as 55 percent of registered users are men. Only 30 percent of users have offspring, while one-fourth of them were not born in Lima. The p-value of F-test for the equality of means across all four randomized groups is above 0.05 for all variables except age.

Panels B and C show the mean distribution for baseline variables related to the prior labor market experiences and ICT exposure. For the computation of the mean values for monthly earnings, hours of work per week and job

Table 6.2 Summary Statistics by Treatment Status

Digital Labor-Market Intermediation Program, Lima 2009–10

Baseline variables	Treatment groups			Control	p-Value of F test
	Traditional	Restricted SMS	Unrestricted SMS		
	D^{T_1}	D^{T_2}	D^{T_3}	D^C	$[D^{T_1} = D^{T_2} = D^{T_3} = D^C]$
A. Sociodemographic					
Sex (1=male)	0.57	0.52	0.55	0.54	0.65
Age	27.04	25.33	26.27	25.55	0.02
Years of schooling	12.15	12.09	12.06	11.94	0.76
Single	0.71	0.76	0.73	0.73	0.52
Have children	0.32	0.26	0.32	0.26	0.22
Number of children					
Migrant	0.27	0.29	0.26	0.25	0.75
Cement floor	0.66	0.69	0.69	0.66	0.80
Cement roof	0.80	0.74	0.75	0.74	0.20
Cement walls	0.91	0.88	0.89	0.89	0.64
Flush toilet	0.93	0.91	0.93	0.95	0.29
Safe water	0.94	0.90	0.93	0.94	0.39
Poverty index	0.06	−0.12	−0.01	0.02	0.66
B. Last labor-market experience					
Worked ever	0.81	0.8	0.82	0.82	0.95
Discouraged worker	0.11	0.14	0.13	0.13	0.65
Monthly income (in soles)	519.82	484.97	490.6	562.00	0.60
Hours work per week	34.15	34.97	34.36	37.28	0.39
Had accident insurance	0.18	0.16	0.16	0.18	0.87

(continued)

Table 6.2 (*Cont.*)

Digital Labor-Market Intermediation Program, Lima 2009–10

Baseline variables	Treatment groups			Control	p-Value of F test
	Traditional	Restricted SMS	Unrestricted SMS		
	D^{T_1}	D^{T_2}	D^{T_3}	D^C	$[D^{T_1} = D^{T_2} = D^{T_3} = D^C]$
Last job matched with skills	0.32	0.33	0.27	0.31	0.62
C. ICT usage					
Use cell phone	0.95	0.95	0.96	0.97	0.43
Cell phone usage for job search	0.51	0.49	0.49	0.46	0.54
Use internet	0.83	0.85	0.84	0.83	0.86
Internet usage for job search	0.6	0.62	0.61	0.62	0.91
D. Job gain expectations					
Very optimistic	0.67	0.71	0.65	0.70	0.12
Somewhat optimistic	0.29	0.24	0.30	0.25	0.21
Only a little optimistic	0.04	0.04	0.05	0.05	0.78
Do not expect to find a job	0.00	0.01	0.00	0.00	0.86
N	345	188	303	354	

Source: Author's own data.

Notes

1. The test of equal means for the experimental sample is based on a regression with treatment indicators on the right-hand side D^{T_1} refers to the standard treatment group, D^{T_2} to the restricted-SMS group, D^{T_3} to the unrestricted-SMS treatment group, and D^C to the control group.

2. We imputed zero values to unemployed individuals when computing the baseline mean values for monthly income, hours worked per week, accident insurance and job matched skills.

accident insurance we input zero to the individuals who did not work. The data show that most individuals in the sample had previous job experience in the private sector, worked on average 35 hours per week, and earned 560 soles per month or US$ 160. Moreover, most jobseekers have experience using mobile phones and the Internet in general, while around half of the sample has used these electronic gadgets for job search purposes. The p-value of the F-test for the equality of means is above 0.05 for all variables considered in these two panels.

Finally, Panel D shows the distribution of future job gain expectations. The baseline survey question is, "Are you optimistic you will find a job in the next three months?" with answers on a Likert scale from one to four, which implies an ordinal measure, not a probabilistic measure, of subjective expectation: "very optimistic," "somewhat optimistic," "only a little optimistic," or "do not expect to find a job."[7] Almost 68 percent of jobseekers were very optimistic, while 26 percent and 5 percent were somewhat and only a little optimistic, respectively. Surprisingly, almost no one expects not to find a job. The p-value of F-test for the equality of means is above 0.05 for all of these categories. In sum, the statistical analyses suggest that the sample of individuals assigned to all of the different groups were drawn from the same population.

6.5 Empirical Framework and Results

The estimation of the causal effects of labor-market intermediation on subjective job expectations is based on a standard difference-in-difference approach as follows:

$$Y_{it+1} - Y_{it} = \beta_0 + \beta_1 D_i^{T_1} + \beta_2 D_i^{T_2} + \beta_3 D_i^{T_3} + X_{it}\beta_4 + \varepsilon_{it} \qquad \text{(Eq. 6.1)}$$

where $Y_{it+1} - Y_{it}$, is the before–after change in subjective expectations; $D_i^{T_1}, D_i^{T_2}$ and $D_i^{T_3}$ denote treatment indicators for the standard, restricted-SMS and unrestricted-SMS experimental groups, respectively; X_{it} denotes a rich set of baseline covariates, while ε_{it} is the error term. The coefficients β_1, β_2 and β_3 represent intent-to-treat parameters of interest that measure the mean gains of offering the treatment to participates. Both Y_{it+1} and Y_{it} are expressed in a binary form, with "very optimistic" =1 and "somewhat optimistic," "only a little optimistic" and "do not expect to find a job"=0. Importantly, the estimation sample is based on individuals who remain unemployed before and

---

7   Manski (2004) provides a detailed analysis of Likert scales with respect to more sophisticated probabilistic measures of subjective expectations. Likert scales do not allow, for instance, for answers in a cardinal scale and thus cannot be used to calculate the moments of a distribution of interest.

after the treatment, as the survey design elicited subjective expectations on future job prospects from unemployed individuals.

6.5.1 Subjective expectations

Table 6.3 presents estimates from the parametric model (1) along with clustered standard errors by date in parenthesis. The upper panel shows the overall impacts of information without considering the specific information channels or information treatment sets. Column 1 presents the unconditional before–after mean differences, while column 2 includes a set of baseline sociodemographic characteristics, column 3 adds previous labor-market covariates and column 4 includes the experimental assignment dates fixed effects. Results show the positive effects of information on before–after changes in subjective job expectations for unemployed individuals. The point estimates range from 6.5 to 8.4 percentage points after controlling for a rich set of baseline covariates and experimental assignment dates fixed effects. These positive impacts are in line with the available evidence that suggests that if individuals update expectations, they do it with a predictable bias toward optimism. In fact, empirical studies show that new valuable information is often read optimistically rather than objectively, since people under-react to negative information and overreact to positive information (e.g., Easterwood and Nutt, 1999; Hirshleifer and Shumway, 2003). However, our estimated coefficients are not statistically significantly different from zero, which might indicate that not necessarily all types of treatments are indeed causing positive before–after changes in job expectations, or some of the particular treatments could be just adding up noise to the conditional average estimates, or both.

Next, we present the intent-to-treat estimated effects for each particular treatment relative to the control group in the lower panel. By comparing the magnitude and significance of β_1 and β_2 in equation (1) we are able to test the impacts of digital intermediation, holding fixed the set of information, while by comparing β_2 and β_3 we test the impacts of expanding the set of information while holding fixed the information technology. Relative to the control group, the traditional (D^{T_1}) and the restricted-SMS (D^{T_2}) treatment groups show small and insignificant impacts on before–after changes in subjective job expectations. As both groups received labor-market information based on the same restricted public information set (i.e., job vacancies only from firms that signed up with the public intermediation system), this result suggest that changes in the information channel, from standard to digital provision of information, are not enough to cause differential impacts in expectations about future job market prospects. Indeed, the resulting p-values of the test for

Table 6.3 Impacts of Digital Labor Market Intermediation on Job Gain Expectations

Labor-Market Intermediation Program, Lima 2009–10

	(1)	(2)	(3)	(4)
Overall treatment	0.065	0.078	0.086	0.084
	(0.059)	(0.060)	(0.060)	(0.073)
N	386	386	386	386

Types of treatment

	(1)	(2)	(3)	(4)
Traditional treatment (D^{T1})	0.015	0.032	0.035	0.037
	(0.070)	(0.071)	(0.072)	(0.103)
Restricted-SMS (D^{T2})	0.026	0.037	0.035	−0.006
	(0.084)	(0.085)	(0.085)	(0.104)
Unrestricted-SMS (D^{T3})	0.144**	0.154**	0.173**	0.179**
	(0.072)	(0.073)	(0.074)	(0.077)
p-value of Ho: $D^{T1} = D^{T2}$	0.89	0.95	0.99	0.72
p-value of Ho: $D^{T2} = D^{T3}$	0.17	0.18	0.11	0.09
p-value of Ho: $D^{T1} = D^{T2}=D^{T3}$	0.16	0.20	0.13	0.10
N	386	386	386	386

Source: Author's own data.

Notes

1. Standard errors in parenthesis.

2. Estimates based on a parametric differences-in-differences estimator. D^{T1} refers to the standard treatment group, D^{T2} to the restricted-SMS treatment group, and D^{T3} to unrestricted-SMS treatment group. Base category is the control group. Column (2) includes socio-demographic covariates, column (3) labor market covariates and column (4) experimental assignment dates fixed effects.

3. The estimation sample is based on unemployed individuals before and after the intervention.

equality of parameters, *Ho:* $D^{T_1} = D^{T_2}$, presented at the bottom of Table 6.3, do not reject the null hypothesis across all columns.

On the other hand, by comparing the estimated parameters associated with the restricted-SMS and unrestricted-SMS treatment groups, we provide evidence that the latter shows positive and statistically significant before–after changes in subjective job expectations. The point estimates for β_3 lie in the range of 14–17 percentage points, showing an approximately 20 percent increase with respect to the baseline measure of job expectations. Moreover, controlling for a rich set of sociodemographic, labor-market variables and experimental date-fixed effects does little to change the positive estimates or their statistical significance, as shown in columns 2–4 in Table 6.3. By looking at the bottom of column 4 (our preferred specification), we observe that the p-value of the test for equality of parameters, H_0: $D^{T_2} = D^{T_3}$, does reject the null hypothesis at the 10 percent level. These results suggest that the scope and size of the information set matter for subjective job expectations rather than the information channel per se. In our view, the distinctiveness between restricted [public] and unrestricted [public/private] information sets involves a novelty factor, since historically, the traditional public intermediation system has operated only with information from a limited group of low-quality firms. Thus, individuals in the unrestricted-SMS treatment group received, on average, not only more information but also qualitatively different information coming from firms that do not normally register with the public system, all of which makes the information received more valuable. Put differently, the value of the information generated by the novelty of the information, along with a higher number of SMS received, might explain the positive impacts on subjective job expectations.

6.5.2 Heterogeneous analysis

We analyze the heterogeneous treatment impacts across multiple policy-relevant variables of interest associated with demographics and labor-market characteristics of individuals in our dataset: gender, age, poverty, education, migration status and prior labor-market experience. Following a parametric specification, we extend Equation (6.1) to incorporate the interactions terms between treatment indicators and the selected variables of interest in the full model that incorporates sociodemographic and labor market covariates as well as the treatment assignment date-fixed effects. No statistically significant differential impacts emerge from this analysis for all but one variable of interest: women show disproportionally higher before–after changes in job expectations relative to men. This result is statistically significant for the overall measure of treatment and for the restricted-SMS and unrestricted-SMS treatment arms. In the case of the overall treatment, the estimated coefficient for the interaction term between the treatment and the male dummy variable is -0.31 with a standard error of 0.13. In the case of the SMS interventions, the corresponding coefficients range between -0.39 and -0.53, both statistically significant at the 1 percent level. These results suggest that, relative to men, women update job expectations with higher bias toward optimism.

Considerable gender gaps still exist in the Peruvian labor market in favor of men who report, on average, not only higher earnings and employment rates but also higher rates of participation in public labor-market intermediation relative to women. Therefore, it is possible that women, who do not have the same experience as men in terms of labor-market trades, might have a different set of expectations than men, which is positively reinforced once they start receiving free SMS information on their cell phones about job opportunities.

6.5.3 Employment

The positive relationship between (unrestricted) information and subjective job expectations matter, as the latter is a meaningful predictor of subsequent work status (Stephens, 2004) and is associated with job search effort (Diagne, 2010) and wage growth (Campbell et al., 2007). We therefore investigate whether labor-market intermediation that alters both the provision of information and subjective job expectations will indeed lead to an increase in employment rates. Two important employment data features need to be highlighted. First, unlike other labor-market interventions (e.g., training) that might have long-lasting effects due to human capital accumulation, the potential impacts of this (information-only) labor-market intermediation mainly happen during the treatment period. Second, we face a short-term intervention, since control group individuals were left out of treatment for only three months, and thus everyone in the sample, regardless of the random assignment, was subject to the same standard non-digital labor-market intermediation beginning in the fourth month.

In contrast to the empirical analysis on subjective expectations based only on the unemployed, we can use a larger sample of individuals as the employment variable is collected for everyone in the survey. Likewise, we provide employment impacts for three different time periods: the first, second and third months after the intervention. A detailed explanation of the employment outcome and measures can be found in Dammert et al. (2015). The upper panel in Table 6.4 shows the overall impacts without considering the differences in the information channel or information set treatment assignment. Clustered standard errors by date are shown in parentheses. Results indicate that public labor-market intermediation has positive and significant employment impacts within the first month of the intervention. These effects are somewhat above 6 percentage points and statistically significant at the 5 percent level for the first month following labor-market intermediation. This impact equals a 17 percent increase with respect to the baseline mean outcome. The magnitude and statistical significance of the impacts, however, lessen at two and three months after treatment. Columns 2 and 3 show that the magnitude of the treatment effects reaches 5.5 percentage points and is statistically significant at the 10 percent level two months following the intervention. For the third month, no statistically significant impacts are observed.

Table 6.4 Labor-Market Intermediation on Employment Outcome

Labor-Market Intermediation Program, Lima 2009–10

	Month # 1		Month # 2		Month # 3	
Overall treatment	0.066**	0.062**	0.056*	0.055*	0.003	−0.002
	(0.032)	(0.027)	(0.032)	(0.031)	(0.031)	(0.033)
Types of treatment						
Traditional treatment D^{T1}	0.041	0.34	0.46	0.40	−0.018	−0.034
	(0.039)	(0.035)	(0.038)	(0.037)	(0.038)	(0.044)
Restricted-SMS treatment D^{T2}	0.081*	0.083*	0.057	0.060	0.034	0.034
	(0.046)	(0.042)	(0.046)	(0.046)	(0.045)	(0.045)
Unrestricted-SMS treatment D^{T3}	0.086**	0.081**	0.067*	0.069*	0.008	0.008
	(0.040)	(0.032)	(0.039)	(0.037)	(0.039)	(0.035)
p-value of Ho: $D^{T1} = D^{T2}$	0.38	0.28	0.810	0.68	0.24	0.14
p-value of Ho: $D^{T2} = D^{T3}$	0.91	0.95	0.830	0.85	0.58	0.54
p-value of Ho: $D^{T1} = D^{T2} = D^{T3}$	0.47	0.38	0.870	0.71	0.49	0.33
N	1118	1118	1118	1118	1118	1118
Covariates	No	Yes	No	Yes	No	Yes
Experimental groups FE	No	Yes	No	Yes	No	Yes

Source: Author's own data.

Notes

1. Standard errors in parenthesis.
2. Estimates based on a parametric cross-sectional estimator.
3. The treatment indicator takes the value 1 for those benefiting from labor-market intermediation, 0 otherwise. Set of control variables include socio-demographic and labor-market characteristics.
4. Clustered standard errors by day are considered when including experimental group fixed effects in columns 2, 4 and 6.
5. *** statistically significant at 1%, ** statistically significant at 5%, * statistically significant at 10%.

To disentangle the role of information channels from the information sets available to jobseekers, the lower panel reports the intent-to-treat parameters for each specific treatment group. Relative to the control group, the traditional treatment group (D^{T_1}) shows positive but not statistically significant treatment effects across all months. On the contrary, the digital channel seems to explain the overall significant employment impacts we found for this labor-market intermediation initiative. By looking closely at rows three and four in Table 6.4, we observe that within the digital channel is the unrestricted-SMS treatment group (D^{T_3}) that shows the strongest impacts in month one (8 percentage points) and month two (7 percentage points), both statistically significant at the 5 and 10 percent levels, respectively. The magnitude of these impacts is equivalent to a slightly above 20 percent increase with respect to the baseline measure of employment. The restricted-SMS treatment group (D^{T_2}), on the other hand, has weaker impacts since it is statistically significant only at the 10 percent level in month one, while in month two it loses statistical relevance. The p-value of the F-test, however, does not reject the null hypothesis of equal coefficients. In month 3, no (statistically) significant effects are found for all individual treatment groups.

We also analyze heterogeneous treatment impacts across the same set of policy-relevant variables of interest: gender, education, migration, age, labor-market experience and poverty status of participants. In contrast to the subjective expectations, we do not find a differential impact by gender. The heterogeneous analysis shows that, one month after the treatment begins, jobseekers who have worked in the past show statistically significant higher employment rates (0.16) relative to those who lack labor market experience. No significant impacts were found for months two or three, however. These results reveal that a lack of labor-market experience constitutes a resilient barrier that is difficult to overcome through public labor-market intermediation. Similar to the heterogeneous analysis for subjective expectations, we do not find differential impacts by age, education, migration status and poverty.

6.6 Conclusion

This study exploits a multi-treatment experimental design implemented as part of the regular (nonexperimental) public intermediation system in Peru to investigate the extent to which digital labor-market intermediation influences subjective job gain expectations. The estimation of intent-to-treat parameters reveals that jobseekers who received unrestricted-SMS intermediation, which is based on public and private information sources, increase their before–after job gain expectations relative to the control group. Independent of the information channel, no significant effects were found when labor-market intermediation is based on a restricted (short) set of information. An analysis of heterogeneous effects did not find any statistically significant differential effects across a set of policy-relevant variables of interest with one exception. Women showed statistically significant higher before–after changes in subjective expectations relative to men.

As subjective job expectations are considered in the literature as a meaningful predictor of subsequent work status, we also assessed the role of labor-market intermediation on employment status. Overall, we found a positive and statistically significant relationship between labor-market intermediation and employment in the very short term, that is, one and two months after the treatment started. These positive effects are mainly driven by the unrestricted-SMS treatment group that shows the largest employment impacts within the first two months of the intervention. In contrast to the subjective expectations outcome, we did not find differential impacts for women relative to men. Instead, the heterogeneous impacts analysis showed that individuals who have labor-market experience benefit more from labor-market intermediation relative to jobseekers who have weak labor-market attachment.

All in all, the unrestricted-SMS treatment group shows sizable and statistically significant effects on job expectations and on employment. Although the differential impacts among treatment groups lack power to be statistically detected, these results suggest that integrating mobile phone technologies into traditional, public labor-market intermediation and extending the set of information available for jobseekers could be a cost-effective initiative as the marginal costs of sending SMS messages are low.

References

Aker, J. (2010). "Information Markets Near and Far: Mobile Phones and Agricultural Markets in Niger." *American Economic Journal-Applied Economics*, 2(3): 46–59.

Autor, D. H. (2001). "Wiring the Labor Market." *Journal of Economic Perspectives*, 15: 25–40.

Bagues, M., and M. Sylos (2009). "Do Online Labor Market Intermediaries Matter? The Impact of Alma Laurea on the University-to-Work Transition." In: *Studies of Labor Market Intermediation*, edited by David Autor. Chicago: University of Chicago Press.

Cahuc, P., and F. Fontaine (2009). "On the Efficiency of Job Search with Social Networks." *Journal of Public Economic Theory*, 11(3): 411–39.

Campbell, D., A. Carruth, A. Dickerson and F. Green (2007). "Job Insecurity and Wages." *Economic Journal*, 117: 544–66.

Chacaltana, J., and D. Sulmont (2004). "Políticas activas en el mercado laboral peruano: el potencial de la capacitación y los servicios de empleo." In Garcia, Chacaltana, Sulmont, Sierra, Sato y Jaramillo (2004), "Políticas de empleo en Perú." CIES–CEDEP–I P–PUCP–UNI. pp. 221–88.

Chong, Alberto (2011). "Development Connections: Unveiling the Impacts of New Information Technologies." New York: Palgrave MacMillan.

Dammert A., J. Galdo and V. Galdo (2013). "Digital Labor-Market Intermediation and Job Expectations: Evidence from a Field Experiment." *Economics Letters*, 120 (1): 112–16.

Dammert A., J. Galdo and V. Galdo. (2014). "Preventing Dengue through Mobile Phones: Evidence from a Field Experiment in Peru." *Journal of Health Economics*, 35: 147–61.

Dammert A., J. Galdo and V. Galdo (2015). "Integrating Mobile Phone Technologies into Labor-Market Intermediation: A Multi-Treatment Experimental Design." *IZA Journal of Labor and Development*, 4(11).

Delavande, A., X. Giné and D. McKenzie (2011). "Measuring Subjective Expectations in Developing Countries: A Critical Review and New Evidence." *Journal of Development Economics*, 94: 151–63.

Diagne, M. (2010). "Information and Job Search Intensity in South Africa." *Mimeo World Bank*.

Easterwood, J. C., and S. R. Nutt (1999). "Inefficiency in Analysts' Earnings Forecasts: Systematic Misreaction or Systematic Optimism?" *Journal of Finance*, 54(5): 1777–97.

Griffin, D., and A. Tversky (1992). "The Weighting Evidence and the Determinants of Confidence." *Cognitive Psychology*, 24(3): 411–35.

Goyal A. (2010). "Information, Direct Access to Farmers, and Rural Market Performance in Central India." *American Economic Journal-Applied Economics* 2(3): 22–45.

Hirshleifer, J., and J. G. Riley (1992). "The Analytics of Uncertainty and Information." *Cambridge Surveys of Economic Literature*. Cambridge: Cambridge University Press.

Hirshleifer, D., and T. Shumway (2003). "Good Day Sunshine: Stock Returns and the Weather." *Journal of Finance*, 58(3): 1009–32.

Jensen, R. (2010). "The Perceived Returns to Education and the Demand for Schooling." *Quarterly Journal of Economics*, 125 (2): 515–48.

Karlan D., M. McConnelly, S. Mullainathan and J. Zinman (2010). "Getting to the Top of Mind: How Reminders Increase Saving." NBER WP 16205.

Kuhn, P., and M. Skuterud (2004). "Internet Job Search and Unemployment Duration." *American Economic Review*, 94(1): 218–32.

Kuhn, P., and H. Mansour (2014). "Is Internet Job Search Still Ineffective?" *Economic Journal*, 124: 1213–33.

Kroft K., and D. Pope (2009). Does Online Search Crowd Out Traditional Search and Improve Matching Efficiency? Evidence from Craigslist." In: Studies of Labor Market Intermediation, edited by David Autor. Chicago: University of Chicago Press.

List, J., and I. Rasul (2010). "Field Experiments in Labor Economics." NBER WP 16062.

Luseno, W., J. McPeak, C. Barrett, G. Getachew and P. Little (2003). "The Value of Climate Forecast Information for Pastoralists: Evidence from Southern Ethiopia and Northern Kenya." *World Development*, 31 (9): 1477–94.

Manski, Charles (2004). "Measuring Expectations." *Econometrica*, 72 (5): 1329–76.

Meyer, B. (1995). "Lessons from the U.S. Unemployment Insurance Experiments." *Journal of Economic Literature*, 33: 91–131.

MTPS (1998). "Programa Red CIL PROEMPLEO." *Ministerio de Trabajo y Promoción del Empleo*.

MTPS (1999). "Programa Red CIL PROEMPLEO." *Ministerio de Trabajo y Promoción del Empleo*.

MTPS (2006). Anuario Estadístico. Ministerio de Trabajo y Promoción del Empleo.

Nakamura, A., K. Shaw, R. Freeman, A. Nakamura and A. Pyman (2009). "Jobs Online." In: *Studies of Labor Market Intermediation*, edited by David Autor, 27–65. Chicago: University of Chicago Press.

Pop-Eleches, C., H. Thirumurthy, J. Habyarimana, J. Zivin, M. Goldstein, D. de Walque, L. Mackeen, J. Haberer, S. Kimaiyo, J. Sidle, D. Ngare and D. Bangsberg (2011). "Mobile Phone Technologies Improve Adherence to Antiretroviral Treatment in a Resource-Limited Setting: A Randomized Controlled Trial of Text Message Reminders." *AIDS*, 25(6): 825–34.

Stephens, M (2004). "Job Loss Expectations, Realizations and Household Consumption Behaviour." *Review of Economics and Statistics*, 86 (1): 253–69.

Stevenson, Betsey (2009). "The Internet and Job Search." In: Studies of Labor Market Intermediation, edited by David Autor. Chicago: University of Chicago Press.

Stinebrickner T., and R. Stinebrickner (2012). "Learning about Academic Ability and the College Dropout Decision." *Journal of Labor Economics*, 30(4): 707–48.

Tversky, A., and D. Kahneman (1974). "Judgement under Uncertainty: Heuristics and Biases." *Science*, 185: 1124–31.

Vera, R. (2006). "La discriminación en los procesos de selección de personal." Geneva: ILO.

World Bank (2012). "Information and Communications for Development: Maximizing Mobile." Washington, DC: World Bank.

Chapter 7

FROM COW SELLERS TO BEEF EXPORTERS: THE IMPACT OF TRACEABILITY ON CATTLE FARMERS

Laura Jaitman

7.1 Introduction

In the past five decades Latin America experienced on average slower growth than the rest of the world but Africa. Within the developing world, Latin America and Africa fell behind the progresses made by Asian countries. Blyde and Fernandez-Arias (2005) documented that these differences are mainly due to total factor productivity changes over time. Most Latin American countries have comparative advantages in agriculture and, therefore, in order to boost growth they should apply techniques that improve agricultural productivity. Developing countries with comparative advantages in agriculture are disadvantaged by the fact that the specificity of their agroecological features and contexts leaves them less able than other regions to benefit from international technology transfers (World Bank, 2008). Therefore, unlike the transfer of industrial technology that is complex but more standardized, agricultural technology often requires local investment in adaptation and innovation.

In this chapter we evaluate the implementation of TRAZ.AR, a traceability system to electronically identify and track the production cycle of cow herds in small/medium rural enterprises (SMEs) in Argentina. Cattle traceability is a requirement to access the high value European market. To the best of our knowledge this is the first attempt to assess the effect of traceability at the farmer level, and more importantly to evaluate an ICT intervention to increase productivity in cattle farms.

There are compelling reasons to expect significant economic development from the adoption of ICTs in cattle activities. First, technology is a means of adding value to production and, therefore, would increase the price consumers pay. Second, the introduction of technology can improve the quantity and quality of information available, reducing asymmetric and imperfect information in markets. The use of this valuable data can increase productivity which might be a driving force for growth in agriculture.[1]

In the particular case of beef production, anonymity of the open market limits the ability to create incentives to improve product quality. Traceability identifies the animals and stores all the information related to them in a central server that could be audited, engendering a differentiation of traced products. Furthermore, traceability systems trigger a "learning by tracing" process because the information generated helps to improve production and trading decisions.

Cattle traceability in the first stage of the beef production chain (ranch-to-slaughterhouse) is particularly challenging as the process is in the hands of thousands of SMEs which usually face barriers to adopt new technology (Banerjee and Duflo, 2011). Individual ranchers may lack the resources, motivation and know-how to track their cattle. Nevertheless, all major beef exporting countries are developing regulations and processes in line with traceability (e.g., Uruguay and Brazil). However, none of these policies have been evaluated.

Traceability is not only applied to cattle. It is a concept utilized in several industries (agriculture, livestock, medicine, for example) in different ways and deepness (degree of tracing back and forward), depending on the needs. Technically it is defined as *the ability to trace the history, application or location of that which is under consideration* (ISO 9000:2000).[2] In the cattle industry traceability, methods improve food security, quality control, product flow, fraud detection and limit potential spillovers in case a sanitary accident occurs. In addition to these, traceability was also used in the past years as a powerful tool to improve management and accountability of stocks.

The scarce literature on the effects of traceability focuses on the demand side. Dickinson and DeeVon (2002), for example, study how much consumers value traceability certificates. Hayes et al. (1995) explore the demand for traceability in a setting where the products are auctioned off. Regarding the supply of traceability, the literature is based on the probability or level of its adoption but not on the consequences of traceability introduction (for instance, Hassan et al., 2006) study the beef producers in Canada or Souza-Monteiro and

---

1   Gains in productivity have been a driving force for growth in US agriculture. Over the second half of the twentieth century the farm output increased on average 12 times. The development of new technology was a primary factor in these improvements (Fuglie et al., 2007).

2   The definition usually applied to food is the one postulated is the one by the European Community: *The ability to trace and follow a food, feed, food-producing animal or substance intended to be, or expected to be incorporated into a food or feed, through all stages of production, processing and distribution* (EC Regulation, 178/2002).

Caswell (2009) the pear producers in Portugal. Concerning the reasons for adoption, diverse studies for the US (Golan et al., 2004) and the EU (European Commission, 2005) show that firms adopt this system to become more efficient in stock managing, to differentiate and to increase the quality of their products.

TRAZ.AR program involved the development of cattle traceability software and the implementation of the system in Santa Fe province, Argentina. The aim of the program was to strengthen the competitiveness of the cattle SMEs in the international meat market through the use of traceability, which would in turn increase their profits. The fieldwork consisted of animal electronic identification with tags employing RFID (radio frequency identification) technology. Farmers were trained to keep records of all the activities related to their herd in hand-computers and to update the data contained in the electronic tags. Apart from the potential efficiency gains due to the useful information generated through traceability, another advantage of the system is that cattle traceability is a requirement to export beef to high value markets, such as the European Union (EU).

We analyze the effects of the TRAZ.AR intervention that took place between 2004 and 2006 in Santa Fe province, Argentina. We evaluated the effects of the treatment at the enterprise level for 2006 and 2010. Unfortunately this evaluation was not planned before the program, so it was carried out ex-post, relying mainly on official administrative records containing annual information on prices, livestock counts, and employment. We complemented these records with surveys to farmers. Treatment assignment was neither random, nor based in any deterministic rule. For this evaluation we constructed a control group matching treated and untreated farmers from the same region in pre-treatment variables in levels and trends to recover the counterfactual of what would have happened to the treated farmers in the absence of treatment. We employed administrative records coupled with surveys and additional sources of information to make sure that there may not be significant differences in the recall bias of the treatment and control group, and to support the idea that the intervention was exogenous to this matched control group.[3]

---

3   We checked for recall bias asking in the surveys for information contained in administrative records, and there were no differences between groups. Also in the surveys, all the questions on the program where asked in the end, and the surveys where carried out within the regular surveys that these farmers are subject to. To define the control group, we also worked with agricultural technicians working in the area and program implementers to find out which farmers were not offered the program (mainly due to the capacity of the implementing NGO), but had similar production processes to mitigate the risk that the treated had differential characteristics as willingness to join cooperatives, to export or expansion plans of their herd.

We assess the causal effect of the program on farm outcomes after the program finished in 2006 and 2010. We consider as treated all the farmers that initially participated in the program, though some did not remain during the whole period. We estimate the effects of the program at the enterprise level by estimating the intention-to-treat of the program using a difference-in-differences estimator employing a panel of treated and matched control groups, including period and farms fixed effects. We are interested in the effects of the intervention at the enterprise level concerning production, innovations, and trading among other relevant aspects of the beef production chain. We also explore changes in the behavior and inter-action of the farmers due to the implementation of this program. The results of this case study suggest that TRAZ.AR proved to be successful. Although the agricultural sector suffered from discouraging public policies and an intense drought, beneficiaries increased their livestock by 15 per-cent and rural skilled employment doubled relative to the non-treated control group. The beneficiaries created a cooperative to commercialize their products and thereby increased their social capital. They thus managed to overcome market failures due to coordination and asymmetric infor-mation problems that mostly affect SMEs. The program also encouraged the farmers to improve their sanitation, animal welfare and meat quality standards, which enabled them to export to the EU, increasing their profits. Treated farms also reported significant improvements in their efficiency and risk management.

7.2 TRAZ.AR Program

Argentina has comparative advantages in the production of quality meat (see Brambilla et al., 2018). However, as in most of the developing countries spe-cialized in primary production, the pace of technology adoption is relatively slow and there is scope to implement ICT innovations that would increase productivity and growth (World Bank, 2008).

Building a global beef export industry not only involves complying with the regulations of importing countries, but it also depends upon maintaining con-sumer confidence and ensuring a competitive and transparent supply chain. Accomplishing these objectives requires investments in traceability, since a traceable supply chain can function as a kind of quality control system: it records every step in the production of beef products and by doing so verifies the production and processing practices based on third-party audits, helps exporters sort beef by type and quality and price it more profitably (EIU, 2008). Outbreaks of foot-and-mouth disease (FMD) and bovine spongiform encephalopathy (BSE) have triggered import bans and regulations in many countries. Among these regulations, traceability is one of the requisites to be able to export to the EU.

The program TRAZ.AR was created at the end of 2003 and was implemented during 2004–6, in Santa Fe province (Argentina) with funding from the Inter-American Development Bank through its Multilateral Investment Fund (FOMIN) and an NGO in Argentina: ACDI (Asociación Cultural para el Desarrollo Integral). The main aim of the program was to strengthen the competitiveness of the SMEs in the international meat market through the use of traceability, which would in turn increase their profits.

The first outcome of the program was the development of a cattle traceability software that stores all the information regarding the beef production chain. In practice the system works as follows: cows are tracked by farm of origin through ear tags that remain in the animal whenever it changes hands. The tags used in this program employ radio-frequency identification (RFID) technology,[4] meaning that they contain a chip that stores the information of the animals. The farmers have to be trained in the use hand-computers with TRAZ.AR application. Those computers are then connected to an antenna which reads the information of the tag. The information so captured in the field is uploaded to a central server through the Internet. With all the data stored, the software produces different kinds of reports which the farmers can use to monitor the evolution of their stock and sanitary situation.TRAZ.AR electronic application also offers the possibility to contact other farmers using it.

The most demanding and time-consuming part of the project was the development of this ICT solution. Meanwhile, there were workshops in different provinces of the country to inform farmers of this new technology (in total 800 farmers attended to these workshops and more than four thousand attended different presentations that TRAZ.AR did in agricultural forums). In Santa Fe (province where the program took place), the field work started with workshops to make the farmers aware of the advantages of the system. More than a hundred cattle farmers attended, and 41 enrolled in the program. Also, more than twenty technicians were trained in the use of this ICT solution. TRAZ.AR program also had a staff of 14 employees (administrative, informatics and agricultural technicians). The 41 beneficiaries received the necessary training and the equipment to use TRAZ.AR system. The intervention also covered the cost of the traceability service for two years (2004 and 2005). The total cost of the program was $830,000. If a treated farmer wanted to continue having the traceability service after the intervention finished (2006 onward), they had to pay $1 per animal per year.

---

4   Another variant for tags is the simplest numbered or bar-coded ones. In this program RFID was used, but the others could also serve traceability purposes.

The program also encouraged the treated SMEs to commercialize together. As a consequence a cooperative called PROGAN was created and joined by 70 percent of the treated farmers. The cooperative could give the framework to achieve a larger scale and closer integration among producers, input suppliers and processors that would improve animal husbandry practices and save on capital, labor and feed. Furthermore, given the isolation of cattle producers in the vast lands of Argentina, the cooperative could turn into a valuable source of social capital that would enable the farmers to profit from information spillovers regarding the best practices in their business.

The expected benefits of this program are twofold. In the first place, the ability to identify and track the animals can provide useful information that would increase the efficiency of the farms: a "learning by tracing" process. For example, farmers would be able to quantify their productivity more accurately, detect problems, set precise targets, commit to sell certain amounts of their production for determined dates and so on. These will engender efficiency gains which eventually translate into an increase in profits (through a decrease in costs).

Second, as traceability is a requisite to export to high value markets (such as EU), the program could enable feeders or complete-cycle farmers to reach those destinations—provided that they also comply with the other quality and sanitation requirements of those buyers. TRAZ.AR program also provided training in other aspects necessary to reconvert the production to export to those markets: cattle managing and feeding techniques, animal welfare, special slaughtering protocols, among others.[5] To achieve the aim of the program regarding exports, the treated group should get a portion of the Argentine Hilton Quota. These quotas are allocated by the EU to various countries[6] that export high-quality fresh, chilled and frozen beef to countries within the EU with a 20 percent import tax, enjoying a duty preference vis-à-vis the EU Most Favored Nation import regime (European Commission Regulation No 936/97). In Argentina the government allocates the Hilton Quota (Decree No 906/09), with 10 percent usually assigned to SMEs. However, the quota is not always fulfilled because of the unavailability of high-quality export animals complying with the required standards.[7]

Finally, it is worth mentioning that TRAZA.AR was the first program to implement cattle traceability in Argentina SMEs. Although in the country

---

5   For instance, the animals should not be hit while transported; they should be led by workers using flags. This is to avoid hematomas that could reduce the meat production and quality.

6   Argentina, Brazil, Uruguay, Paraguay, the United States, Canada, Australia and New Zealand.

7   For example in 2007–10, 13,222 tons were not delivered according to official statistics.

there are improvements regarding animal identification requirements, tracking backwards their life cycle is not mandatory yet. Regarding identification, the official institution in charge of Sanitation and Agro-food Quality—SENASA[8]—established through the resolution N°15/03 in 2003 that official registration and identification were compulsory for all the animals held in farms that supply cattle to exports. Later, through the resolution N°103/06 in 2006, SENASA implemented a Nation System of Cattle Identification, extending mandatory identification to all the calves and heifers born since January 2006.

7.3 The Argentine Livestock Sector

In this section we discuss the outlook for the livestock sector in 2003 and the policies affecting it thereafter. Understanding the context in which this program took place is very important as its targets can be affected by macro shocks impacting the livestock industry as a whole.

Historically, the livestock sector has been 20 percent of the agricultural GDP, and 3 percent of the national GDP. Argentina was among the main world meat exporting and consumer countries.[9] On average in 2000–3, the export levels were around 400,000 tons of meet per year. The context for the livestock sector in 2003–4 was promising and suitable for a program to boost exports. Theoretically it was a good time to enable the farmers to experience a qualitative leap in their production for the following reasons: (1) increasing international beef prices; (2) reopening of the external markets (after closure due to foot-and-mouth outbreaks) and (3) adverse sanitary conditions for competitors in the international market (foot-and-mouth in Brazil, BSE in the United States).

Despite these favorable international conditions, the past years were very difficult for the Argentine beef industry. Since 2004 the government has been interfering especially in the cattle and beef markets with a wide range of uncoordinated and disruptive policies. The intervention was partly justified with the argument that it would contribute to stop the inflationary process evidenced in Argentina after the rapid recovery from the last crisis and devaluation of the local currency. Another argument was to preserve the purchasing power of the salaries of the unskilled workers (Galiani et al., 2010). The livestock sector was especially distorted because beef is the main item in the consumer basket and consequently in the Consumer Price Index of Argentina.[10] Those

8   Servicio Nacional de Sanidad y Calidad Agroalimentaria.
9   In 2005 Argentina was the third beef exporting country, behind Brazil and Australia.
10 Meat weights 7.639 percent, and beef is the subgroup with the highest weight: 61 percent within meats; 4.513 percent of the Consumer Price Index.

measures comprised setting caps to retail prices and livestock, changing the slaughtering minimum weight, raising export taxes and finally setting quotas to beef exports and even banning beef exports during some periods.

This context was really adverse for a program that promotes ICT to increase exports and access high-value markets. The change in rules came completely unexpected. In fact, in 2005, when the cooperative was preparing the first shipments, the export taxes for beef increased from 5 percent[11] to 15 percent and in March 2006 to 25 percent. In addition to this, in February 2006 there was a foot-and-mouth episode in Corrientes province (Argentina), which suspended Argentine beef exports temporarily during 2006 (the exports from Corrientes province remained banned). Nevertheless, after Argentina accessed again the international markets when the outbreak was over, the government decided to ban meat exports. These policies not only did not achieve their objectives, but instead affected negatively the entire beef production chain. On top of the inaccurate public policies, by the end of 2008 and early 2009, the worst drought in the last 50 years affected a vast area of the most productive crop and cattle land in Argentina.

These unexpected shocks which occurred after the program started engendered an alteration in the normal cattle cycle. In general, the cattle cycle is determined by the combined effects of cattle prices, the time needed to breed, birth and raise cattle to market weight, and climatic conditions. Fluctuations in the cattle herd over time arise because biological constraints prevent producers from instantly responding to price (Murphy et al., 1994). If profits are expected to be high, producers slowly expand their herd size;[12] similarly they contract their herd size to cut expected losses.

The combination of uncoordinated policies and severe drought generated the deepest herd liquidation phase since livestock records are available (1875): Argentine livestock decreased 20 percent (10 million animals) in 2006–10.

Table 7.1 shows that in 2003 there were 55.9 million animals and in 2010 the livestock decreased to 48.9 million (after having peaked in 2006 reaching 59 millions). In Santa Fe province the negative trend in livestock was also evident with its livestock decreasing from 6.8 million in 2006 to 6 million in 2010. In light of the aggregate shocks (public policies and climate) that experienced the Argentine livestock industry, it is very important to have a control group in this study to which compare the outcomes of the treated group. Thus, in

---

11 They were 5 percent since 2002.
12 Cow-calf producers respond to profitable calf prices by holding back more replacement heifers and not culling as many cows. The increase in cow numbers leads to more calves the next year. But additional heifers held back for entry in the cow herd do not increase beef production for at least three years.

Table 7.1 Livestock Sector Evolution in Argentina

Evolution of livestock

	2003	2006	2010
Total Argentina (Millions)	55.9	59.2	48.9
Santa Fe Province (Millions)	6.8	6.5	6.0
Control group	867	840	715
	(826.0)	(820.0)	(595.1)
Treatment group	865	941	840
	(929.1)	(899.8)	(859.9)

Source: TRAZ.AR administrative records including SAGPyA statistics and INTA estimates, as well as own survey to farmers.

this context, the control group is very likely to play its role of estimating the secular trend (i.e., what would have happened to the treatment group in the absence of the program).

Table 7.1 shows that the control and treatment groups were balanced in 2003 in terms of herd size with an average of 865 animals per farm. During the program (2004–6), the treated group increased their cattle herd by 8.8 percent, while the control group started a herd liquidation phase. After the program, the initial beneficiaries also decreased their livestock on average (11 percent), but to a lesser extent than the control group (15 percent). Overall, between 2003 and 2010, the livestock showed a contraction of 3 percent in the initial beneficiaries group and of 17.5 percent in the control group.

Another explanation of the reduction in the livestock is that throughout 2003–10 there was also an expansion of the agricultural frontier in Argentina in view of the high prices of commodities like the soybean.[13] This expansion sometimes led to a substitution of cattle land for agriculture. However, we can rule out the possibility of substitution in our sample because neither the control nor the treated groups experienced significant changes in the proportion of land use for the different activities or in the income from livestock and crops.

7.4 Methodology

To identify the effect of TRAZ.AR program on relevant farm-level outcomes we built a panel with observations for 2003, 2006 and 2010. The treatment

---

13 The external market for grains was also intervened by the government, with increases in export taxes and export rationing.

group comprises the initial beneficiaries of the intervention and the farmers in the control group were never offered TRAZ.AR program. For most outcomes of interest, we estimate the following model:

$$Y_{it} = \alpha_i + \beta T_{it} + \gamma X_{it} + \text{»}_t + \varepsilon_{it} \qquad \text{(Eq 7.1)}$$

We estimate the intention-to-treat (ITT) parameter by regressing the dependent variable on a treatment dummy which indicates treatment assignment to TRAZ.AR program and a vector of control variables. Some farmers that adopted the program did not continue using traceability after the program ended in 2006 (see section on compliance). But since this decision is endogenous and given our reduced sample size, we can only recover the intention-to-treat effect of the program (on those initially treated). We also include in the model two-time varying control variables at the farm level: the productive activity of the farm (breeding, feeding or complete cycle) and the percentage of the farm's income derived from agriculture. Changes over time in these two variables are uncorrelated with treatment assignment and all the results are robust to including both, one or none of these controls. Finally, we condition the analysis on both farmer and year fixed effects.

Another concern is that the equation error terms might be correlated across time and space. Therefore, to address this issue, we allow for an arbitrary covariance structure within farms by computing our standard errors clustered at the farm level.

The internal validity of the design relies on the fact that the control and treatment groups were balanced before the program on pretreatment levels and trends and on the reasonable assumption that the time evolution of the outcomes studied in the absence of the intervention is well captured by the control group. Since this appears to be dominated by the aggregate shocks suffered by the livestock sector—rather than by specific trends, which is also true for pretreatment years in Argentina-, this assumption seems plausible. Therefore, the control group very likely replicates what would have happened to the treated in the absence of the program.

Another concern is on the difference in unobservable variables between the treatment and control groups, like differential motivations to innovate, which can drive the results. As explained before, the allocation of treatment was not random and the control group was matched in observable variables, so we cannot rule out this possibility. However, the balance in observed characteristics related to cattle figures and in pretreatment assessments of efficiency, profits and risk-management, support the exogeneity of the treatment.

As per external validity, it is important to emphasize that the program was developed in a very adverse context for the beef industry. Thus, if the results of the program are positive even despite the adverse conditions (export bans, when the main aim of the program was to promote exports), it is conceivable to think that in a more favorable situation the gains could be larger.

7.4.1 Data collection

To evaluate the impact of traceability at the farm level, we should ideally compare the performance of the treated group with what would have happened to them in the absence of the program. As the allocation of treatment was not random, we recreated the counterfactual selecting a control group conformed by 41 farmers from Santa Fe with similar pretreatment characteristics and trends.[14] We constructed this control group working with local technicians from the National Institute of Agricultural Technology (INTA) who have been surveying and monitoring the activities of the farmers of the province for decades. We chose a control group by matching the treated farmers in observable characteristics for 2003, such as scale, income, socioeconomic status, use of technology, land use, region, productive activity, agricultural income, herd size and pretreatment assessments of growth in productivity, efficiency and risk management before 2003. The matching process was performed with official records from INTA and surveys to farmers.

As mentioned before, given that no baseline survey was held before the program, for the evaluation we employed data from official administrative records complemented with individual surveys to the treated group (41 beneficiaries) and a control group (40 farmers), conducted in 2010. The interviews were performed by local technicians who are usually in charge of surveying that population for the agricultural and population Census, and periodic surveys. This was the only way to get total compliance with the survey, given that farmers usually do not provide information to strangers about their activities and income. The farmers where contacted once by phone or in person (either in their farms or in the village, where most of them live) and were asked to gather information regarding the relevant variables for 2003, 2006 and 2010 about which we would ask in a second personal interview arranged by appointment. No question was asked about the program, except for the very last ones where beneficiaries had to explain advantages and disadvantages of TRAZ.AR. Aware of the concerns regarding retrospective evaluations, we checked for differential recall biases through the comparison of the answers provided and the official registers from INTA of that region

---

14 Given our results showed later, we suggest a randomized evaluation of a traceability program, maybe targeted at poorer farmers to use technology to take them out of poverty.

for all the period surveyed (2003–10). We found that the answers are consistent with the on-time recorded data for both groups and with the trends experienced by other farmers of the region. Nevertheless, the retrospective characteristic of this evaluation was a constraint in terms of the deepness and precision of the questions we could ask.

Another source of information was TRAZA.AR system and the registers of PROGAN (the cooperative created through the program). We profited from the fact that a considerable part of the intervention had to do with registering and storing information in the system. To complement the individual records and the information regarding the cooperative, we employed data from the main meat processing firm of the area (FRIAR) and available statistics from INTA and SENASA.

7.4.2 Balance checks

In Table 7.2 we provide summary statistics of relevant variables for the control and treatment groups corresponding to the year 2003 (pretreatment). We can see that most of the variables were balanced before the treatment, which does not reject the assumption that the control group is comparable to the treated farmers in these observable levels and trends.

Regarding the farm characteristics, we notice that this program targeted SMEs, with an average size of 865 animals per farm, 1,172 hectares for cattle-related activities, which gives a density of 0.8 animals per hectare.[15] There are no statistically significant differences with the control group in all these important variables. The average number of animals is greater in those farms that develop complete-cycle activities, followed by feeders and breeders. The main source of income of these farms is cattle breeding or feeding. Only 10 percent (9 percent) of their income comes from agriculture. Regarding employment, the treated (control) farms have approximately 3 (2) unskilled employees on average and 0.68 (0.25) skilled workers. This variable is not balanced (at the 10 percent significance level) between the two groups, as treated farms employ more workers (especially skilled).

As far as qualitative variables are concerned, we enquired from the farmers how they perceived the evolution of efficiency, profits and risk management in the three years previous to 2003. This is a proxy for the perceived pretreatment trends in these variables. Table 7.2 shows that most of the farmers claimed that these three variables remained unchanged or worsened, while

15 It has been estimated that 95 percent of the treated and control farmers had a livestock of less than six hundred animals, entering the category of SMEs. However, 5 percent of the treated had more than two thousand animals (large enterprises).

Table 7.2 Summary Statistics

	Control group	Treatment group	Difference
	2003	2003	Control-treat
Cattle farm characteristics			
Livestock	867	865	2.023
(Number of Animals)	(826.0)	(929.1)	(195.5)
Hectares for cattle activities	1347	1172	175.1
(Number of Hectares)	(1219.0)	(1171.2)	(265.6)
Density of livestock	0.750	0.800	−0.050
(Number of animals per Hectare)	(0.297)	(0.397)	(0.0780)
Agriculture	0.325	0.415	−0.090
(Dummy=1 if also does	(0.474)	(0.499)	(0.108)
agriculture)			
Agriculture income	9.000	10.122	−1.122
(total farm income (%))	(14.106)	(17.975)	(3.596)
Breeders	883.7	746.6	137.1
(Number of animals in breeding	(886.2)	(915.9)	(275.7)
farms)			
Feeders	409.5	646.3	−236.8
(Number of animals in	(409.4)	(409.4)	(317.1)
backgrounding farms)			
Complete-cycle farmers	939.2	1090.9	−151.7
(Number of animals in	(463.3)	(1133.9)	(541.2)
complete-cycle farms)			
Employment			
Unskilled employees	1.900	2.780	−0.880
(Number of workers)	(0.8102)	(2.987)	(0.489)*
Skilled employees	0.250	0.683	−0.433
(Number of workers)	(0.438)	(0.907)	(0.008)***
Perception of evolution in the previous three years			
Efficiency improved	0.000	0.049	−0.049
(Dummy=1 if improved; 0 otherwise)	(0.000)	(0.218)	(0.0345)
Profits improved	0.000	0.024	−0.024
(Dummy=1 if improved; 0 otherwise)	(0.000)	(0.156)	(0.0247)
Risk management improved	0.000	0.000	0.000
(Dummy=1 if improved; 0 otherwise)	(0.000)	(0.000)	(0.000)
Observations	40	41	81

Source: TRAZ.AR administrative records including SAGPyA statistics and INTA estimates, as well as own survey to farmers.

Notes

* Significant at 10%; ** significant at 5%; *** significant at 1%.

very few declared an improvement in efficiency (5 percent of treatment group) and in profits (2 percent of the beneficiaries). The pretreatment differences in these qualitative variables across groups are not statistically significant.

7.5 Results

The results in Table 7.3 suggest that the adoption of the new technology generated firstly a change in inputs. The treated group increased on average 15 percent the number of animals in the farm throughout the period. This would suggest that in the absence of the negative unexpected shocks mentioned (drought and inaccurate policies for the beef industry), the beneficiaries may have experienced a net increase in their livestock (contrary to the slight reduction of Table 7.1). Apart from the increase in the cattle herd, Table 7.3 shows that assignment to TRAZ.AR increased employment in treated farms by one worker on average. This is the result of adding one skilled employee, while the program does not seem to have a significant effect on the number of unskilled workers.[16] This suggests the presence of complementarities between technology adoption and skilled workers. These changes in input quantities and management, together with the adoption of traceability enabled the treated farmers to meet the strict standards demanded by high value markets. Indeed in 2005 PROGAN was allocated 40 tons of the Hilton quota increasing to 78 tons in 2006 (constituting the group of cattle farmers with the highest portion of the quota). For 2011 they were assigned 100 tons, the largest amount since the beginning of their exports in 2005.

The improved international competitiveness in turn had a positive effect on the profitability of the SMEs involved. In fact, the members of PROGAN would either commercialize their cattle through the cooperative or sell their animals to the nearest meat processing firm (what their neighbors in the control group do). This alternative represents the opportunity cost of selling to the cooperative. We compared the prices received monthly by those that traded through PROGAN with the price the main meat cold-storage firm in the region[17] paid per kilogram of high-quality export steer. The price PROGAN

16 Employment was the only unbalanced variable in 2003 (Table 7.2), with more workers reported in treated firms. In this case the main concern is that those in the treatment (control) had a particularly high (low) employment level in 2003 that would revert in the future (regression to the mean). However in this case the effect goes in the opposite direction because the treated farms that had more workers registered before the implementation of the program are the ones showing an increase in employment.

17 According to the surveys, most of the feeders sell their animals to FRIAR (mainly), Quickfood and Finexcor firms, or alternatively to intermediaries who pay them less than the firms. Thus, these estimations of price differential are conservative.

Table 7.3 TRAZ.AR on Production Inputs

	Livestock		Employment		
	Ln number of animals	Animals per Ha.	Unskilled workers	Skilled workers	Total workers
Treatment (*Dummy=1 if treated*)	0.140 (0.083)*	0.131 (0.059)**	0.048 (0.060)	0.997 (0.169)***	1.018 (0.186)***
Productive activity	YES	YES	YES	YES	YES
Percent agricultural income	YES	YES	YES	YES	YES
Observations	243	243	243	243	243

Source: TRAZ.AR administrative records including SAGPyA statistics and INTA estimates, as well as own survey to farmers.

Notes

1. Robust standard errors clustered by farmer in parentheses.

2. * Significant at 10%, ** significant at 5%, *** significant at 1%.

paid includes the dividends that were distributed after each year. Figure 7.1 shows that the beneficiaries received a positive price differential when trading through PROGAN since the second year of the program, and it increased until the 2008–9 period (peak of price differential of 20 percent). Therefore, TRAZ.AR was successful in achieving its objectives: enable SMEs to export their production to high value markets[18] and hence increase their profits. In addition, we explored the effect of this program on a set of variables on the assessment of the production process (Table 7.4). Farmers were asked whether in the previous three years their efficiency, profits and risk management improved or not. They answered the questions for 2003, 2006 and 2010. Here we do not employ a difference-in-differences approach since the farmers already report changes in the variables and the interpretation of the dummy equal to one (variable improved) is different in 2006 and 2010 according to the previous evolution of it. Therefore, we estimate a linear probability model for each year for the cross-section of farmers.[19]

18 The destinations of exports include Germany, Netherland, Spain, Italy, United Kingdom, Chile and Russia.
19 The results we obtain are similar to those of a difference-in-differences analysis considering the following pairs of years: 2003 with 2006 and 2003 with 2010.

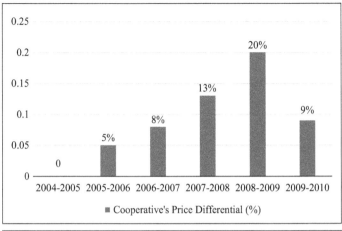

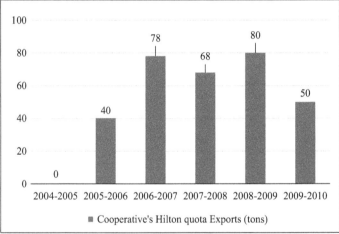

Figure 7.1 The evolution of price differentials and high-value exports for beneficiaries
Source: PROGRAN and FRIAR (main cold-storage plant of the area).

In the first place, note that the estimation for 2003 in Table 7.4 constitutes a falsification test to explore whether treatment assignment is correlated with the pretreatment trend in the qualitative variables reported. As already reported in Table 7.2, we find that the coefficient of the treatment estimator is not different from zero at conventional significance levels.

Second, Table 7.4 confirms that the treated group experienced efficiency gains of similar magnitudes in the period 2004–6 and 2007–10: the probability of reporting that efficiency improved is 78 percent and 84 percent higher respectively for the treated group. The treatment raised the probability of

Table 7.4 TRAZ.AR on Perceptions of Efficiency, Profits and Risk Management

	Dep. Var.: Efficiency			Dep. Var.: Profits			Dep. Var.: Risk management		
	2003	2006	2010	2003	2006	2010	2003	2006	2010
Treatment assignment (Dummy=1 if belongs to treatment group)	0.031 (0.023)	0.784 (0.090)***	0.844 (0.074)***	0.016 (0.016)	0.412 (0.102)***	0.815 (0.075)***	0.000 (0.000)	0.447 (0.107)***	0.506 (0.119)***
Productive activity	YES	YES	YES	YES	YES	YES	YES	YES	YES
% Agricultural income	YES	YES	YES	YES	YES	YES	YES	YES	YES
Observations	81	81	81	81	81	81	81	81	81

Source: TRAZ.AR administrative records including SAGPyA statistics and INTA estimates, as well as own survey to farmers.

Notes

1. Robust standard error in parentheses.

2. * Significant at 10%, ** significant at 5%, *** significant at 1%.

reporting that profits improved by 41 percent in the first period and by 82 percent in the second. This might be due to two reasons: first, in the beginning the cooperative did not pay significantly higher prices and second because it takes time for the efficiency gains to translate into higher profits. Finally, Table 7.4 indicates that the program increased significantly the probability of experiencing an improvement in risk management of around 50 percent for both periods. The channel through which this progress operates is the commercialization through the cooperative which increases the scale of production and the possibilities of diversification. For example, in light of the constant changes in export regulations the associated beneficiaries opened in 2007 a high-quality butcher shop in Santa Fe to also serve the domestic market in the event that exports are caped or discouraged by other public policies.

In addition to analyzing these effects, we also explored the probability that the farmers introduced further changes in the way they produce as a consequence of this ICT program. Table 7.5 shows the results of the linear probability models where we regress the dummy variable equal to one if there was a change in the determined category (zero otherwise) on treatment assignment and control variables (in brackets we report the changes mostly mentioned by the farmers in the surveys). TRAZ.AR increased 42–45 percent the probability of adopting changes in animal sanitation (upgrade standards to enable exports), marketing strategies (mainly trading through the cooperative) and management of problems (traceability provides information for a better diagnosis of problems and planning solutions, also consultation within the cooperative helped). The program raised the probability of improving meat quality by 58 percent (through better pastures, reproduction selection, better cattle managing practices to avoid stress and hematomas that downgrade the meat quality) and raised the chances of changing the way in which the activities of the farm were registered by 75 percent (direct consequence of TRAZ.AR).

We find no significant effect of the program on the probability of changing the animal identification techniques used. This seems paradoxical a priori because an important component of TRAZ.AR is the electronic identification of the animals. However, in the control group there were also changes in identification in this period due to the new official regulations of SENASA that made it compulsory to identify all the animals (see Section 2). It is important to perform cost-benefit analysis to assess the sustainability of programs of this kind. TRAZ.AR program costs were mainly fixed costs to pay for the software development, workshops with farmers to promote the program, and the project organization and implementation of the treatment. Once the system was set, the costs per treated farmer was the RFID identification technology infrastructure (u$s1, 000) plus the cost per animal (u$s1 per year). At the aggregate level, this program was originally planned for a minimum number of 70,000

Table 7.5 TRAZ.AR on the Probability of Implementing Other Changes

Improvements in	Animal sanitation	Animal identification	Registry	Meat quality	Cattle/ Mear marketing	Management of problems
Treatment	0.452	−0.109	0.749	0.577	0.419	0.415
(Dummy=1 if in Treatment group)	(0.109)***	(0.075)	(0.107)***	(0.106)***	(0.107)***	(0.124)***
Productive activity	YES	YES	YES	YES	YES	YES
Agricultural income	YES	YES	YES	YES	YES	YES
Observations	81	81	81	81	81	81

Source: TRAZ.AR administrative records including SAGPyA statistics and INTA estimates, as well as own survey to farmers.

Notes

1. Robust standard errors in parentheses.

2. * Significant at 10%, ** significant at 5%, *** significant at 1%.

traced animals (around 90 SMEs). However, given the discouraging outlook for beef exports in the first years of the program only half of that amount was traced and 41 SMEs were treated. Therefore, the program would have not been sustainable if other income generating activities were not started. In response to this adverse scenario, TRAZ.AR expanded to other countries (like Nicaragua) and other provinces in Argentina. According to sustainability analysis, TRAZ.AR could operate with fewer personnel to serve 40,000 animals without losses but with no possibility of expansion.

If we take into account the marginal cost per farmer, as the program increased their income per livestock kilogram sold in an average of 10 percent (weighted average for feeders, breeders and complete-cycle farmers, of the present value of the markup of PROGAN firm), the net-benefit of the program was on average an annual 6 percent per dollar invested. The net profits reached 13 percent for the larger enterprises, and for the small enterprises, the net profits were almost 2 percent. This is due to the fact that traceability alone does not allow to export to high-value markets. Other investments were also necessary, in terms of sanitation procedures, pastures improvement, infrastructure, Internet connection, computer, skilled personnel, which are expensive fixed costs for small scale farmers. In terms of marginal price for the future, once these investments are made, all size enterprises would get net gains from spending u$s1 per animal to keep the system.

There are two additional issues that are very interesting to explore: compliance and take-up after the program finished. During the program, there was *full compliance* among the treated farmers: the program took place between 2004 and 2006, period during which 41 farmers decided to take part in the program receiving traceability for free for two years. Almost forty thousand animals were traced in that period. There was complete compliance, which was mainly demand-driven as without traceability (animals' identification and periodically uploading of information), there would not be differential market value for the cattle. Finally, we would like to point out some additional effects related to associability. The formation of the cooperative seems to have been very important to gain social capital. Before the treatment most of the farmers used to sell cattle to the nearest meat-processing plant or to intermediaries, but after TRAZ.AR was implemented the beneficiaries who were associated to PROGAN started to participate in all the links of the meat production chain: primary sector, industrialization, commercialization and distribution to final consumers (either domestic or in external markets).[20]

---

20 For example, the members of the cooperative claim in the surveys that now they "*understand the business*" and "*while in the past they used to sell animals, now they decide where to sell high quality meat*". They also reported that the contact with other farmers produced information spillover that allowed them to improve their production practices.

Regarding the evolution of the cooperative, in 2006, after the program finished 24 farmers continued using the traceability system, 22 of them where the members of the cooperative (53 percent of the initial beneficiaries). This finding suggests that technology adoption might be more likely within a context of a group of adopters (Bandiera and Rasul, 2006; Foster and Rosenzweig, 1995). Another interesting finding is that despite the loss of members, the cooperative does not want to grow in size but prefers doing agreements with other groups of farmers (other similar cooperatives that emerged after the replication of TRAZ.AR in other Argentine provinces: Chaco, Corrientes and Entre Rios[21]). The reason for not expanding the number of members is twofold: first, commercializing together implies a basis of mutual trust about the compliance with the predefined standards of animal sanitation, feeding and welfare[22] not compatible with a large group of farmers; and second, this group wants to keep the decision making within their committee dispensing with a manager.

Finally, although TRAZ.AR program would be profitable, it is interesting to analyze the take-up rate after the free period. In 2006, the beneficiaries could choose to continue having the traceability service for $1 per year per animal or quit. After 2006, 24 farmers continued paying for traceability (60 percent of the initial beneficiaries). We estimate a linear probability model of a dummy equal to one if the farm continued employing the traceability system after 2006 on different observable farm-level covariates. Table 7.6 shows that those farms that developed breeding activities in 2003 (pretreatment) are 45–47 percent less likely to continue using this service, and those enterprises that are relatively small (smaller than average in 2003) are 30 percent less likely to remain under traceability. Breeders did not export directly, so they did not experience higher profits in the beginning. Moreover, those breeders that experienced relatively low efficiency gains, very likely dropped. The same happened to smaller farmers (breeders and feeders) that on average had lower efficiency gains.[23] This last result is consistent with those of De Janvry and Sadoulet (2002) and World Bank (2008) that show that technology adoption depends on firm size.

21 For the production cycle 2010–11 the three cooperatives achieved a portion of the Hilton Quota: the cooperative in Entre Rios 32 tons, in Corrientes 55 tons and in Chaco 41 tons.
22 They had rules that prohibit trading with any farmer that did not comply with the required standards in a sense the formation of this group with its optimal relatively small size could be comparable to the case of the Maghribi Traders (Greif, 1993).
23 In the surveys those leaving the program reported that *"as they do not export directly (breeders) they do not have the need of keeping so many records,"* or *"the cost of the equipment is too high relative to the profits they get."* Some also reported problems to get Internet connection in their areas.

Table 7.6 Probability of Demanding Traceability after the Program

Dep var: Continue using TRAZAR			
(Dummy=1 if user after 2006)			
Breeder in 2013	−0.455		−0.473
(Dummy=1 if user after 2003)	(0.151)***		(0.137)***
Small farm in 2003		−0.269	−0.299
(Dummy=1 if number of animals		(0.154)*	(0.142)**
< average in 2003			
Observations	41	41	41

Source: TRAZ.AR administrative records including SAGPyA statistics and INTA estimates, as well as own survey to farmers.

Notes

1. Robust standard errors in parentheses.

2. * Significant at 10%, ** significant at 5%, *** significant at 1%.

7.6 Conclusions

In this chapter we evaluated the implementation of TRAZ.AR, a traceability system to electronically identify and track the production cycle of cow herds in small/medium rural enterprises (SMEs) in Argentina. The analysis of this case study suggests that overall TRAZAR program had promising results. The initial beneficiaries of this program experienced an increase in livestock of 15 percent and doubled the number of skilled workers. Those participating in the cooperative also received a higher price for their high-quality beef as they complied with strict standards that enabled them to export to the EU among other regions. Treated farmers also reported improvements in efficiency, profits and risk managements.

The effects of TRAZ.AR depended on the farm's characteristics. From the treated group, after the program finished, in 2006, 60 percent of the farmers continued demanding traceability services (90 percent of them belonged to the cooperative). Those more likely to drop out were breeders and small-scale farms. The breeders quitted as they did not perceive any price differential (cannot export directly) and experienced efficiency gains that still were not enough to compensate the cost of the service. The relatively smaller enterprises were more likely to stop demanding traceability because on average the efficiency gains of traceability are positively correlated with the size of the cattle herd. It might have been the case that the smaller ones could not wait until their efficiency gains reduced their costs given other restrictions that they may have had—such as credit constraints. Small feeders were more likely to continue with traceability than small breeders.

TRAZ.AR shows that traceability is a source of product differentiation which receives a price premium in the export market. The trends of the last years in the cattle industry suggest that beef export opportunities will continue to grow for producers in countries which respond to the demand for consistent supplies of safe, quality beef. With continued support for traceability and product verification, improvements in production efficiency and attention to quality, beef exporters will be able to improve their positions in the global marketplace (EIU, 2007). Thus traceability could be an intervention that may boost Latin American agriculture competitiveness and growth.

Programs of this type could also be useful for Latin America and Africa because agricultural productivity growth is a very powerful tool for development, food security and poverty reduction (Byerlee et al., 2009). Agricultural technology can help reduce poverty through direct and indirect effects (de Janvry and Sadoulet, 2002). Direct effects are gains for the adopters while indirect effects are gains derived from adoption by others leading to lower food prices, employment creation and growth linkage effects.

References

Bandiera, O., and I. Rasul (2006). "Social Networks and Technology Adoption in Northern Mozambique." *Economic Journal*, 116(514): 862–902.

Banerjee, A., and E. Duflo (2011). "Poor Economics: A Radical Rethinking of the Way to Fight Global Poverty." Public Affairs.

Blyde, J., and E. Fernández-Arias (2005). "Why Latin America Is Falling Behind?." In: *Sources of Growth in Latin America: What Is Missing?*, edited by J. Blyde, E. Fernández-Arias and R. Manuelli, Ch. 1. Washington, DC: Inter-American Development Bank.

Brambilla, I., S. Galiani and G. Porto (2018). "Argentine Trade Policies in the XX Century: 60 Years of Solitude." *Latin American Economic Review*, 27: 4. https://doi.org/10.1007/s40503-017-0050-9 (accessed September 2019).

Byerlee, D., A. de Janvry and E. Sadoulet (2009). "Agriculture for Development: Toward a New Paradigm." *Annual Review of Resource Economics*, 1(1): 15–31.

De Janvry, A., and E. Sadoulet (2002). "World Poverty and the Role of Agricultural Technology: Direct and Indirect Effects." *Journal of Development Studies*, 38(4): 1–26.

Dickinson, D., and B. DeeVon (2002). "Meat Traceability: Are U.S. Consumers Willing to Pay for It?" *Journal of Agricultural and Resource Economics*, 27(2): 348–64.

The Economist Intelligence Unit-EIU (2008). "Improving the Beef Supply Chain: Ensuring Quality in a Demanding World." *Discussion Paper from EIU*.

European Commission (2005). "Food Supply Chain Dynamics and Quality Certification." *Sustainability in Agriculture, Food and Health Review Paper*. Institute for Prospective Technological Studies.

European Community Regulation (178/January 28, 2002). "General Principles and Requirements of Food Law." https://eur-lex.europa.eu/legal-content/EN/ALL/?uri=CELEX:32002R0178 (accessed September 2019).

Foster A., and M. Rosenzweig (1995). "Learning by Doing and Learning from Others: Human Capital and Technical Change in Agriculture." *Journal of Political Economy*, 103(6): 1176–209.

Fuglie, K., J. MacDonald and E. Ball (2007). *Productivity Growth in U.S. Agriculture*. Economic Brief Number 9, September 2007. USDA.

Galiani, S., D. Heymann and N. Magud (2010). "On the Distributive Effects of Terms of Trade Shocks: The Role of Non-Tradable Goods." IMF Working Paper 10/241. Paper available at: https://www.imf.org/external/pubs/ft/wp/2010/wp10241.pdf (accessed September 2019).

Golan, E., B. Krissoff, F. Kuchler, L. Calvin, K. Nelso and G. Price (2004). "Traceability in the U.S. Food Supply: Economic Theory and Industry Studies." Agricultural Economic Report Number 830. Economic Research Service, U.S. Department of Agriculture.

Greif, A. (1993). "Contract Enforceability and Economic Institutions in Early Trade: the Maghribi Traders' Coalition." *American Economic Review*, 83(3): 525–48.

Hassan, Z., R. Green and D. Hearth (2006). "An Empirical Analysis of the Adoption of Food Safety and Quality Practices in the Canadian Food Processing Industry." In: *Exploring the Frontiers in Applied Economic Analysis: Essays* in Honor of Stanley R. Johnson, edited by M. Holt and J. P. Chavas, 23. Berkeley, CA: BE Press.

Hayes, D., J. Shogren, S. Shin and J. Kliebenstein (1995). "Valuing Food Safety in Experimental Auction Markets." *American Journal of Agricultural Economics*, 77: 40–53.

Murphy, K., Rosen, S. and J. Scheinkman (1994). "Cattle Cycles." *Journal of Political Economy*, 102(3): 468–92.

Souza Monteiro, D., and J. Caswell (2009). "Traceability Adoption at the Farm Level: An Empirical Analysis of the Portuguese Pear Industry." *Food Policy*, 34(1): 94–101.

World Bank (2008). "Agriculture for Development." *World Bank Development Report*. World Bank.

Chapter 8

THE LABOR MARKET RETURN TO ICT SKILLS: A FIELD EXPERIMENT

Florencia Lopez-Boo and Mariana Blanco

8.1 Introduction

The labor market is characterized by search costs, mismatches and asymmetric information. In this context, the use of PCs and the Internet promise to improve and make more efficient worker-firm communications (Autor, 2001; Pissarides, 2000). Internet job search, which involves navigating the web, online job searching, filling forms, writing Word documents and attaching them to an e-mail, is indeed already commonplace.[1] Still, no research examines how Information and Communication Technologies (ICT) skills of workers might play a role in their likelihood of employment.[2] This chapter concentrates on the question of whether people with High ICT skills are more likely to be successful in this new "wired" labor market or not. Specifically, we design an experiment to study whether people with high knowledge of ICT skills (i.e., a line in their resume self-reporting an advanced level of knowledge of various software) are more likely to be contacted after submitting a resume, in the context of two middle-income Latin-American cities.

---

1   Estimates place the number of online job boards at over three thousand, the number of (unique) active resumes online at over 7 million, and the number of job postings (not necessarily unique) at 29 million (Boyle and Koby, 1999; Computer Economics, 2000).
2   Three categories of ICT competencies are usually distinguished in the literature (OECD, 2005): (1) ICT specialists: those who have the ability to develop, operate and maintain ICT systems. Therefore, ICTs constitute the main part of their job. (2) Advanced users: competent users of advanced, and often sector-specific, software tools. Here, ICTs are not the main job but a tool and (3) Basic users: competent users of generic tools (e.g., Word, Excel, Outlook, PowerPoint) needed for the information society, e-government and working life. In this chapter, basic ICT skills are defined as those needed to perform common tasks associated with (almost) any clerical-type of job in the spirit of the third definition.

Our experimental design follows the empirical strategy utilized in the seminal works of Riach and Rich (2002), and Bertrand and Mullainathan (2004) to address the issue of not observing the full set of relevant variables determining individual's labor market productivity. The former study gives an overview of this type of field experiments, while the latter investigates potential discrimination of non-whites (against whites). Since then a host of other studies have been done each focusing on a dimension of discrimination: gender (Booth and Leigh, 2010), immigrants (Carlsson and Rooth, 2007), homosexuality (Ahmed et al., 2011) and beauty (López Bóo, Rossi and Urzúa, 2010). The common element in these studies is that fake applications are send to real vacancies. These fake applications—within a group—are similar in all except one characteristic, which is the one being randomized. This is the characteristic that defines whether or not there is discrimination. The studies find that males, immigrants, homosexuals and plain looking applicants receive fewer callbacks than females, natives, heterosexuals and good-looking applicants. This is evidence that employers discriminate in the first step of the hiring process since all the characteristics associated with productivity are the same by design. In our study, we will not define this as discrimination because our theoretical framework will be one of "digital alphabetization" or basic skills (such as knowing how to read and write or speaking a foreign language) and, therefore, skills, such as ICT, *do* matter for employers. We then interpret our results as the unbiased return to High ICT skills, as we define it in this study (see Section 8.2).

We sent approximately eleven thousand fictitious resumes for real job vacancies in Buenos Aires, Argentina and Bogota, Colombia. We find that people with high knowledge of ICT receive 11–12 percent more responses (callbacks) than people with low knowledge of ICT (i.e., those self-reporting a basic level of PC use, Internet and e-mail). These results are robust to an important set of covariates, including vacancy and employer fixed effects. Interestingly we also show that the effect of ICT skills is de-linked from actually using those skills on the job as the effect is not present when restraining the sample to those ads that did require ICT skills. We also find that effects are quite similar between the two cities once we control for vacancy (i.e., ad) fixed effects.

8.2 The Literature

While numerous studies have documented the effects on labor market outcomes for high-end ICT skills (programmers and other IT specialists), surprisingly little research has been conducted on basic ICT skills, especially in a developing country. The evidence on ICT skills and employment is scant (maybe due to the lack of representative micro-data on the variable of interest, ICT skills). From studies on macro-data and some household surveys evidence is mixed on the sign of the ICT-labor markets relationship. In terms of the wages-ICT relationship, the evidence generally shows a positive correlation, with a premium of around 4–7 percent. However, Atasoy (2011) uses households surveys from Turkey in the late 2000s to show that ICT skills do not have any effect on the probability of being employed once they control for the difference between individual's years of education and average years of education of his age cohort (a variable that aims to capture skill-biased jobs) and the interaction term between ICT skills and the place where the ICT abilities were acquired (at work, at the library or from a book).[3] Walton et al. (2009) found that while ICT skills seems a predictor of employment and higher income in Kazakhstan, the levels of ICT skills required to obtain these jobs are not as high as one may expect in a developed country. Lastly, Borghans and Ter Weel (2003) found no effect of ICT skills on wages using British data, while writing and math skills do have an effect. They, therefore, conclude that knowing how to use a computer cannot be considered a new basic skill.

For Latin-America in particular, the evidence is also scarce. In Argentina the graduates of an ICT training program (Entra21 in Cordoba) held higher quality jobs,[4] while Ruffo, Nahirñak and Brassiolo (2006) use 2005 household surveys to show that lower educated workers benefit more from the use of PCs (the ICT-wage premium is 25 percent for a lower educated, while it is 10 percent for the more educated workers). Moreover, Silvero (2009) finds that a better access to ICTs increases the labor income of the individuals in Paraguay. Unfortunately, none of these studies go beyond establishing correlations. The contribution of this chapter is that we will tackle this issue by adopting the experimental design described in the next section.

8.3 Defining ICT Skills and Experimental Design

The first step of the experimental design is to generate fictitious CVs for real job vacancies published weekly in three top job search web sites in each city. The challenge is to produce a set of realistic and representative resumes

---

3   This last variable aims to capture reverse causality, from employment to acquisition of ICT skills.

4   Chapple (2006) has similar findings in relation of an ICT training program offered by several NGOs in the United States. They found that 76 percent of the interviewed retain their job for at least three years (although they have no control group nor counterfactual) and that, on average, wages of the "intervened" group were 56 percent higher than those that did not participate in the training; with higher returns for the less educated group.

without effectively using resumes that belong to actual jobseekers. To achieve this goal, we created a CV template for each city. The template had to represent the average actual jobseeker for each of the occupational categories that were considered in the study, but we altered them sufficiently to create distinct resumes. Therefore, we begin by performing an additional study of the CVs posted by jobseekers in the Bumeran job search engine for both cities and we created a dataset of CVs corresponding to the main occupational categories as the basis for our artificial resumes.[5] Additionally, one template was created for each of the four occupational categories considered in the study. While the resumes posted in this web site may not be completely representative of the average job seeker, they provide a practical approximation.

We only included the CVs of people seeking employment in the two cities under analysis, Buenos Aires and Bogotá.[6] We also restrict our analysis to two occupational categories: Sales/Commercial and Administrative/Accountancy. Finally, we only consider two educational categories: high school and undergraduate ongoing. Professionals (such as lawyers, doctors, engineers) were left out of the analysis as they perform in a different labor market. Since they are supposed to have at least a medium level of ICT skills, the skills relevant for the job application are other than those of this study such as foreign languages, experience in the field of interest, etc. On the other hand, low skilled workers (less than high school education) are not required to have ICT skills to perform their daily job activities. Therefore, they are also irrelevant for this study.

8.3.1 Signaling information and communication technologies (ICTs) skills

Given the main interest of the study, we defined two variables of interest that were taken into account when putting together the fictitious CVs. The first variable is *ICT skills*, which was set either as *High ICT* skills or *Low ICT* skills. The second variable was *Gender*. These define four demographic cells. The definition of the variable *ICT skills* is the crucial point of our experimental design. For the Low ICT Skills CVs, in the "Computer Skills" section, we selected only Office Tools with *Basic* knowledge (where the options were *Basic*,

---

5   This study was conducted in both cities independently. That is, the Buenos Aires' CV template and database were created using the CVs posted by jobseekers in Buenos Aires and the template and database for Bogotá were developed using the CVs posted by jobseekers in Bogotá.

6   Given that the City of Buenos Aires (Capital Federal) is very well integrated with the suburbs in terms of geography, transport, media, information and so on; both the city and the suburbs were included in the experiment. However, in Bogotá, the suburbs are not as well integrated and this translates to the labor market itself; that is why we only took the City of Bogotá as the unit of interest.

Medium and *Advanced*). In the description window we wrote: Basic Knowledge of PC. On the other hand, for the same section of the High ICT Skills CVs, we stated *Advance* knowledge of Office Tools, while in the description windows for Office Tools we listed: Word, Excel, PowerPoint, Outlook, Internet. Additionally, if the ad required Management Software, Database Software or Operative System we stated *Advance* knowledge in the corresponding category. Moreover, in the description window we listed the specific software that was specific to the occupational category and country.[7]

8.3.2 Our bank of CVs

As indicated above, job vacancies were grouped into two occupational categories: Sales/Commercial and Administration/Accountancy. Two research assistants were assigned responsibility for each specific category. They were in charge of selecting the weekly vacancies, as well as the production, sending and supervision of the CVs sent. For each of these categories, we generate a database of fictitious CVs (half for Administration/Accountancy and half for Sales/Commercial). In producing the required CVs, we intended to comply with the most competitive profile. For each ad, four CVs were chosen from the bank of CVs. In order to comply with the particular profile requested in the ad, features such as education, employment experience, and addresses were adjusted for each CV. Then, the CVs were uploaded in the websites considered in this study.[8] Once uploaded to the website, every CV acquired the same layout. When a candidate applies for a job, the website sends the CV on to the firm on his behalf. Each set of four CVs is constructed so that its qualification levels (human capital) and employment experience are equivalent in order to ensure that the applicants are equally eligible for the job in question.

8.3.3 Ensuring the equivalence of fictitious applicants between cells

In each set of four fictitious CVs sent to each ad, we systematically varied gender and ICT skills level, so that we obtained one male and one female

---

7   For Administration/ Accountancy, in Buenos Aires we listed Tango and BEJERMAN as Management Software and SAP as Database software. In Bogotá, the additional programs were: SIIGO, SAP, NOVASOFT and SISTEMA UNO. For Sales/ Commercial, in Buenos Aires we listed Maria Operative System and Fox and Fridman in Database software. In the case of Bogotá, none of the ads in this occupational category required additional software, so we did not list any.

8   In Argentina, we used zonajobs.com.ar, empleosclarin.com.ar and bumeran.com.ar. In Bogotá the websites used were: elempleo.com, zonajobs.com.co and bumeran.com.co.

candidate for each of the possible ICT skill level. All other categories in the CV are assigned randomly, in the following way:

1. Age: For each occupational category, the age of the applicants was set between 22 and 30 years of age in the case of Argentina and between 20 and 35 in Bogotá. These intervals were chosen following the mean age and standard deviation of the data set of real CVs surveyed for each city.

2. ID Number: each fictitious applicant had a different ID number according to his age (and gender, in the case of Bogotá). In Argentina every ID number belongs to a real person, in order not to compromise anyone, eight numbers were obtained under permission of the people that owned them. As we had the availability of only eight ID numbers corresponding to individuals of 22, 23, 26 and 27 years old, we used real CVs from people of those ages to generate the fictitious CVs. These numbers were sufficient to create all the CVs needed without repeating any ID number. For Bogotá, ID numbers are assigned according to the region that issues the ID. Therefore, there is no straightforward link between the age and the ID number of a person. There is, however, a link between the ID number and the gender of the person. We did take care of that by assigning ID numbers that correspond to women to a fictitious female candidate and those that correspond to men to a fictitious male candidate. Overall 94 people agreed to sign a consent form allowing us to use their ID numbers.

3. Names and Surnames: We used name frequency data by age range calculated from the actual CVs uploaded at the Bumeran website for the corresponding city. The database for Buenos Aires consisted of 200 CVs while for Bogotá we had 280 CVs uploaded by real applicants aged between 17 and 32 that were looking for a job in the corresponding city. We calculated the most frequent names that appeared for man and woman. In the case of Bogotá we used the same procedure to generate the surnames as well. For Argentina, we used the most common surnames in the country according to an article published in an Argentinean newspaper and from World Names Profiler.[9] Once we selected the most common/neutral names and surnames, they were randomly matched in order to avoid the use of a name belonging to a real person.

4. E-mails: For each fictitious combination of name and surname we generated one e-mail address, either at hotmail.com, gmail.com or yahoo.com.

---

9 Herrera, Silvana "El origen y la historia de los apellidos en Argentina," *Diario Perfil*, 2008.

5. Neighborhoods: In order to facilitate the fieldwork, the study is concentrated in the biggest and most populated metropolitan urban region in Argentina, Buenos Aires and also the most populated in Colombia, Bogotá. Buenos Aires is the capital, and largest city of Argentina, currently the second largest metropolitan area in South America, after São Paulo. Buenos Aires is divided in four regions: North GBA, South GBA, West GBA and Capital Federal. Capital Federal is again divided in 15 neighborhoods (Centros de Gestiones Personales Comunales, CGPC) and each region of GBA is also divided into several districts. We constructed fictitious residential areas based on the neighborhoods and districts of Buenos Aires. The randomized selection of the residential areas was done in the following way: for example, for a job vacancy located in Capital Federal, we choose at random four different neighborhoods, each corresponding to one of the four different resumes. The process of randomization was carried out without replacement. Bogotá is the capital city of Colombia. According to the 2009 census, Bogotá has 8,566,926 inhabitants in its metropolitan area (47.5 percent of the population are male and 52.5 percent women), while the city houses about 7,362,520. The neighborhoods of Bogotá are categorized in six different strata, which are positively and highly correlated with the economic level of the population living there, being one the lowest and six the highest. Based on the information obtained in the Bogotá CVs' survey, we overall used 80 real addresses: for strata one, two, five and six we used 10 real addresses for each of them, and 20 for strata three and four.

6. Marital Status: Applicants in both categories aged between 22 and 23 were assigned the marital status *Single*, while the marital status of applicants aged between 26 and 27 was randomly selected between *Single* and *Married* because in Argentina the individuals of these ages could be married or single. In Colombia is not that unusual to get marry at a young age, therefore, the marital status of all fictitious applicants was randomized.

7. Education: Following previous literature from Latin-America (Galiani and Sanguinetti, 2003; among others) we considered semi-skilled individuals with complete high school and skilled individuals with undergraduate degree ongoing. For all the undergraduate applicants we listed *Universidad de Buenos Aires* (UBA) as the institutional education because it is the most representative of the Argentinean population, and various universities from Colombia as a whole, being the source again Bumeran.[10]

---

10 According to the last Argentine Student Census (October 2008), *Universidad de Buenos Aires* (UBA) is the biggest argentine university, with 253,260 undergraduate students.

On the other hand, the selection of the high schools for the semi-skilled individuals as for the skilled ones was made according to the applicant's neighborhood of residence. A bank of public high schools was constructed for this purpose. Using the official website of Capital Federal and the one of the Ministry of Education, we randomly selected public schools for each of the 15 CGPC of Capital Federal and also for each of the districts of GBA. In Bogotá, high school quality is assessed yearly by the Colombian Institute to Promote Higher Education (ICFES, from the Spanish acronym Instituto Colombiano de Fomento a la Educación Superior), the high school dataset used for the randomization process was built using the ICFES records for schools in Bogotá and considered public and private schools of different quality.[11]

8. Employment Experience: The employment experience of the applicants is equivalent within occupational categories but different between categories. We constructed a bank of employment experience for each occupational category from our CV survey. The descriptions were sufficiently altered to create distinct sets that would not be associated with real applicants, but the original overall content was maintained. Using the database of real CVs we found that the undergraduate applicants, who spend more time in the educational system, have fewer years of employment experience; meanwhile, the high school graduates have a longer track record in the labor market. Thus, the number of previous jobs was set to two for undergraduate applicants and to four for the high school graduates. Considering this, for each set of CVs we choose at random job experiences from the banks settled.

9. Telephone Number: Each CV of the set of four sent out to a single ad had a unique cell phone number. Applicants in each gender/ICT skills cell were allocated the same phone number. This guaranteed that we could precisely track employer callbacks in each of these cells and ensured that recruiters did not encounter repeated phone numbers.

10. Pay Expectations: The pay expectations, which generally had to be included in job applications, were also based on the information gathered on our CVs survey. We used the average pay level required for each category. So, each set of four CVs sent for a vacancy stated the same expected pay. For Bogotá this information was not required, therefore we selected the neutral option given by the job search engine, which was the "to be negotiated" category.

11 All high school students that are about to graduate have to take the same exam, then the school receives a mark according to its students' performance. In the assessment each school receives an overall grade, which can be either: Very Inferior, Inferior, Low, Medium, High, Superior, Very Superior.

11. Languages: Following the results of our CVs survey, in Buenos Aires we selected advanced English knowledge for the undergraduate applicants and basic knowledge of English for the remaining ones for both occupational categories. For Bogotá we randomly varied the level of English among intermediate, basic and none, which were the levels identified in the survey.

12. References: Giving a reference in each CV implies the creation of other fictitious identities (at least e-mail addresses and telephone numbers for those referenced). Since none of the ads asked for this and given that almost none of the CV available at bumeran.com included this feature, we left this information blank in our fictitious CVs.

This procedure left us with a bank of names, surnames, neighborhoods and high schools that we could assign to the template resumes when responding to the employment ads.

8.3.4 Responding to ads

We eliminated any ad where applicants were asked to call or appear in person or where the gender of the applicant is markedly specified. For each ad, we used the bank of resumes to sample four resumes (two High ICT skills and two Low ICT skills) that fitted the job description and requirements as closely as possible. In some cases, we slightly altered the resumes to improve the quality of the match, such as by adding the knowledge of a specific software or experience in a particular field. One of the men and one of the women resumes generated were then drawn at random to receive High ICT skills, the other women and men resumes received Low ICT skills.

8.4 Econometric Model and Results

We are interested in estimating the causal effect of having competency on ICT (i.e., high level of skills) on callback rates. It is worth noting that by callback we mean being contacted by a potential employer, either by phone or e-mail. Formally, we estimate the following equation:

$$Callback_i = \alpha + \beta ICTskills_i + \gamma X_i + \varepsilon_i \tag{Eq. 8.1}$$

where i indexes resumes; Callback is a dummy variable that takes the value of one when the fictitious applicant is contacted (she/he receives a callback) and zero otherwise; ICT is a dummy variable that takes the value of one for resumes that state high level of ICT skills applicants and zero otherwise (i.e., when level of ICT skills is basic use of PC, Internet and e-mail); X is the set of control variables, such as age, gender, marital status, education, dummies for residential area and occupational category, and it includes whether or not ICT was required by the ad; and ε_i is an error term. The main parameter of interest is β. Given the random assignment of the ICT skills described in the experimental design, Equation (8.1) can be estimated straightforwardly by Ordinary Least Squares.[12]

Table 8.1 presents the descriptive statistics of our sample. The average response rate (which we refer to as callback) of the experiment was 14 percent. The rate of response in Argentina is 19 percent, while the one in Colombia is 12 percent.[13] Overall, 22 percent of the ads or vacancies considered in the experiment required some kind of ICT skill in their listing; and 3 percent of those ads were highlighted in the website. With respect to education, we can see that 66 percent of the applicants are still pursuing undergraduate studies, while the rest have completed high school.[14]

Table 8.2 reports the difference in the means of the variables that were reported in the CVs. In this Table we compare the Low ICT CVs with the High ICT ones and also the CVs that correspond to a male candidate with the ones that correspond to women. There is only one characteristic that is not balanced in each comparison: the average Low ICT candidate is older than the High ICT one, the difference is small, though significant; and the average male candidate is more likely to be married than the average female candidate. Our sample is balanced across all other characteristics. Nevertheless, in the regressions reported we control for these characteristics.

Table 8.3 presents the number of resumes sent by occupational category and country in each experimental cell. This table shows that the number of resumes sent was approximately the same in all the demographic cells. Adding

12 A previous version of this chapter also used probit models and results were very similar (Lopez Boo and Blanco, 2010).

13 It is worth noting that we only had 154 responses by e-mail in Argentina and 180 in Colombia, which is not a big enough sample to run our specification separately for the cases contacted by phone and the ones contacted by e-mail. That is why we use the response rate without distinguishing how the candidate was contacted.

14 Moreover, for both countries the distribution of the residential areas is concentrated in Capital Federal (83.9 percent of the ads corresponds to this geographical area) and Bogotá (100 percent). Note that the resumes were also sent to the GBA area, 9 percent to North GBA, 3.4 percent to South GBA and 3.2 percent to West GBA. The proportion of resumes sent to the GBA area is much lower compared to Capital Federal, but this is due to the fact that vacancies for these areas are much less than those of Capital Federal (9.22 percent of the vacancies correspond to North GBA, 1.19 percent to South GBA and 3.42 percent to West GBA).

Table 8.1 Descriptive Statistics

Variable	Pool sample		Argentina		Colombia	
	Mean	**Std. Dev.**	**Mean**	**Std. Dev.**	**Mean**	**Std. Dev.**
Callback	0.14	0.35	0.19	0.39	0.12	0.32
High ICT	0.50	0.50	0.50	0.50	0.50	0.50
Argentina	0.31	0.46	—	—	—	—
Adm./Account	0.38	0.49	0.55	0.50	0.31	0.46
Male	0.50	0.50	0.50	0.50	0.50	0.50
Married	0.34	0.47	0.27	0.45	0.37	0.48
Age	25.00	3.78	24.82	2.04	25.07	4.33
Undergraduate ongoing (baseline = high school)	0.66	0.47	0.57	0.49	0.70	0.46
ICT required	0.22	0.41	0.26	0.44	0.20	0.40
Highlightened ad	0.03	0.16	0.09	0.29	0.00	0.00
Webpage	1.25	0.75	2.00	0.00	0.92	0.68
Buenos Aires Capital Federeal	—	—	0.84	0.37	—	—
GBA Norte	—	—	0.09	0.29	—	—
GBA Oeste	—	—	0.04	0.19	—	—
GBA Sur	—	—	0.03	0.18	—	—
Strata 1	—	—	—	—	0.16	0.37
Strata 2	—	—	—	—	0.20	0.40
Strata 3	—	—	—	—	0.19	0.39
Strata 4	—	—	—	—	0.30	0.46
Strata 5	—	—	—	—	0.08	0.27
Strata 6	—	—	—	—	0.06	0.23
Number of observation	7903		2412		5491	

Source: Authors' calculations.

up Buenos Aires and Bogota, we sent around one thousand and seven hundred resumes in each demographic sell of Sales/Commercial occupational category and 1,050 resumes in each demographic cell of Administration/ Accountancy occupational category.

Table 8.4 shows the number of callbacks by occupational category, gender and country.[15] Callbacks in Colombia are higher for the Sales category, while in Argentina callbacks are similar across occupation categories. Also, on average, females are contacted more often than males in both categories, but

---

15 It is important to note that the average callback rate by week was maintained relatively stable during all the experiment.

Table 8.2 Check for Sample Balancing

	ICT			Gender		
	Low ICT	High ICT	Difference	Female	Male	Difference
Callback	0.133	0.144	-0.011	0.145	0.131	0.014
	(0.005)	(0.005)	(0.007)	(0.005)	(0.005)	(0.007)
High ICT	—	—	—	0.500	0.499	0.001
				(0.005)	(0.005)	(0.007)
Argentina	0.305	0.306	-0.001	0.304	0.307	-0.003
	(0.007)	(0.007)	(0.010)	(0.007)	(0.007)	(0.010)
Adm./Account	0.382	0.380	0.002	0.380	0.382	-0.001
	(0.007)	(0.007)	(0.010)	(0.007)	(0.007)	(0.010)
Male	0.498	0.497	0.001	—	—	—
	(0.007)	(0.007)	(0.011)			
Married	0.339	0.338	0.001	0.303	0.374	-0.072
	(0.007)	(0.007)	(0.010)	(0.007)	(0.007)	(0.010)
Age	25.130	24.865	0.265	25.016	24.979	0.036
	(0.059)	(0.060)	(0.085)	(0.061)	(0.059)	(0.085)
Undergraduate ongoing (baseline = high school)	0.659	0.663	-0.004	0.658	0.664	-0.005
ICT required	0.221	0.221	0.001	0.221	0.220	0.001
	(0.006)	(0.006)	(0.009)	(0.006)	(0.006)	(0.009)
Highlightened ad	0.028	0.028	0.000	0.028	0.028	0.000
	(0.002)	(0.002)	(0.003)	(0.002)	(0.002)	(0.003)
Webpage	1.252	1.254	-0.002	1.252	1.254	-0.002
	(0.011)	(0.012)	(0.003)	(0.011)	(0.012)	(0.016)
Number of observations	3958	3945	13	3969	3934	35

Source: Authors' calculations.

Table 8.3 Number of CVs Sent by Country, Occupational Category, Gender and ICT Skills Level

	Sales/commercial		Adm/account	
	Colombia	Argentina	Colombia	Argentina
Female				
Low ICT	1,405	300	680	372
High ICT	1,404	300	673	372
Male				
Low ICT	1,402	300	674	372
High ICT	1,397	300	669	372

Source: Authors' calculations.

Table 8.4 Number of Callbacks by Country, Occupational Category, Gender and ICT Skills

	Sales/commercial		Adm/account	
	Colombia	Argentina	Colombia	Argentina
Female				
No callback	1,627	448	802	515
Callback	284	100	50	143
Male				
No callback	1,631	449	796	542
Callback	254	99	47	116

Source: Authors' calculations.

in Colombia (Administrative/Accountancy) and in Argentina (Sales category) this is not the case.

Table 8.5 shows the main results of OLS regressions. Huber–White standard errors are reported in parentheses to account for heteroskedasticity and are clustered at the employer-level in all specifications.[16] The regression reported in the first column of this table only includes the ICT skills dummy, while the second shows the specifications with all the control variables (including area of residence, not reported in the table) and the third column adds vacancy fixed effects to check whether after controlling for all the unobserved vacancy-specific requirement, ICT skills matter within job categories. It is worth noting that the area of residence differs in each city. As mentioned in Section 8.2,

16 Clustering at the vacancy or regional level gives similar results, which are available upon request.

Table 8.5 OLS Regression Results, Pooled Sample

Variables	(1)	(2)	(3)
	Callback	**Callback**	**Callback**
High ICT	0.011*	0.036***	0.026**
	(0.003)	(0.012)	(0.011)
Male		−0.009	−0.013
		(0.008)	(0.009)
High ICT* Male		−0.013	−0.002
		(0.010)	(0.010)
Undergraduate ongoing		−0.005	−0.005
(baseline = high school)		(0.015)	(0.015)
High ICT* Undergr.		−0.031**	−0.024*
		(0.015)	(0.013)
Age		−0.009***	−0.002*
		(0.002)	(0.001)
Argentina		−0.117**	0.027
		(0.048)	(0.087)
Adm/Account		−0.034**	−0.051
		(0.016)	(0.046)
Married		−0.018*	−0.005
		(0.010)	(0.008)
ICT required		0.006	−0.92*
		(0.015)	(0.051)
Highlightened ad		0.067	0.060**
		(0.053)	(0.027)
Webpage		0.039***	0.060**
		(0.011)	(0.027)
Constant	0.133***	0.313***	0.073
	(0.019)	(0.056)	(0.062)
Controls	N	Y	Y
Vacancy FE	N	N	Y
Observations	7903	7903	7903
R-squared	0.000	0.041	0.428

Source: Authors' calculations.

Notes

1. Controls: Area of residence.
2. Robust standard errors in parentheses.
3. Significance at *** p<0.01, ** p<0.05, * p<0.1.

Bogotá's neighborhoods are classified in six different strata that are correlated with income. In this sense, Bogotá differs from Buenos Aires, where socio-economic status is correlated with the geographical location of the neighborhood. For the Pooled sample regressions, we control for area of living using geographical location in both cities. But for the country-specific regressions we use geographical location for the case of Argentina and strata for Bogotá. Additionally, in all the regressions we include the interaction between gender and High ICT skill to estimate the differential impact of reporting high ITC skills by gender. We are also interested in learning whether having High ICT skills impacts differently according to the years of education, so we also include the interaction between High ICT skills and Undergraduate ongoing.

In all specifications the coefficient of the variable of interest (ICT skills) is statistically significant and very stable in magnitude. The probability of being contacted for an interview is about 1.2 percentage point higher for those who have High ICT skills, or 11 percent higher chances of receiving a call-back. Among the candidates with High ICT skills, male are not contacted significantly more often than women but being an undergraduate students seems to be a handicap, since the interaction between High ICT skills and undergraduate ongoing is negative and significant. Results also suggest that age, marital status, webpage visited and occupational category are statistically significant and with the expected sign. Older applicants are less likely of being contacted for a job interview compared to younger applicants; married applicants are also less likely to be contacted, as well as candidates applying for an Administration and Accountancy job. These last two effects are not robust to the introduction of vacancy fixed effects.

It is interesting to note that the fact that ICT skills were required by the ad is not significant in explaining the callback rate. This suggests that having ICT skills in the resume is relevant even when the ad does not specifically require it. Results shown in column 3 suggest that even when controlling for the unobserved vacancy effects by adding a dummy for each vacancy name, the ICT effect remains unchanged and explanatory power of the regression increases substantially.

In the experiment there are 16 "cells" stratified according to country, occupation, gender and ICT skills. In the analysis in Table 8.5 all these groups are combined. However, as seen in the descriptive statistics, the callback rate in Argentina was 19 percent while in Colombia it was only 12 percent. This suggests that the labor market in these countries differ substantially. Moreover, while there are many similarities between the designs of the two audit studies, there are also some few differences that make hard to compare the results from one city and the other. Therefore, we analyze each city separately. Table 8.6 reports results by country for the whole sample and also restricting the analysis to the ads that explicitly required ICT knowledge. For the case of Argentina, for vacancies where ICT knowledge is not explicitly required, we can only conclude that female candidates are contacted more often than male. Being an undergraduate student decreases the likelihood of contact from an employer,

Table 8.6 OLS Regression Results for Receiving Callback, by Country and ICT Required

Variable	Full sample				ICT required			
	Argentina		Colombia		Argentina		Colombia	
High ICT	−0.005	−0.008	0.023	0.023	−0.011	−0.002	0.064**	0.049
	(0.014)	(0.015)	(0.014)	(0.014)	(0.045)	(0.048)	(0.027)	(0.037)
Male	−0.28**	−0.28*	−0.006	−0.008	−0.043	−0.044	0.004	0.003
	(0.015)	(0.015)	(0.010)	(0.011)	(0.033)	(0.035)	(0.019)	(0.022)
High ICT*Male	0.011	0.011	−0.017	−0.008	0.011	0.012	−0.040*	−0.028
	(0.014)	(0.015)	(0.012)	(0.013)	(0.033)	(0.036)	(0.023)	(0.024)
Undergraduate ongoing (baseline = high school)	−0.092*	−0.076	−0.005	0.011	−0.263**	−0.080	0.008	−0.014
	(0.055)	(0.050)	(0.013)	(0.010)	(0.111)	(0.154)	(0.029)	(0.027)
High ICT*Undergr.	0.028	0.028	−0.014	−0.015	0.023	0.012	−0.029	−0.016
	(0.017)	(0.018)	(0.012)	(0.011)	(0.044)	(0.047)	(0.021)	(0.021)
Constant	0.766***	0.114	0.247***	0.118**	1.007**	−1.325***	0.330***	0.102
	(0.184)	(0.289)	(0.058)	(0.052)	(0.443)	(0.393)	(0.117)	(0.097)
Controls	Y	Y	Y	Y	Y	Y	Y	Y
Vacancy FE	N	Y	N	Y	N	Y	N	Y
Observations	2,412	2,412	5,371	5,371	636	636	1,108	1,108
R-squared	0.044	0.457	0.029	0.422	0.055	0.573	0.056	0.497

Source: Authors' calculations.

Notes

1. Controls: Age, occupational category, marital status, ICT required, webpage, strata for Colombia and area of residence for Argentina.
2. Robust standard errors in parentheses.
3. Significance at *** p<0.01, ** p<0.05, * p<0.1.

though this effect is not significant when we introduce vacancy fixed effects. For the whole sample in Bogotá, none of the variables of interest explain the likelihood of being contacted by an employer. However, when we restrict the analysis to the ads that explicitly required ICT knowledge, reporting High ICT skills significantly increases the callback rate. Additionally, the male candidates with High ICT skills are contacted less often. However, both of these effects are not robust to the introduction of vacancy fixed effects. For the Argentinean case, when ICT is required, the only effect that remains is that the undergraduate students are contacted less, though it is not robust to the introduction of vacancy fixed effects.

Table 8.7 reports regression by country and occupation category. Results suggest that ICT knowledge has no differential impact between the occupational categories included in our experiment. Results are very similar to the previous analysis.

Results shown above should not be surprising as the High ICT group of applicants has more human capital to offer. They may have invested more in themselves or have a higher ability, and, therefore, that pays off in terms of invitations to interviews. It is already a currently accepted assertion is that ICT skills are becoming a new basic skill as literacy and numeracy are and our chapter seems to be in-line with this assertion. We cannot compare the magnitude of the effects with those of the returns to, for instance, speaking English as a foreign language as no study before has used an experimental approach to assess the returns to particularly skills as we do here.[17] However, looking at our own dataset, we can say that this effect compares to one extra year of experience in the labor market.

Our contribution is twofold: the first is methodological, as we can estimate the causal relation between ICT skills and the likelihood of callbacks without biases. Second, and given the design, we can somehow suggest what the origin of the differential effect from High and Low ICT knowledge is, given that when ICT is required the coefficient is not significant. This is, we are able to suggest that firms looking to fill vacancies will pay special attention to ICT skills *regardless* of the fact that those skills are actually being used on the job. However, when we analyze each country separately and use a more accurate measure of socioeconomic status for the case of Bogotá, most of our results do not hold. A possible explanation for this is that our sample does not have enough power to detect small effects, thus, when we

---

17 Azam (2010), for instance, have found that knowing English meant 34 percent higher wages for men and 22 percent higher wages for women in India, but this is based on correlations from wage equations.

Table 8.7 OLS Regression Results for Receiving Callback, by Country and Occupational Category

Variable	Administrative/accountancy				Commercial/sales			
	Argentina		Colombia		Argentina		Colombia	
High ICT	0.234	−0.255	0.014	0.023	−0.008	−0.015	0.021	−0.013
	(0.178)	(0.194)	(0.032)	(0.032)	(0.016)	(0.017)	(0.029)	(0.026)
Male	−0.039**	−0.040*	−0.037	−0.039	−0.010	−0.014	0.012	0.009
	(0.019)	(0.021)	(0.037)	(0.036)	(0.021)	(0.023)	(0.015)	(0.013)
High ICT*Male	−0.002	0.000	−0.025	−0.007	0.017	0.025	−0.018	−0.011
	(0.021)	(0.022)	(0.039)	(0.039)	(0.021)	(0.023)	(0.020)	(0.020)
Undergraduate ongoing (baseline = high school)	−0.156*	−0.093	−0.015	0.010	−0.072	−0.022	−0.008	−0.009
	(0.085)	(0.201)	(0.021)	(0.020)	(0.068)	(0.068)	(0.012)	(0.014)
High ICT*Undergr.	−0.203	−0.227	0.007	−0.020	−0.009	−0.013	−0.015	0.012
	(0.181)	(0.198)	(0.024)	(0.023)	(0.030)	(0.034)	(0.021)	(0.016)
Constant	0.410*	0.020	0.573***	0.313**	1.281***	0.536	0.076	0.030
	(0.227)	(0.417)	(0.146)	(0.139)	(0.279)	(0.390)	(0.059)	(0.109)
Controls	Y	Y	Y	Y	Y	Y	Y	Y
Vacancy FE	N	Y	N	Y	N	Y	N	Y
Observations	1,316	1,316	1,437	1,437	1,096	1,096	1,399	1,399
R-squared	0.043	0.483	0.075	0.539	0.060	0.433	0.023	0.473

Source: Authors' calculations.

Notes

1. Controls: Age, occupational category, marital status, ICT required, webpage, strata for Colombia and area of residence for Argentina.
2. Robust standard errors in parentheses.
3. Significance at *** p<0.01, ** p<0.05, * p<0.1.

attempt to draw conclusions for each country separately, we do not observe significant results.

8.5 Conclusion

This chapter contributes to the literature on labor markets in a developing country, particularly in the relationship between ICT skills and hiring practices. We use an experimental approach to identify for the first time the effect of High ICT skills on the likelihood of being called for a job interview in two Latin-American cities. Our results suggests that an individual stating a High level of ICT skills in his resume can increase the probability of receiving a callback by around 12 percent. We are also able to suggest that firms will pay special attention to ICT skills *regardless* of the fact that those skills are actually being used on the job, indicating some signaling effect of the ICT skills. Of course, one important limitation of our results is that we are only analyzing one step in the complex process behind a hiring decision, namely being contacted for an interview. Future research should try to identify the causal effect between ICT and wages as well as compare this effect with those of other basic skills such as English, writing and reading.

References

Acemoglu, D. (1999). "Patterns of Skill Premia." *NBER Working Paper 7018*.

Ahmed, A., L. Andersson and M. Hammarstedt (2011). "Are Homosexuals Discriminated Against in the Hiring Process?" *IFAU Working Paper 21*.

Atasoy, H. (2011). *ICT Use and Labor: Firm-Level Evidence from Turkey*. Working Papers 11–23, NET Institute.

Autor, D. H. (2001). "Wiring the Labor Market." *Journal of Economic Perspectives*, 15(1): 25–40.

Autor, D. H., F. Levy and R. J. Murnane (2003). "The Skill Content of Recent Technological Change: An Empirical Exploration." *Quarterly Journal of Economics*, 118(4): 1279–334.

Azam, M. (2010). "India's Increasing Skill Premium: Role of Demand and Supply." *BE Journal of Economic Analysis & Policy*, 10(1).

Bertrand, M., and S. Mullainathan (2004). Are Emily and Greg More Employable than Lakisha and Jamal? A Field Experiment on Labor Market Discrimination." *American Economic Review* 94(4): 991–1013.

Booth, A., and A. Leigh (2010). "Do Employers Discriminate by Gender? A Field Experiment in Female-Dominated Occupations." *Economic Letters*, 107: 236–38.

Borghans, L., and B. Ter Weel (2003). *Are Computer Skills the New Basic Skills? The Return to Computer, Writing and Math Skills in Britain*. Discussion Paper Series 751. Institute for the Study of Labor.

Boyle, H. P. Jr., A. S. Lynn and B. Koby (1999). E-Cruiting: From Job Boards to MetaMarkets. Thomas Wiesel Partners (May).

Bravo, D., C. Sanhueza and S. Urzua (2008). "Estudio experimental de discriminación de mercado de trabajo: Sexo, clase social y vecindario en chile." *Research Network Working Paper #R-541*. Inter-American Development Bank.

Carlson, M., and D. Rooth (2007). "Evidence of Ethnic Discrimination in the Swedish Labor Market Using Experimental Data." *Labour Economics*, 14: 716–29.

Cecchini, S. (2005). *Oportunidades digitales, equidad y pobreza en América Latina: ¿Qué podemos aprender de la evidencia empírica?*. CEPAL, Serie Estudios Estadísticos y Prospectivos.

Chapple, K. (2006). *Moving beyond the Divide: Workforce Development and Upward Mobility in Information Technology*. PolicyLink and the institute of Urban and Regional Development (IURD). https://www.policylink.org/sites/default/files/MOVINGBEYONDTHE DIVIDE_FINAL.PDF (accessed September 30, 2019).

Computer Economics (2000). "Resume Renaissance: Projected Number of Resumes from 2000 to 2003." *Internet Marketing & Technology*, 6(7): 101–16.

Galiani, S., and P. Sanguinetti (2003). "The Impact of Trade Liberalization on Wage Inequality: Evidence from Argentina." *Journal of Development Economics*, 72(2): 497–513.

Herrera, S. (2008). "El Origen y la Historia de los Apellidos en Argentina." *Diario Perfil*. Buenos Aires.

Katz, L., and A. Krueger (1999). *The High-Pressure US Labor Market of the 1990s*. Working Paper 795. Industrial Relations Section, Princeton University, Department of Economics.

Kremer, M., and E. S. Maskin (1996). *Wage Inequality and Segregation by Skill*. Working Paper 5718. Massachusetts Institute of Technology, Department of Economics.

Lopez-Bassols, V. (2002). "ICT Skills and Employment." *OECD Science, Technology and Industry Working Papers 2002/10*. OECD, Directorate for Science, Technology and Industry.

López Bóo, F., and M. Blanco (2010). "ICT Skills and Employment: A Randomized Experiment." *IZA Discussion Papers No. 5336*.

López Bóo, F., M. Rossi and S. Urzua (2013). "The Labor Market Return to an Attractive Face: Evidence from a Field Experiment." *Economic Letters*, 118(1): 170–72.

López Bóo, F., and I. Trako (2010). "Labor Market Discrimination Based on Gender and the Place of Residence: A Randomized Experiment in Argentina." Available at SSRN: https:// ssrn.com/abstract=1784985 or http://dx.doi.org/10.2139/ssrn.1784985.

OECD (2005). "New Perspectives on ICT Skills and Employment." *OECD Digital Economy Papers (96)*, OECD, Directorate for Science, Technology and Industry.

Pissarides, C. A. (2000). Equilibrium Unemployment Theory. Second Edition. Cambridge, MA: MIT Press.

Riach, P. A., and J. Rich (2002). "Field Experiments of Discrimination in the Market Place." *Economic Journal*, 112(483): 480–518.

Ruffo, H, P. Nahirñak and P. Brassiolo (2006). Uso y adopción de tecnología informática en el mercado laboral de Argentina. Unpublished manuscript presented at AAEP annual meeting.

Silvero, Jorge (2009). "El impacto de las TICs en el ingreso laboral de las personas: El caso de Paraguay." Available at: http://www.jorgesilvero.com/ (accessed July 10, 2010).

Walton, R., C. Putnam, E. Johnson and B. Kolko (2009). "Skills Are Not Binary: Nuances in the Relationship between ICT Skills and Employability." *Information Technologies and International Development*, 5(2): 1–18.

Chapter 9

SOAP OPERAS FOR FEMALE MICRO ENTREPRENEUR TRAINING

Eduardo Nakasone and Máximo Torero

9.1 Introduction

There is an increasing interest in understanding the role of micro enterprises in developing countries. First, they constitute the vast majority of firms in developing countries. For example, Li and Rama (2012) find that this group comprises 61 percent of firms in Chile; 83 percent in Turkey; 95 percent in South Africa; 85 percent in India and 84 percent in Pakistan. While certainly some of them will disappear, some others may transition into larger companies and will provide the foundation for a modern private sector. Second, they are also the most important source of employment: 72 percent of jobs are created in micro enterprises in developing countries.[1] Third, they have relatively low productivity levels, and this is especially concerning given their large share of employment. In this line, Angelelli, Moudry and Llisterri (2006) calculate that, even though 77 percent of total employment is generated by micro and small enterprises in Latin America, they only contribute to 30–60 percent of GDP.

The economic literature provides a long list of potential culprits for low levels of productivity of micro enterprises. A considerable proportion of

---

[1] There are some other calculations of the share of jobs in micro enterprises in developing countries (e.g., see Ayyagari, Demirguc-Kunt and Maksimovic (2011)). However, most of these estimates are based on either business surveys (which exclude usually exclude firms in the informal sector) or are calculated for a single sector (e.g., manufacturing). We construct the average of the share of employment in micro enterprises for a sample of developing countries in the World Development Report 2013. (See WRD's Online Appendix.) The World Bank's (2012) estimates are based on household surveys and, therefore, do include the informal sector. We estimate the average share of employment in micro enterprises (weighted by the size of their labor force) for 27 developing countries that collected household surveys *c.* 2005 or 2010.

previous studies have focused on the challenges that financial constraints can impose on small businesses: if firms are unable to borrow, they would be unable to finance optimal levels of capital (e.g., Banerjee, Duflo, Glennerster and Kinnan, 2013; de Mel, McKenzie and Woodruff, 2008; Evans and Jovanovic, 1989; Fafchamps, McKenzie, Quinn and Woodruff, 2014). Restuccia and Rogerson (2008) argue that policies that create other distortions in the input or output markets can lead to misallocation of resources and reductions in productivity. Low levels of human capital (at least, measured through formal schooling) has been another candidate to explain low levels of productivity in small firms in developing countries. De Soto (1989) argues that the regulatory framework in developing countries creates an unnecessary burden for businesses in developing countries and promote informality. More recently, another potentially constraining factor in micro enterprise development has gained attention: managerial capital (Bruhn, Karlan and Schoar, 2010). For example, Bloom and Reenen (2010) argue that persistent differences in firm productivity can be explained by management practices. The authors surveyed around six thousand firms in 17 countries and measure their practices in three broad areas: monitoring (e.g., production process tracking), targets (e.g., goal setting) and incentives (e.g., promotion workers with high performance). Their findings suggest that there is considerable variation in firms' practices within and between countries, and that better management is associated with stronger performance (in terms of size, productivity and survival). The idea that managerial capital can spur firms' growth has powerful policy implications: even within their capital limitations or adverse regulatory environment, micro enterprises can improve if they put their inputs to a better use. Not surprisingly, this notion has promoted a large number of business training programs in developing countries (Cho and Honorati, 2013).

In this chapter, we assess the impact of a large-scale program that provided short-term training to female micro entrepreneurs in Peru. The project "Strengthening Women Entrepreneur-ship in Peru (SWEP)" was implemented by the Inter-American Development Bank's (IADB) Multilateral Investment Fund (MIF), who partnered with APRENDA (a local institution who provides business training for micro entrepreneurs) and the Thunderbird School of Global Management (a US-based business school). The general objective of the project was to improve the contribution of women-headed MSEs to family incomes and the economy of Peru, by providing assistance aimed at broadening access to business training.

Since its deployment in 2010, SWEP has provided business training to one hundred thousand women in Peru. Training sessions were free for participants, short (one afternoon) and provided only once. They relied on a combination of media, games, practical exercises and take-home guides. Contents were designed by APRENDA and Thunderbird for the needs of female Peruvian micro entrepreneurs using a soap opera format. This soap opera depicts the struggles of the owner of a cash-strapped grocery shop who decides to open a catering business when her husband gets fired from his job. The idea is that trainees could relate to the main character's problems.[2] Among other topics, it illustrates the advantages of timely cash flows, setting a fixed salary for the owners (rather than using the business's cash for personal needs), keeping record of important business clients/suppliers to develop a business net-work and better work–life balance. This soap opera was complemented with instructors' in-class instructions for group activities and workbook exercises.

We designed a field experiment where we reproduced SWEP's recruiting process and conducted a baseline survey with around 2,500 female micro enterprise owners. Participants were randomly assigned participants to one of two groups: 60 percent were assigned to the treatment group, who were immediately invited to participate in SWEP's training, while the remaining 40 percent were assigned to the control group and received the training a year later, at the end of the experiment. We conducted follow-up surveys six and twelve months after the baseline to investigate whether women who attended the SWEP sessions implemented the business management practices taught by the program and if these improved practices had any impact on their business outcomes (sales, expenditures, profits, size and productivity). Given that the program should affect resources under women's control, we examine if changes in business outcomes translate to their household. Therefore, to some extent, we also analyze if enhanced business profitability induces improvements of broad household welfare indicators and female bargaining power.

Papers that analyze the impact of business training on micro entrepreneurial outcomes have found mixed results.[3] For example, Calderón, Cunha and Giorgi (2013) find that a 48-hour business-training program in rural Mexico increased beneficiaries' profits, revenues and clients. Karlan and Valdivia (2011) conduct a field experiment program among clients of a microfinance institution (MFI) in Peru to analyze the impact of training. The training was

---

2   Previous evidence have shown that access to television and media contents can alter women's behavior. For example, Jensen and Oster (2009) show that access to cable TV increased female autonomy and lower tolerance of domestic violence. La Ferrara, Chong and Duryea (2012) show that areas where soap operas (novelas) are broadcasted experience reductions in fertility rates. The authors argue that the more "modern" attitude that female characters have in the novelas generate changes in women's role models and aspirations.

3   For a more detailed review of the available evidence on the impact of training programs for small firms in developing countries, see McKenzie and Woodruff (2014) and Cho and Honorati (2013).

provided in 30–60 minutes sessions after the clients' regular banking meetings over a period of one to two years. While they find that participants in the program improved their knowledge on business practices, they do not find changes in their business performance (i.e., revenue, profits or employment). Field, Jayachandran and Pande (2010) implement a similar field experiment with poor female bank clients in India, where a group of them participated in a two-day training on financial literacy, business skills and aspirations. They find differential effects of the program for different castes: while Hindu women in upper castes increased their borrowing and business incomes, there was no effect among Muslims or Hindu women from historically disadvantaged castes. Bruhn et al. (2010) investigate the impact of a training program in Bosnia and Herzegovina and find increased financial basic knowledge among its beneficiaries. However, they also find that this increased knowledge did not translate into increases in the probability of business survival, business start-up, performance, or sales.[4]

This somewhat disappointing evidence led many to believe that training by itself would not suffice for businesses to thrive. One possibility is that, even with more entrepreneurial skills, financial constraints might still hinder firms' growth. de Mel, McKenzie and Woodruff (2014) test this hypothesis by analyzing the impact of a program that provided a group of women with either training alone or a combination of training and a cash grant. Their results suggest that training by itself led to the adoption of enhanced business practices but did not improve firms' profitability.[5] In contrast, the combination of human and financial capital led to increases in short-run improvements in business performance, but this effect dissipates a couple of years later. However, this effect was not found by Berge, Bjorvatn and Tungodden (2011) and Giné and Mansuri (2011) in Tanzania and Pakistan, respectively. In their studies, male and female MFI clients were offered a combination of training and financial capital. Training increased business knowledge among participants, but this only translated into higher sales for males' business sales, and no such effect was found among women. Additionally, both studies find that financial capital did not have any effect on firms' performance.

Another possibility is that the contents or methods of traditional business training are not suitable for micro entrepreneurs in developing countries. In

---

4   The authors do find some improvements on sales and performance among entrepreneurs with ex ante higher financial literacy. But, overall, they do not find any average effects of the program.

5   Karlan, Knight and Udry (2012) conduct a similar field experiment with tailors in urban Ghana, where they test the impact of a training program (business consultancy) and of a cash grant among tailors. They find that the training led to a temporary change in business practices (which disappeared a year later) and that the cash grant led to business investments. However, neither intervention increased firms' profitability.

this spirit, Valdivia (2011) tests whether general entrepreneurial training needs to be complemented with more personalized technical assistance to unleash firm growth. In his study, a group of female participants attended a traditional training program (36 three-hour sessions over 12 weeks), while a subgroup receives additional technical assistance during three months. He finds that business performance effects were concentrated among those who received technical assistance (whose sales increased by at least 18 percent), suggesting a need to tailor the approach of traditional training programs. Drexler, Fischer and Schoar (2014) take a different approach: rather than providing a more comprehensive training, they compare the effect of traditional training vis-à-vis one based on simplified rule-of-thumb business rules. They find that the latter had a positive impact on business performance, while the former did not have any significant effect.

This chapter presents three contributions to the existing literature. First, it provides new experimental evidence of the impact of training on female entrepreneurs' adoption of improved business practices and firm performance, an area in which there is no consensus in the available literature. Second, we provide evidence on alternative training methodologies to deliver business training. In the lines of Drexler et al. (2014), we investigate the role of a simplified training program provided through SWEP. Training was provided throughout an afternoon at a relatively low cost.[6] Because the program was short, simple and cheap; it was able to reach more than one hundred thousand female micro entrepreneurs. Third, to our knowledge, this is the first impact evaluation of a training program that extensively used classroom media. It included motivational videos and a soap opera about a struggling micro entrepreneur. The media contents were tailored to the needs of female micro entrepreneurs and highlighted many daily life aspects with which participants could identify themselves.

Our results suggest that SWEP increased the adoption of business practices taught by the program. In particular, we find that participants were significantly more likely to assign themselves a fixed salary (rather than take cash from the business based on household needs). We also find larger shares of entrepreneurs that implement bookkeeping practices and keep lists of potential contacts (i.e., clients, suppliers etc.) for networking, though these results are

---

6   The implementation of the cost was about $27 per participant. This estimation considers the following four components of the original budget: (1) design of training model and curriculum, (2) development of training tools, (3) annual training of trainer and coordinators and (4) implementation of training. The budget for these four components was $2.75 million. This excludes other indirect costs, such as promotion & outreach campaigns, creation of linkages with trade associations and markets and so on. The program trained 102,401 female micro entrepreneurs.

not robust in all of our specifications. We also find that participants were quite satisfied with the training program: the average ranking was 7.8/10 points and, in general, reported that they were able to understand well the course contents. This leads us to believe that this media-based program was quite successful as a teaching strategy for micro entrepreneurs. However, we do not find that the implementation of these practices translates into enhanced firm performance. We find no significant treatment impact on sales, payroll or other business expenditures.

9.2 Experimental Design and Data Collection

Ideally, we would have conducted an experiment with participants of the SWEP program. However, this was unfeasible for several reasons. First, many participants in the training events were already clients or potential clients of local MFIs, who referred them to SWEP. These institutions were reluctant to have their clients disclose their business and contact information in our surveys.[7] Second, this would have implied additional costs and delays for APRENDA. The program had to meet ambitious targets for the number of trained women. To maximize their recruiting effectiveness, the SWEP team would intensively recruit women in a certain area, train as many as they could and move to the next area. A randomized controlled trial would have required the SWEP team to recruit participants in an area, only train those randomly allocated to the treatment group, wait for an appropriate time span for the impact evaluation and go back to the same area to train the remaining women in the control group.

Due to these obstacles, we implemented an alternative experimental design that would replicate APRENDA's recruiting process in a smaller scale. Between February and May 2011, we canvassed the most important ferias, markets, industrial clusters and areas with dynamic commercial activity in two cities (Lima and Piura).[8] This enabled us to create a roster of 4,024 female micro enterprises, which constitute a sample of the target universe

---

7   APRENDA is part of ACP, a local business holding that also owns an important share of an MFI (Mi Banco). Other MFIs referred their clients to SWEP as a complimentary business service but feared that Mi Banco would contact their clients if they disclosed their personal information. Even when we guaranteed that we would not share any personal information with neither APRENDA nor Mi Banco, they were reluctant to participate in this experimental design.

8   In Lima, our sample was concentrated in the following districts: Villa El Salvador (14 percent), Cercado de Lima (11 percent), San Juan de Lurigancho (7 percent), Comas (5 percent), Los Olivos (5 percent), Santa Anita (5 percent) and San Martin de Porres (5 percent). In Piura, the sample was highly concentrated in the district of Piura (64 percent).

of SWEP and the population from which APRENDA could have recruited participants for its business training program. We collected a roster of 4,024 female micro enterprises. Legally, micro enterprises are defined as those with at most 10 employees and with yearly sales of less than 150 tax units (about US$ 200 thousand). When business duties were shared by more than one household member, we asked that the primary decision-maker be a woman. To mitigate attrition problems that have been prevalent in previous studies, we restricted our sample to businesses that had been operating for at least a year at the time of the roster collection. Additionally, we explicitly asked micro entrepreneurs if they would be willing to participate in a free one-afternoon business training between July and September. Our roster was restricted to those who agreed to attend the business training.

We randomly sampled 2,600 micro entrepreneurs from our roster to partic-ipate in the evaluation: 1,500 were randomly assigned to the treatment group, while the remaining 1,100 were part of the control group. Each micro entre-preneur in the treatment group was invited to attend one out of twelve training sessions in our experimental design between July and August 2011. The ones in the control group did not receive the business training for the duration of the field experiment but would be invited to participate at the end of it (October and November 2012). We collected some very basic information of women in the treatment and control groups during the collection of our roster. The first three columns of Table 9.1 show some of these characteristics: 61 per-cent of them worked in retail (e.g., bodegas, clothing stores etc.), 27 percent in services (e.g., beauty parlors, photocopy services, catering etc.) and 12 percent in manufacturing (e.g., textile workshops, artisan jewelry and crafts etc.). Their average age was around 42 years (65 percent of them were 30–50 years old), 30 percent had a bank account and 70 percent owned a mobile phone.

Our treatment group was intentionally larger than the control group. We were concerned about entrepreneurs in the treatment group canceling or not showing up for the trainings. Previous recruiting experience of the APRENDA team suggested that many invitees would eventually decide not to attend the training.[9] Following APRENDA's approach, we included incentives for micro entrepreneurs to attend the training sessions. We hired buses to pick women from certain predetermined locations and provided them lunch, a coffee break and a symbolic present for their participation. Attendants would also enter a lottery where they could win appliances and other prizes. In order to

9   Imperfect compliance is usual in field experiments for training programs. Considerable no-show rates among micro entrepreneurs offered business training have also been documented by Bruhn et al. (2010)—61 percent, Drexler et al. (2014)—50–52 per-cent), Calderón et al. (2013)—35 percent, Valdivia (2011)—49 percent and Karlan and Valdivia (2011)—12–24 percent.

Table 9.1 Characteristics of Micro Entrepreneurs (Original Design versus Effective Sample[a])

	Design (original sample)			Effective sample		
	Treatment	**Control**	**Diff**	**Treatment**	**Control**	**Diff**
City (Lima = 1)	0.79	0.79	0.00	0.74	0.80	−0.05
	(0.40)	(0.40)	(0.02)	(0.44)	(0.40)	(0.02)
Services	0.27	0.26	0.01	0.28	0.26	0.02
	(0.44)	(0.44)	(0.02)	(0.45)	(0.44)	(0.02)
Retail	0.61	0.62	−0.01	0.57	0.61	−0.04
	(0.49)	(0.49)	(0.02)	(0.50)	(0.49)	(0.02)
Manufacturing	0.12	0.12	0.00	0.15	0.12	0.02
	(0.32)	(0.32)	(0.01)	(0.35)	(0.33)	(0.02)
Age	41.78	41.58	0.20	43.07	41.66	1.40
	(11.18)	(11.58)	(0.45)	(10.63)	(11.52)	(0.55)
Has bank account	0.30	0.30	0.01	0.31	0.30	0.01
	(0.46)	(0.46)	(0.02)	(0.46)	(0.46)	(0.02)
Has mobile phone	0.70	0.69	0.01	0.72	0.69	0.03
	(0.46)	(0.46)	(0.02)	(0.45)	(0.46)	(0.02)
Has home land line	0.48	0.49	−0.02	0.51	0.50	0.01
	(0.50)	(0.50)	(0.02)	(0.50)	(0.50)	(0.02)
Has business land line	0.20	0.18	0.02	0.19	0.19	0.00
	(0.40)	(0.39)	(0.02)	(0.39)	(0.39)	(0.02)
Observations	1,500	1,100		703	1,035	

Source: Authors' own calculations.

Notes

[a] The effective sample is comprised of women who attended the training in the treatment group and of the ones that completed the baseline questionnaire in the control group.

Standard deviations in parentheses. Significance levels of differences denoted by: *** $p<0.01$, ** $p<0.05$, * $p<0.1$.

maximize attendance, the training venues were carefully chosen considering the availability of public transportation, their centric location and closeness to the areas where the roster was collected.[10] Despite all of our efforts, only 703 (47 percent) out of the fifteen hundred women invited to the trainings attended.

We collected a much more detailed baseline with the characteristics of the micro entrepreneurs in our field experiment. Our questionnaire included information of both the women's micro enterprise (i.e., business practices, sales, costs, number of employees, payroll, access to credit etc.) and household (i.e., composition, household expenditures, women's role in household decision-making etc.). The survey was administered in Android-based tablets to facilitate data collection. We took two approaches for the baseline collection. In one approach, women in the treatment group were interviewed in the training venues. Upon their arrival—but prior to the beginning of the training—the enumerators administered the survey. In the other approach, enumerators visited women in the control group either at their houses or businesses to gather their information. Because enumerators were able to visit micro entrepreneurs multiple times and (re)schedule appointments as needed, 1,035 out of the 1,100 women in our evaluation sample completed the baseline survey.

We were not able to collect data (neither baseline nor follow-ups) for invited micro entrepreneurs who did not attend the training nor from the women in the control group who refused to be interviewed.[11] Therefore, our impact evaluation will be based on an effective sample of 703 micro entrepreneurs who did attend the training and 1,035 women in the control group. Because our sample and allocation deviated from our original random design, this creates some challenges to interpret our results. While the refusal rate (6 percent) in the control group was fairly small, the significantly larger no-show rates in the treatment group poses a problem: while women were randomly invited to the training, the actual decision of attending was not random. The last two columns of Table 9.1 shows that women in our final treatment group were 1.4 years older and more likely to work in retail. Table 9.2 presents more detailed characteristics of our effective sample at baseline. Women in both groups are similar in several dimensions (e.g., business value, education, access to formal credit etc.). Importantly, they also have similar business outcomes

10 There were 10 training sessions in Lima in eight districts: Chorrillos (2), El Augustino (1), Independencia (2), Breña (2), Magdalena (1), Independencia (1) and Villa El Salvador (1). There were two training sessions in Piura.

11 This prevents us from calculating standard Intention-to-Treat estimates as other papers in the literature (de Mel et al. 2014; Drexler et al. 2014; Karlan and Valdivia, 2011; Karlan et al., 2012; Valdivia, 2011).

Table 9.2 Baseline Characteristics by Treatment Status

	Control	Treatment
A. Business characteristics		
Age of business (in months)	98.8	101.7
	(91.8)	(91.4)
Own store	0.48	0.52
	(0.50)	(0.50)
Business value (self-reported, in soles)	26,674	25,780
	(34,008)	(33,796)
B. Business performance (in soles)		
Yearly sales	43,887	42,003
	(41,364)	(39,925)
Yearly payroll	1,736	1,863
	(4,024)	(4,068)
Yearly expenditures (excl. payroll)	27,615	24,869
	(36,266)	(32,354)
C. Employment		
Total number of workers	0.81	1.10
	(1.17)	(1.36)
Number of permanent salaried workers	0.44	0.52
	(0.99)	(1.15)
Number of permanent non-salaried workers	0.28	0.42
	(0.63)	(0.72)
Number of salaried temporary workers[a]	0.06	0.10
	(0.24)	(0.34)
Number of temporary non-salaried workers[a]	0.03	0.06
	(0.15)	(0.20)
D. Credit		
Received formal loan in last 12 months	0.28	0.31
	(0.45)	(0.46)
Size of most important formal loan[b]	6,193	5,691
	(7,476)	(9,403)
Received informal loan in last 12 months	0.16	0.23
	(0.37)	(0.42)
Size of most important informal loan[a]	1,331	1,377
	(1,724)	(1,792)
D. Household variables		
Monthly per capita HH expenditure (soles)	358.5	363.7
	(216.2)	(220.2)
Value of household assets	4,132	4,927
	(5,998)	(6,220)

Table 9.2 (*Cont.*)

	Control	Treatment
D. Micro entrepreneur's characteristics		
Married	0.62	0.63
	(0.49)	(0.48)
Head of household	0.42	0.44
	(0.49)	(0.50)
Years of education	10.96	11.08
	(3.36)	(3.28)
E. Does woman decide?[c]		
How to spend money	0.70	0.73
	(0.46)	(0.44)
Food purchases	0.83	0.85
	(0.38)	(0.36)
Furniture purchases	0.68	0.71
	(0.47)	(0.46)
Family outings	0.67	0.68
	(0.47)	(0.47)
Children's education	0.70	0.73
	(0.46)	(0.44)
Family discipline	0.66	0.71
	(0.47)	(0.45)
What to do if any HH member is sick	0.82	0.82
	(0.38)	(0.39)
Observations	1,035	703

Source: Authors' own calculations.

Notes

[a] Number of temporary workers was adjusted by the number of months worked, that is, number of temporary workers × (number of worked months)/12.
[b] For the sample of those who received a loan in the last 12 months.
[c] Whether each of these decisions is primarily made by the micro entrepreneur.

Standard deviation in parentheses. Significance levels denoted by: *** p<0.01, ** p<0.05, * p<0.1.

in terms of sales, payroll, and other business expenditures. However, our effective treatment group has larger firms in terms of number of workers, has more access to informal credit and are more likely to own their own stores. This seems to suggest that, if anything, women who attended the training were better-off (and likely better able) than their counterparts in the control group. Therefore, the results of our chapter constitute an upper bound of the actual effects of the training.

The APRENDA training sessions were typically 4–5 hours long. During these sessions, attendants watched a soap opera about Vicky, a struggling bodega owner. The soap opera depicted wrongful management practices that are common among micro entrepreneurs. Vicky's bodega was not able to keep up with the increasing household expenditures of her son and younger sister, and usually she covers these personal expenses with the bodega's day-to-day sales. Her situation turns critical when her husband is fired from his job and her sister gets unexpectedly pregnant. With the help of a friend, she decides to start a catering business and get better organized. She sets a salary for herself (separating her personal expenses from the business's profits); sets a cash flow to decide any new investments and collects a list of potential clients. These changes in practices eventually pay off and she is able to open a successful restaurant after a few months.

The soap opera was divided in six parts. After each part, the instructor reinforced the concepts the video illustrated with other examples and group games. Participants also received a workbook with exercises. After the soap opera and the instructor's explanations, they would start working on exercises. For example, the workbook would provide a hypothetical list of business sales, expenditures and personal expenses. Participants would need to determine the cash flow, potential investments and the salary they could assign themselves. The workbook also included take-home exercises where micro entrepreneurs were encouraged to work on their own cash flows and to create a list of potential clients to expand their business. To measure the impact of the program, we collected two follow-up surveys. The first one was collected six months after the training (January and February 2012) and the second one was collected another six months later (August–September 2012). This survey was collected among those in the effective evaluation sample (703 in the treatment and 1,035 in the control groups). Enumerators visited micro entrepreneurs either at their home or business, depending on their availability. The questionnaires were similar to those in the baseline for comparability reasons.

9.3 Empirical Approach and Results

Our results focus on four main aspects on which the program might have affected micro entrepreneurs. First, we analyze whether training led to the adoption of the business practices that were taught to participants. The contents of the training prioritized three rules: (1) rather than taking cash based on the needs of their households, micro entrepreneurs should assign themselves a fixed salary every month; (2) they should register all sales and expenses in a cash flow to aid them in their investment and credit decisions and (3) they should build a list of potential contacts (i.e., buyers, suppliers etc.) to network. Second, we analyze if there were any changes in business outcomes. In particular, we investigate if the training affected firms' sales, payroll and other expenses. Third, we analyze if the program had any impact on micro entrepreneurs' household welfares measured by participants' increased expenditures and the degree of the micro entrepreneurs' empowerment in the family.

We analyze the data with several specifications. Our basic specifications exploit the difference in outcomes Yit for the post-intervention rounds of the data through a simple regression analysis:

$$Y_{i,t=T} = \beta Treat_i + \varepsilon_{it} \qquad \text{(Eq. 9.1)}$$

where $Treat_i$ is an indicator variable for the treatment group and $T=1$ for the first follow-up (six months after the intervention) and $T=2$ for the second follow-up (a year after the intervention). We also estimate the average effect over the impact evaluation period by pulling together both post-intervention rounds and estimating:

$$Y_{i,t=T} = \beta Treat_i + \theta D_{t=2} + \varepsilon_{it} \qquad \text{(Eq. 9.2)}$$

where $D_{t=2}$ is an indicator variable for the twelve-month follow-up round of the data. Because our effective sample deviated from the original random design we also estimate two additional versions of Equation (9.1) where we control for a set of characteristics of women in the control and treatment groups. In this spirit, we estimate ANCOVA (Analysis of Covariance) estimators, by including the baseline value of the dependent variable ($Y_{i,t} = 0$) as a regressor. We also estimate Equation (9.1) conditioning on a set Xi of micro entrepreneur's characteristics. This set Xi includes sector (i.e., services, manufacturing or retail), city, age, head of household at baseline, whether the micro entrepreneur had received previous business training and marital status.

$$Y_{i,t=T} = \beta Treat_i + \gamma Y_{i,t=0} + \varepsilon_{it} \qquad \text{(Eq. 9.3)}$$

$$Y_{i,t=T} = \beta Treat_i + \delta X_i + \varepsilon_{it} \qquad \text{(Eq. 9.4)}$$

Table 9.3 shows the results of our estimation framework for business practices. We find a strong significant impact of the program on the probability that the micro entrepreneur assigns herself a fixed salary. The coefficient is highly significant across all specifications and is large in magnitude: there is an increase of 5 percentage points with an average of 5 percent in the control group (doubling the share of women who implement this practice). In most specifications, we also find a positive impact of the program on the other two practices: bookkeeping (between 4 and 6 percentage points, with an average of 43 percent in the control group) and networking list (between 6 and 10 percentage points, with an average of 28 percent in the control group).

While we find a general positive impact on the adoption of business practices, we do not find that these changes translate into any improvements in business performance. Table 9.4 shows the results for firms' sales, payroll and business expenditures (excluding payroll). Our results suggest that firms did not experience any improvements and are, in general, consistent with previous results in the literature. As suggested by McKenzie and Woodruff (2014), most studies find some changes in business practices taught to training participants but no effects on outcomes.

Finally, we estimate the impact of the program on household outcomes. First, we estimate whether there were any increases in household per capita expenditures (which is commonly used as a general measure of well being). The results are shown in the top panel of Table 9.5 and suggest that the program did not have any significant impact on household expenditures. The coefficients are not statistically significant and are rather small in magnitude compared to the means in the control group.

Next, we also test the impact of the program on women's empowerment. To capture the female micro entrepreneur's degree of empowerment in the household, we captured a set of questions to determine whether she, her husband or other family member decides.[12] (1) how to spend household's income; (2) food purchases; (3) furniture purchases; (4) family outings; (5) children's education; (6) family discipline and (7) what to do if a household member gets ill. Our analysis includes the estimation of seven empowerment measures. Independently testing such a large number of outcomes of the same family can lead to over-rejection: if we test a sufficiently large number of empowerment variables, we would considerably increase the probability that the treatment effect will be significant in at least one dimension (Duflo et al., 2007; Schochet, 2008).

We are really more interested in the effect of the training on women empowerment, in general, rather than the strengthening of their bargaining power on specific household decisions. Therefore, we aggregate all of our seven decisions on a single index for this "family" of outcomes to avoid estimating too many outcomes. We adopt the framework proposed by Kling, Liebman and Katz (2007). Consider G household decisions, each denoted by the subscript g. let σg be the standard deviation of the control group for each decision Dg. We

12 Admittedly, measurement of women's empowerment is a complex issue and presents several challenges. While we did not design a set of original questions for this purpose, we used several items from the Mexican Intrahousehold Violence Survey (Encuesta

Table 9.3 Impact of Training on Business Practices

Estimation	(1) Post[a]	(2) Post[a]	(3) Avg Post[b]	(4) ANCOVA[c]	(5) Post[d]	(6) ANCOVA[c]	(7) Post[d]
Rounds[5]	1	2	1,2	1	1	2	2
Controls	No	No	No	No	Yes	No	Yes
N	1,480	1,371	2,851	1,480	1,480	1,371	1,371
A. Assigns herself a fixed salary							
Treat	0.040***	0.059***	0.049***	0.040***	0.039***	0.058***	0.057***
	(0.013)	(0.014)	(0.011)	(0.013)	(0.013)	(0.014)	(0.014)
Treat x $D_{t=1}$							
Treat x $D_{t=2}$							
$\hat{\gamma}_{ctl,\,t=1}$	0.051		0.051	0.051	0.051		
$\bar{\hat{\gamma}}_{ctl,\,t=2}$		0.044	0.044			0.044	0.044
B. Bookkeeping							
Treat	0.055**	0.046*	0.051**	0.038	0.044*	0.036	0.037
	(0.026)	(0.027)	(0.021)	(0.025)	(0.026)	(0.026)	(0.026)
Treat x $D_{t=1}$							
Treat x $D_{t=2}$							
$\hat{\gamma}_{ctl,\,t=1}$	0.413		0.413	0.413	0.413		
$\bar{\hat{\gamma}}_{ctl,\,t=2}$		0.446	0.446			0.446	0.446
C. Networking							
Treat	0.090***	0.111***	0.100***	0.063***	0.075***	0.090***	0.099***
	(0.024)	(0.026)	(0.020)	(0.023)	(0.023)	(0.025)	(0.025)

(continued)

Table 9.3 (*Cont.*)

Estimation	(1) Post[a]	(2) Post[a]	(3) Avg Post[b]	(4) ANCOVA[c]	(5) Post[d]	(6) ANCOVA[c]	(7) Post[d]
Treat x $D_{t=1}$							
Treat x $D_{t=2}$							
$\hat{\gamma}_{ctl,\,t=1}$	0.254		0.254	0.254	0.254		
$\hat{\gamma}_{ctl,\,t=2}$		0.306	0.306			0.306	0.306

Source: Authors' own calculations.

Notes

[a] Post Estimators: $Y_{i,t} = \beta Treat_i + \varepsilon_{it}$ for each $t = 1$ and $t = 2$.

[b] Average Post Estimator: $Y_{i,t} = \beta Treat_i + \theta D_{t=2} + \varepsilon_{it}$.

[c] ANCOVA (Analysis of Covariance) estimators: $Y_{i,t} = \beta Treat_i + \gamma Y_{i,t=0} + \varepsilon_{it}$ for each $t = 1$ and $t = 2$.

[d] Post Estimators including baseline controls: $Y_{i,t} = \beta Treat_i + \delta X_i + \varepsilon_{it}$ for each $t = 1$ and $t = 2$. X_i includes sector, city, age, head of household at baseline, whether the micro entrepreneur had received previous business training, and marital status.

[e] Rounds: baseline (0), Jan–Feb 2012 Follow-up (1), and Aug–Sep 2012 Follow-up (2).

Standard errors in parentheses. Standard errors are clustered at the micro entrepreneur level in Column (3). Significance levels denoted by: *** p<0.01, ** p<0.05, * p<0.1.

Table 9.4 Impact of Training on Business Outcomes

Estimation	(1) Post[a]	(2) Post[a]	(3) Avg Post[b]	(4) ANCOVA[c]	(5) Post[d]	(6) ANCOVA[c]	(7) Post[d]
Rounds[e]	1	2	1,2	1	1	2	2
Controls	No	No	No	No	Yes	No	Yes
N	1,468	1,366	2,834	1,453	1,468	1,361	1,366
A. Yearly sales							
Treat	−1,673.3	−1,786.4	−1,728.0	−2,064.4	236.5	−525.9	−543.5
	(3,660.0)	(3,174.7)	(2,751.4)	(2,234.5)	(3,629.1)	(3,028.6)	(3,159.3)
Treat x $D_{t=1}$							
Treat x $D_{t=2}$							
$\bar{Y}_{ctrl,\,t=1}$	52,243.7		52,243.7	52,243.7	52,243.7		
$\bar{Y}_{ctrl,\,t=2}$		45,950.3	45,950.3			45,950.3	45,950.3
B. Payroll							
Treat	394.2	−153.6	129.4	436.8	372.5	−175.0	−221.8
	(397.0)	(235.4)	(269.0)	(360.3)	(395.5)	(220.7)	(233.6)
Treat x $D_{t=1}$							
Treat x $D_{t=2}$							
$\bar{Y}_{ctrl,\,t=1}$	1,977.8		1,977.8	1,977.8	1,977.8		
$\bar{Y}_{ctrl,\,t=2}$		1,937.8	1,937.8			1,937.8	1,937.8
C. Business expenditures (excluding payroll)							
Treat	−1,532.5	−2,164.4	−1,837.0	−1,747.2	−144.2	−691.9	−1,272.4
	(2,869.3)	(2,554.2)	(2,085.6)	(1,265.7)	(2,854.2)	(1,220.7)	(2,551.2)

(continued)

Table 9.4 (*Cont.*)

Estimation	(1) Post[a]	(2) Post[a]	(3) Avg Post[b]	(4) ANCOVA[c]	(5) Post[d]	(6) ANCOVA[c]	(7) Post[d]
Treat x $D_{t=1}$							
Treat x $D_{t=2}$							
$\bar{Y}_{ctl,\,t=1}$	27,469.6		27,469.6	27,469.6	27,469.6		
$\bar{Y}_{ctl,\,t=2}$		24,665.4	24,665.4			24,665.4	24,665.4

Source: Authors' own calculations.

Notes

[a] Post Estimators: $Y_{i,t}=\beta Treat_i+\varepsilon_{it}$ for each $t=1$ and $t=2$.

[b] Average Post Estimator: $Y_{i,t=1,2}=\beta Treat_i+\theta D_{t=2}+\varepsilon_{it}$

[c] ANCOVA (Analysis of Covariance) estimators: $Y_{i,t}=\beta Treat_i+\gamma Y_{i,t=0}+\varepsilon_{it}$, for each $t=1$ and $t=2$.

[d] Post Estimators including baseline controls: $Y_{i,t}=\beta Treat_i+\delta X_i+\varepsilon_{it}$, for each $t=1$ and $t=2$. X_i includes sector, city, age, head of household at baseline, whether the micro entrepreneur had received previous business training, and marital status.

[e] Rounds: baseline (0), Jan–Feb 2012 Follow-up (1), and Aug–Sep 2012 Follow-up (2).

Standard errors in parentheses. Standard errors are clustered at the micro entrepreneur level in Column (3). Significance levels denoted by: *** p<0.01, ** p<0.05, * p<0.1.

	(1)	(2)	(3)	(4)	(5)	(6)	(7)
Estimation	Post[a]	Post[a]	Avg. Post[b]	ANCOVA[c]	Post[d]	ANCOVA[c]	Post[d]
Rounds[e]	1	2	1,2	1	1	2	2
Controls	No	No	No	No	Yes	No	Yes
N	1,498	1,418	2,916	1,454	1,498	1,376	1,418

A. Household per capita expenditure (monthly, in Soles)

	(1)	(2)	(3)	(4)	(5)	(6)	(7)
Treat	5.69	7.79	6.72	−1.94	6.77	4.56	9.01
	(12.17)	(10.07)	(9.33)	(11.35)	(11.77)	(9.36)	(9.72)
Treat x $D_{t=1}$							
Treat x $D_{t=2}$							
$\bar{Y}_{ctrl,\,t=1}$	380.37		380.37	380.37	380.37		
$\hat{Y}_{ctrl,\,t=2}$		337.60	337.60			337.60	337.60

B. Empowerment index

	(1)	(2)	(3)	(4)	(5)	(6)	(7)
Treat (t)	−0.031	−0.052	−0.042	−0.036	−0.017	−0.057	−0.051
	(0.037)	(0.039)	(0.032)	(0.034)	(0.037)	(0.037)	(0.038)

Source: Authors' own calculations.

Notes

[a] Post Estimators: $Y_{t,i} = \beta Treat_i + \varepsilon_{it}$, for each $t = 1$ and $t = 2$.

[b] Average Post Estimator: $Y_{t,i=2} = \beta Treat_i + \theta D_{t=2} + \varepsilon_{it}$.

[c] ANCOVA (Analysis of Covariance) estimators: $Y_{t,i} = \beta Treat_i + \gamma Y_{t,i=0} + \varepsilon_{it}$, for each $t = 1$ and $t = 2$.

[d] Post Estimators including baseline controls: $Y_{t,i} = \beta Treat_i + \delta X_i + \varepsilon_{it}$, for each $t = 1$ and $t = 2$. X_i includes sector, city, age, head of household at baseline, whether the micro entrepreneur had received previous business training, and marital status.

[e] Rounds: baseline (0), Jan–Feb 2012 Follow-up (1) and Aug–Sep 2012 Follow-up (2).

We calculate the impact on a set of household decision variables. In particular, we asked micro entrepreneurs whether they decide: (a) how to spend household's income; (b) food purchases; (c) furniture purchases; (d) family outings; (e) children's education; (f) family discipline and (g) what to do if a household member gets ill. We estimate a SUR system of decisions: $Y_{i,t} = \beta Treat_i + \epsilon_{it}$ with decisions $g = 1,...,G$. We estimate the overall impact on this family of outcomes through $\tau = \dfrac{1}{G}\sum_{g=1}^{G}\dfrac{\theta_g}{\sigma_g}$.

Standard errors in parentheses. Standard errors are clustered at the micro entrepreneur level in Columns (3) and (8). Significance levels denoted by: *** p<0.01, ** p<0.05, * p<0.1.

estimate regressions $D_{ig} = \theta_g Treat_i + \varepsilon_{ig}$ for each $g = 1, \ldots, G$. To account for the covariance of estimates θ_g across equations, Kling et al. (2007) propose to estimate them as a system of Seemingly Unrelated Regressions (SUR) rather than estimating the parameters individually.[13] We then aggregate the effect on the family of decisions based on the treatment effects of each outcome and the control group standard deviations:[14]

$$\tau = \frac{1}{G} \sum_{g=1}^{G} \frac{\theta_g}{\sigma_g} \qquad \text{(Eq. 9.5)}$$

The sample variance of τ (used to test its significance level) is based on the full variance–covariance matrix of θ estimated through the SUR system. Kling et al.'s (2007) estimation on a family of outcomes allows us to tell whether women experience any positive effect on the set of decisions as a whole. We find no statistically significant differences in the normalized aggregate empowerment index.

sobre Violencia Intrafamiliar): https://www.inegi.org.mx/contenidos/programas/envif/1999/doc/cuest_envif99.pdf (see page 3, accessed December 2014).

13 Evaluation of business training usually entails a large number of outcomes and is prone to family-wise error (FWE) problems. Karlan and Valdivia (2011) and Valdivia (2011) also analyze the impact of training programs on aggregate indexes of outcomes. Their approach is somewhat different: they normalize each outcome with the mean and standard deviations and the control group and aggregate the normalized variables:

$$\frac{1}{G} \sum_g \frac{\left(Y_{ig} - \mu_g \right)}{\sigma_g}.$$

They use this index as the dependent variable in a regression. This method is suitable when there are no missing variables in the analysis. In particular, Kling and Liebman (2004, p. 9) argue that "when an individual is missing data on an outcome however, the other non-missing outcomes implicitly are given more weight when the index is based on a simple average of non-missing standardized outcomes. The formulation described above based on the mean of estimated effects is a more direct summary of the estimates for each outcome." Some of our decisions are prone to missing data problems. For example, the question of whether women decide about their children's education is only answered by women with school-aged sons/daughters. Therefore, we prefer to normalize the coefficients for different decisions rather than to create a single regress and based on normalized individual decisions.

14 Because we use different samples in our estimations, σ_g varies between specifications. In the cross-sectional post regressions—with and without controls (i.e., Equations 9.1 and 9.4)—we use the standard deviations of the control group in the period for which we estimate the regression (either $t=1$ or $t=2$). In the ANCOVA regressions, we standardize τ using the standard deviations in $t = 1$. Standardization in the ANCOVA model is based on the baseline values of σ_g.

9.4 Discussion of Results

We discuss three threats to the validity of the above findings: (1) missing data in the treatment group due to selective attendance to the training; (2) attrition in follow-up surveys; statistical power limitations and (3) low quality of the training and levels of practice adoption.

9.4.1 Selective Attendance to Trainings

First, our identification strategy can be compromised by the high no-show rates among the invitees to the trainings. Because of the random assignment, had all the invitees attended the trainings, we would have expected very similar treatment and control groups. However—despite all of our efforts to increase attendance and our previous screening of the micro entrepreneur's interest—only 703 (47 percent of invited women) attended the trainings. We could not interview the remaining 797 of women in the treatment group who did not attend, and they were not part of the impact evaluation sample. This leaves us with an unbalanced composition of the treatment and control groups. However, as suggested by Table 9.2—relative to the control group—it seems that our effective treatment group was comprised of women with larger businesses, somewhat more access to credit and more household assets. This would suggest that the effective treatment group ended up having "better" business women and that, if anything, our estimates are an upper bound of the true impact.

Positive selection makes it improbable that those who did not show up (and for whom we do not observe outcomes) performed better than those in our sample. Nevertheless, even if that were the case, their performance would have needed to be exceedingly large compared to the ones who attended. We can do some back-the-envelope calculations to assess how much larger their outcomes would have needed to be to find an overall positive impact of the program. We illustrate this calculation for business sales. Take the first column of Panel A of Table 9.4. Average sales of the control group in $t=1$ were $S/.52,244$, and average sales in the treatment group were $S/.50,570$ (i.e., $S/.52,244 + \beta_{Treat}$). We can estimate what the average among those without data in the treatment group would have needed to be to generate, for example, an overall 10 percent impact of the program on sales is:

$$\left[\frac{(1.1 \times 52,244 \times 1,500) - (703 \times 50,570)}{757} \right].$$

This would imply that those who did not attend would need to have had 26 percent larger sales than those who did to have a 10 percent effect in $t=1$. Similarly, their sales should have been 29 percent higher than those who attended in $t=2$. The magnitude of these estimates seems rather implausible.

9.4.2 Attrition in Follow-Up Surveys

The results in Section 9.3 show that there are different number of observations in each round of the survey. There were 1,738 observations in the baseline that we tried to reinterview in the first and second follow-ups. However, only 80 percent of micro entrepreneurs participated in all three rounds of the survey. Table 9.6 shows the distribution of the sample attrition across rounds. Attrition is a usual problem in entrepreneurship studies because they take place in urban settings and among relatively mobile individuals. For example, Karlan and Valdivia (2011), Valdivia (2011) and Berge et al. (2011) experienced attrition rates of 24 percent, 28 percent and 18 percent, respectively. There were several reasons why we were not able to locate the micro entrepreneurs for follow-up interviews. Some of them were peddlers and street vendors (who could easily move their businesses) or went out of business.[15] We tried to locate them at home, but many of them had moved. A small share of them refused to cooperate with our survey. In general, sample attrition would not represent a problem for our analysis if it were uncorrelated with the treatment. However, Table 9.6 suggests that, in our case, our program was indeed associated with the attrition: the share of micro entrepreneurs who participated in the three rounds of our evaluation was 9 percentage points higher among those who received the training.

Because attrition is correlated with the treatment, we need to further investigate how it could affect our results. In particular, we would like to get an idea of what would have happened had those who did not participate in our follow-up surveys (and for which we do not have information after the intervention) remained in our estimation sample. For example, it is possible that those who dropped from the control group had smaller sales. This would imply an underestimation of the impact of the program, because the actual effect would have been larger if we were able to incorporate the missing information for those who did not participate in the follow-up surveys.

Table 9.7 presents some baseline characteristics of the attrited micro entrepreneurs. The first four columns present some baseline variables within the treatment and control groups for those who attrited and those who remained in our estimation sample in the first follow-up. Columns 5–8 perform a similar analysis for the second follow-up survey ($t = 2$). In general, micro entrepreneurs that attrited in the treatment group are similar to those who were reinterviewed. However, those who dropped from the sample in

---

15 Some of the micro entrepreneurs in our sample had their shops located in Plaza Villa Sur, a market that experienced a large fire while we were gathering the data for the first follow-up (Diario Correo 2012). While we tried to interview them at home, many of them had moved away after the fire.

Table 9.6 Attrition Rates across Rounds

Round[a]			Control		Treatment		All	
t = 0	t = 1	t = 2	N	%	N	%	N	%
X	X	X	792	76.5	604	85.9	1,396	80.3
X			89	8.6	21	3.0	110	6.3
X	X		107	10.3	49	7.0	156	9.0
X		X	47	4.5	29	4.1	76	4.4
Total			1,035	100.0	703	100.0	1,738	100.0

Source: Authors' own calculations.

Notes

[a] Baseline ($t = 0$), first follow-up ($t = 1$), and second follow-up ($t = 2$).

the control group appear to be better-off than those who remained: their businesses' values are larger, they have higher sales and payrolls, are more educated and have larger per capita household expenditures. Although we cannot know with certainty what would have happened to those who attrited in the follow-up surveys, their baseline characteristics suggest that, if anything, attrition would have created an upward bias in our estimates. Because those missing in the control group were likely to have better businesses, we would be comparing the treatment group against a control group that had been artificially deflated.

Attrition may have biased our estimates of business performance (i.e., sales, payroll and business expenses) and household outcomes (i.e., household expenditures and women's empowerment). In these cases, we do not find that the program had any positive impact, because these effects were likely to have been overestimated in Tables 9.3, 9.4 and 9.5; so the program had at most no positive impact.

Therefore, we are less worried about the impact of the program on business performance and household outcomes, where we do not find any positive effects. However, we are somewhat more concerned about the robustness of the positive and significant impacts we find on the adoption of business practices. If less skilled entrepreneurs were dropped from the control group (as suggested from Table 9.7), they could have been less likely to have implemented any business practices and we would have overestimated the impact of the program. Alternatively, this could happen if those in the treatment group who dropped from the sample were those who would not have adopted the business practices taught during the training (i.e., the "actual" proportion of micro entrepreneurs in the treatment group that adopted a business practice would be smaller than the observed one).

Table 9.7 Baseline Characteristics of Attrited and Non-Attrited Micro Entrepreneurs

| | First follow-up ($t = 1$) | | | | Second follow-up ($t = 2$) | | | |
| | Control | | Treatment | | Control | | Treatment | |
	Sample[a]	Attrition	Sample[a]	Attrition	Sample[a]	Attrition	Sample[a]	Attrition
Age of business (in months)	98.3 (92.0)	102.4 (91.0)	103.2 (92.5)	83.0 (73.3)	97.8 (90.2)	103.4 (98.6)	103.3 (91.8)	87.6 (86.6)
Own store	0.49 (0.50)	0.43 (0.50)	0.52 (0.50)	0.50 (0.51)	0.49 (0.50)	0.45 (0.50)	0.53 (0.50)	0.46 (0.50)
Business value (self reported, S/.)	25,700.1 (33,010.6)	33,132.8** (39,539.2)	25,548.9 (33,351.9)	29,005.6 (39,780.6)	25,757.8 (32,723.6)	30,621.7 (38,914.2)	25,734.3 (33,284.9)	26,197.3 (38,468.3)
Yearly Sales (S/.)	42,816.1 (40,203.0)	51,117.0** (48,047.3)	41,785.0 (40,294.4)	44,900.2 (34,910.9)	43,050.2 (41,115.8)	47,523.5 (42,353.3)	41,806.7 (40,033.8)	43,842.7 (39,164.3)
Yearly Payroll (S/.)	3,063.1 (8,850.3)	5,401.4*** (14,356.0)	3,700.4 (9,934.5)	2,688.2 (5,098.6)	2,967.7 (8,547.7)	5,093.7*** (13,748.9)	3,709.4 (10,020.4)	2,895.5 (5,607.9)
Yearly Expenditures (excl payroll, S/.)	27,434.9 (36,393.5)	28,799.2 (35,535.0)	24,642.1 (32,259.2)	27,828.8 (33,775.0)	27,639.6 (36,921.8)	27,512.4 (33,418.1)	24,902.2 (32,320.6)	24,567.0 (32,907.3)
Total number of workers[b]	0.81 (1.19)	0.80 (1.03)	1.11 (1.39)	1.03 (0.89)	0.79 (1.17)	0.86 (1.19)	1.10 (1.38)	1.10 (1.25)
Head of household	0.43 (0.50)	0.37 (0.48)	0.45 (0.50)	0.34 (0.48)	0.42 (0.49)	0.42 (0.50)	0.43 (0.50)	0.50 (0.50)
Years of education	10.9 (3.4)	11.6** (2.9)	11.1 (3.3)	11.5 (3.0)	10.8 (3.4)	11.6*** (3.1)	11.0 (3.3)	11.6 (2.9)

Table 9.7 (*Cont.*)

	First follow-up (*t* = 1)				Second follow-up (*t* = 2)			
	Control		Treatment		Control		Treatment	
	Sample[a]	Attrition	Sample[a]	Attrition	Sample[a]	Attrition	Sample[a]	Attrition
HH Per-capita monthly expenditure (S/.)	352.9 (208.7)	395.7** (258.4)	360.0 (216.1)	414.9 (267.7)	351.2 (204.5)	390.2** (259.7)	358.4 (212.8)	413.1 (276.2)
Observations	899	136	653	50	839	196	633	70

Source: Authors' own calculations.

[a] Those who we were able to interview and remain in the estimation samples.

[b] Number of total workers: permanent workers + adjusted temporary workers. Temporary workers were adjusted by the number of months worked, that is, the number of temporary workers × (number of worked months)/12.

Standard deviation in parentheses. Significance levels (for differences between the sample and attrition groups) denoted by: *** p<0.01, ** p<0.05, * p<0.1.

Although both situations can happen simultaneously (i.e., the attrited controls can have larger adoption rates and the attrited treated micro entrepreneurs can have smaller adoption rates), we quantify both factors separately. First, we estimate how large the adoption rate in the control group would need to be to wipe out any significant impact of the program. Assume a total sample of N (with N_c observations in the control group and $N - N_c$ observations in the treatment group). Suppose that n_c^A micro entrepreneurs attrited from the control group. Based on the availadata for the $N_n - n_c^A$ micro entrepreneurs that we observe in the post-intervention survey, denote the estimated rate of adoption in the control group as p_c^0. The actual rate of adoption in the control group would be $\dfrac{n_c^A}{N_c} p_c^u + \left(\dfrac{N_c - n_c}{N_c} \right)$, where p_c^u is the rate of adoption among the attriters. The actual treatment effect would then be $\beta = p_T^0 - \left[\dfrac{n_A}{N} p_0^u + \left(\dfrac{N - n_A}{N} \right) p_c^0 \right]$[16],

where p_T^0 is the observed rate of adoption in the treatment group. Of course, we do not know p_c^u, but we can simulate different scenarios.

We would like to determine how large the rate of adoption among attriters in the control group would need to be to have a zero-effect of the program. To do so, we calculate the impact of the program through a regression, where we impute a rate of $p_c^u = \left(p_c^0 + \delta \right)$ among attrited micro entrepreneurs in the control group for alternative positive values of δ (i.e., 1 percent, 2 percent and so on). To preserve the dichotomous nature of the variable, we impute either 0s or 1s to the attrited control group to simulate each hypothetical rate p_c^u. For each value of δ, we assign 1s to $\left\lceil n_c^A \left(p_c^0 + \delta \right) \right\rceil$ (rounded up) observations and assign 0s to the remaining $\left\lfloor n_c^A \left(1 - p_c^0 - \delta \right) \right\rfloor$ observations. We are able to determine the value of δ for which the program no longer has any statistically significant effect and calculate how much larger p_c^u would need to be with respect to p_c^0 for this to happen $\left(\text{i.e.,} \dfrac{p_c^0 + \delta}{p_c^0} \right)$.

This procedure can also be accommodated for the treatment group. In this case, instead of increasing the proportion of adopting micro entrepreneurs in the control group, we could simulate decreasing rates of adoption among the treatment group. Suppose that n_T^A micro entrepreneurs attrited from the treatment group and that their (unobserved) adoption rate is p_T^u, where $p_T^u = \left(p_T^0 - \delta \right) < p_T^c$. We can calculate the impact of the program for

16 Note that the treatment effect for the estimations that consider only the micro entrepreneurs that were included in the follow-up survey would be $p_T - p_u^0$. This would overestimate the impact of the program as long as $p_c^u > p_c^0$.

alternative values of $\beta = \left(\dfrac{n_T^A}{N - N_c} \right)\left(p_T^0 - \delta \right) + \left(\dfrac{N - N_c - n_T^A}{N - N_c} \right) p_T^0 - p_c^0$. We impute 1s in $\left\lceil n_T^A \left(p_T^0 - \delta \right) \right\rceil$ observations in the attrited treatment group and impute 0s for the remaining $\left\lfloor n_T^A \left(1 - p_T^0 - \delta \right) \right\rfloor$ observations. Again, this procedure will tell us the critical value of $\tilde{\delta}$ and how much smaller the adoption rate would need to be among the attrited group to eliminate the effect of the program.

We followed the same procedures for both post-intervention cross-sectional data sets ($t = 1$ and $t = 2$). The estimates for assigning the micro entrepreneur a fixed salary (A), keeping records of network contacts (B) and bookkeeping (C) are reported in Table 9.8. We find that it is very unlikely that attrition could eliminate the positive effect of the program on assignment of a fixed salary. For this to happen, the proportion of micro entrepreneurs that assigned themselves a fixed salary among attriters in the control group would need to be 3.1–5.3 times the proportion of those that we observe in the control group. Alternatively, even if no micro entrepreneurs in the attrited portion of the treatment group would have adopted this practice, the effect of the program would still be 3–4 percent. The case is similar for keeping a record of potential network contacts: the proportion of micro entrepreneurs that adopt this practice among attriters in the control group would need to be twice of what we observe in the data. We also find that even if no one among attriters in the treatment group adopts this practice, we would still get a 5 percent impact. All in all, we believe that it is very unlikely that those who attrited would be so substantially different that we would not find a positive impact of the program anymore.

However, our results for bookkeeping are not as robust. If those that attrited in the control group were 7–23 percent more likely to have a bookkeeping system (compared with those in the control group who remained in the sample), we would not be able to find a significant positive effect any longer. Alternatively, this would also happen if the micro entrepreneurs in the attrited sample of the control group were 11–29 percent less likely to adopt this practice. Although this does not necessarily imply that the program did not have a positive impact on the adoption of bookkeeping practices, it could be the case that the positive effect that we previously found does not hold under some relatively plausible conditions.

9.4.3 Quality of the Training and Practice Adoption

A possible explanation for our results is that the training was not useful for the participants. This could happen if the training did not explain how to implement their proposed business practices clearly enough or if it was unable to convey their usefulness. It could also be the case that even when participants

Table 9.8 Sensitivity of Business Practice Adoption to Attrition

t = 1			t = 2		
Adjustment $(\delta)^a$	Mean imputed group^b	Effect	Adjustment $(\delta)^a$	Mean imputed group^b	Effect
A. Micro Entrepreneur Assigns Herself a Fixed Salary					
Impute missing observations in control					
0% $(p_c^0)^d$	0.056	0.040*** (0.012)	0% $(p_c^0)^d$	0.047	0.059*** (0.012)
5%	0.102	0.033** (0.013)	5%	0.097	0.047** (0.013)
10%	0.153	0.024* (0.013)	10%	0.144	0.035* (0.013)
15%	0.203	0.015 (0.014)	15%	0.187	0.023 (0.014)
20%	0.254	0.006 (0.014)	20%	0.195	0.010 (0.015)
No effect $(\delta = 12\%)^e$	0.175	0.020 (0.013)	No effect $(\delta = 14\%)^e$	0.245	0.025 (0.014)
$(p_c^0 + \delta)/p_c^0$ f	3.10		$(p_c^0 + \delta)/p_c^0$ f	5.25	
Impute missing observations in treatment					
0.0% $(p_c^0)^d$	0.099	0.040*** (0.012)	0.0% $(p_c^0)^d$	0.109	0.059*** (0.012)
−2.5%	0.074	0.037*** (0.012)	−2.5%	0.082	0.055*** (0.012)
−5.0%	0.049	0.035*** (0.012)	−5.0%	0.055	0.051*** (0.012)

0.025	0.032***	−7.5%	0.036	0.048***	
	(0.012)			(0.012)	
0.000	0.029**	−10.0%	0.009	0.044***	
	(0.012)			(0.012)	
NA	NA	No effect[e]	NA	NA	
NA		$(p_T^0+\delta)/p_T^{0}$[f]	NA		

B. Keeps Records of Network

Impute missing observations in control

0.258	0.089***	0% (p_c^0)[d]	0.310	0.111***	
	(0.022)			(0.023)	
0.355	0.072***	10%	0.407	0.087***	
	(0.022)			(0.023)	
0.457	0.053**	20%	0.508	0.062***	
	(0.023)			(0.024)	
0.559	0.035	30%	0.609	0.037	
	(0.023)			(0.024)	
0.656	0.018	40%	0.709	0.011	
	(0.023)			(0.024)	
0.548	0.037	No effect ($\delta = 29\%$)[c] / No effect ($\delta = 30\%$)[c]	0.609	0.037	
	(0.023)			(0.024)	
2.12		$(p_c^0+\delta)/p_c^{0}$[f]	1.96		

Impute missing observations in treatment

0.345	0.089***	0% (p_T^0)[d]	0.421	0.111***	
	(0.022)			(0.023)	

(continued)

Table 9.8 (*Cont.*)

t = 1			t = 2		
Adjustment (δ)[a]	Mean imputed group[b]	Effect	Adjustment (δ)[a]	Mean imputed group[b]	Effect
−10%	0.250	0.078***	−10%	0.325	0.095***
		(0.022)			(0.023)
−20%	0.155	0.066***	−20%	0.219	0.078***
		(0.022)			(0.023)
−30%	0.048	0.054**	−30%	0.123	0.063***
		(0.022)			(0.023)
−35%	0.000	0.048**	−40%	0.026	0.047**
		(0.022)			(0.023)
No effect[e]	NA	NA	No effect (δ = −5%)[c]	NA	NA
$(p_T^0 + \delta)/p_T^0$ [f]	NA	NA	$(p_T^0 + \delta)/p_T^0$ [f]	NA	NA

C. Bookkeeping

Impute missing observations in control

t = 1			t = 2		
Adjustment (δ)[a]	Mean imputed group[b]	Effect	Adjustment (δ)[a]	Mean imputed group[b]	Effect
0% (p_c^0) [d]	0.418	0.054**	0% (p_c^0) [d]	0.447	0.047*
		(0.024)			(0.024)
5%	0.463	0.047*	5%	0.498	0.035
		(0.024)			(0.024)
10%	0.514	0.038	10%	0.549	0.022
		(0.024)			(0.024)
15%	0.565	0.029	15%	0.599	0.010
		(0.024)			(0.024)

	Rate	β	β		Rate	β	β
20%	0.616	0.021 (0.024)	0.038 (0.024)	20%	0.650	−0.003 (0.024)	0.039 (0.024)
No effect (δ = 10%)[e]	0.514			No effect (δ = 3%)[e]	0.479		
$(p_c^0+\delta)/p_c^0$[f]	1.23			$(p_c^0+\delta)/p_c^0$[f]	1.07		

Impute missing observations in treatment

	Rate	β		Rate	β
0% (p_T^0)[d]	0.469	0.054** (0.024)	0% (p_T^0)[d]	0.500	0.047* (0.024)
−5%	0.420	0.049** (0.024)	−5%	0.445	0.039 (0.024)
−10%	0.370	0.043* (0.024)	−10%	0.400	0.032 (0.024)
−15%	0.321	0.037 (0.024)	−15%	0.345	0.023 (0.024)
−20%	0.272	0.032 (0.024)	−20%	0.300	0.016 (0.024)
No effect (δ = −13%)[e]	0.333	0.039 (0.024)	No effect (δ = −5%)[e]	0.445	0.039 (0.024)
$(p_T^0+\delta)/p_T^0$[f]	0.71		$(p_T^0+\delta)/p_T^0$[f]	0.89	0.024

Source: Authors' own calculations.

a Simulated rates of adoption of $p_c^0+\delta$ (or $p_T^0-\delta$) among attrited households in the control (or treatment) group.

b We estimate a linear regression of the imputed variable on the treatment status and report the effect β and standard errors.

c While we impute a rate of adoption of $p_c^0+\delta$ (for the control group) or $p_T^0-\delta$ (for the treatment group), the rate in this column is not exactly the same because of rounding up when assigning 1s and 0s to the attrited observations. The rates reported here are: $\left\lceil n_c^A\left(p_c^0+\delta\right)\right\rceil/n_c^A$ and $\left\lceil n_T^A\left(1-p_c^0-\delta\right)\right\rceil/n_T^A$ respectively.

d When δ=0, the coefficient of the adjusted estimate is the same as the one calculated on the non-attrited sample.

e δ is the minimum value of δ for which the effect of the program is not significant.

f This ratio indicates how much larger (smaller) the adoption of practices should be among the attrited micro entrepreneurs in the control (treatment) group with respect to the observed mean in the control (treatment) group to yield a statistically insignificant effect.

did understand what they were taught, the contents of the training were not helpful for their businesses or were difficult to implement.

It does not seem to be the case that micro entrepreneurs did not understand the training. In general, program participants seemed highly satisfied with the training they received. At the endline, we asked the women in the treatment group (that had participated in the program about a year earlier) to rate their satisfaction with the training from 0 to 10 (with 0 being highly dissatisfied and 10 being highly satisfied). On average they assigned a score of 7.8; 68 percent of them rated the training 8 or more. Albeit subjective, this score does not support the idea that participants did not value the training or that they did not find it useful.

If participants understood the training and considered there were any benefits from the contents they were taught, it might be that the contents of the programs were not practical for their businesses. Among micro entrepreneurs in the treatment group who did not adopt each business practice in the endline, we did ask why they did not do so. This allowed us to present some qualitative evidence and explore why the training did not yield larger adoption rates. The results of this analysis are presented in Figure 9.1. In all the cases, there were few women who did not perceive any benefits from the business practices taught by the program or who did not understand the training (between 3.7 and 5.3 percent). There are some specific reasons for not assigning themselves a fixed salary: entrepreneurs might prefer to take a percentage of the profits (rather than a fixed sum) or they might just want to take all business profits. Also, there are some particular reasons to avoid keeping a client list (arguably they rely on other informal mechanisms, although they were not specified).[17]

However, in all cases, lack of time was an important reason to not adopt the business practices recommended by the program (between 29 and 69 percent, depending on the practice). This is an interesting finding, as it suggests that micro entrepreneurs value their time very highly and may be reluctant to pay the opportunity costs associated with taking on a particular practice. It may simply be the case that the training did not adequately convey the benefits associated with adopting the recommended practices relative to the perceived cost. Equally possible, however, is that we do not have a sufficiently rich understanding of the time constraints that female micro entrepreneurs face. If this is indeed the case, future

---

17 More than 20 percent of women mentioned other reasons not to adopt each practice. The "Other Reasons" category includes many distinct answers. Some of the reasons not to assign themselves a fixed salary were: particular and unexpected economic shocks, businesses that were not profitable enough, husbands taking away all business profits, neglect, etc. Examples of reasons not to keep a record of business contacts were: blurry vision, clients/suppliers coming anyway, single buyer/seller, etc. Other examples of reasons not to keep a record of sales and expenditures were: low levels of sales and expenditures that did not require bookkeeping, reluctance to know when business declines because it would demoralize them, entrepreneurs who forget to do so by the end of the day, etc.

(a) Reasons for not monitoring cash flow

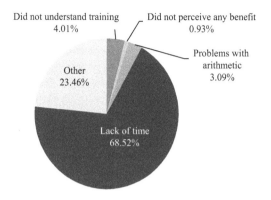

(b) Reasons for not maintaining a client list

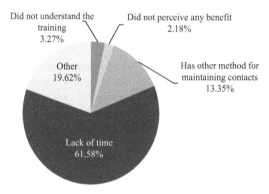

(c) Reasons for not assigning self a fixed

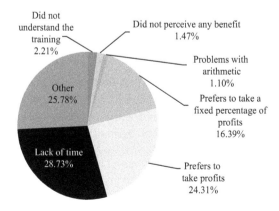

Figure 9.1 Reasons for not adopting business practices

interventions could be tailored to focus on how one might adopt these practices in a busy environment without taking up too much of the individual's time.

9.5 Conclusion

We analyze the impact of a large-scale program (SWEP) that provided business training to female micro entrepreneurs in Peru. It is estimated that more than one hundred thousand women benefited from SWEP during its four years of operation. The program's innovative approach was to teach business practices based on a soap-opera format, where women could identify with the struggles and daily problems of the main character. This soap opera was complemented with games and practical exercises conducted by an instructor. The cost of this media-based intervention was relatively low, providing a potentially cost-effective vehicle for entrepreneur trainings.

To assess the impact of the program, we conducted a field experiment in two cities in Peru (Lima and Piura). We collected a roster of female microenterprises in three sectors (services, retail and manufacturing) who would be willing to receive business training within a time frame of one year. From this roster, we randomly assigned 1,500 women to a treatment group and 1,100 women to a control group. Those in the treatment group were invited to participate in the training sessions immediately, while those in the control group would only be invited after our field experiment. Even when we anticipated cancellations and no-shows, the rate of attendance among those invited to the training was unfortunately only 47 percent (703 entrepreneurs).

We evaluate the adoption of three particular business practices emphasized by the program: assigning themselves a fixed salary (rather than taking money from the businesses based on their households needs), keeping a record of potential clients and contacts and bookkeeping (registering business sales and expenditures to determine their cash flow). We find that the program increased the adoption rate of the first two practices by about 4–6 percentage points and 6–11 percentage points, respectively. These results were significant across multiple specifications. We also find that there were some increases in the rate of adoption of bookkeeping (between 4–5 percentage points). However, this result is not robust in all our regressions. While positive and (for the most part) significant, these relatively modest levels of adoption did not translate into improvements of average business performance (measured through sales, expenditures and payrolls), household outcomes (per capita household expenditures) or women empowerment (measured through a set of questions regarding women's decision-making within their households).

All in all, we find that women who benefited from the program were highly satisfied with the trainings (the average rating was 7.8 out of maximum of 10 points). Women who did not adopt the business practices emphasized by the program were asked their reasons not to. Only a few of them did not adopt business practices because they did not feel they were important or did not understand the training. Instead, most of them indicated that they lacked the time to implement them in their businesses. This suggests the importance of understanding women's time constraints when designing business-training curricula.

References

Alderman, H., J. R. Behrman, H.-P. Kohler, J. A. Maluccio and S. C. Watkins (2001). "Attrition in Longitudinal Household Survey Data." *Demographic Research*, 5: 79–124.

Angelelli, P., R. Moudry and J. J. Llisterri (2006). *Institutional Capacities for Small Business Policy Development in Latin America and the Caribbean*. Sustainable Development Department Technical Paper Series. Washington, DC: Inter-American Development Bank.

Ayyagari, M., A. Demirguc-Kunt and V. Maksimovic (2011). "Small vs. Young Firms across the World: Contribution to Employment, Job Creation, and Growth." *Policy Research Working Paper 5631*. Washington, DC: The World Bank.

Banerjee, A., E. Duflo, R. Glennerster and C. Kinnan (2013). "The Miracle of Microfinance? Evidence from a Randomized Evaluation." Working Paper 18950. Cambridge, MA: National Bureau of Economic Research.

Berge, L. I. O., K. Bjorvatn and B. Tungodden (2011). "Human and Financial Capital for Microenterprise Development: Evidence from a Lab and Field Experiment." Discussion Paper 1/2011. Bergen: NHH Department of Economics.

Bland, J. M., and D. G. Altman (1995). "Multiple Significance Tests: the Bonferroni Method." *BMJ: British Medical Journal*, 310 (6973): 170.

Bloom, N., and J. V. Reenen (2010), "Why Do Management Practices Differ across Firms and Countries?." *Journal of Economic Perspectives*, 24(1): 203–24.

Bruhn, M., D. Karlan and A. Schoar (2010). "What Capital Is Missing in Developing Countries?." *American Economic Review*, 100(2): 629–33.

Calderón, G., J. M. Cunha and G. D. Giorgi (2013). "Business Literacy and Development: Evidence from a Randomized Controlled Trial in Rural Mexico." Working Paper 19740. Cambridge, MA: National Bureau of Economic Research.

Cho, Y., and M. Honorati (2013). "Entrepreneurship Programs in Developing Countries: A Meta Regression Analysis." *Policy Research Working Paper 6402*. Washington, DC: World Bank.

Correo, Diario (2012). "Incendio consume cientos de puestos en mercado de Villa El Salvador." Online Newspaper Version. Published February 17, 2012.

de Mel, S., D. McKenzie and C. Woodruff (2008). "Returns to Capital in Microenterprises: Evidence from a Field Experiment." *Quarterly Journal of Economics*, 123(4): 1329–72.

de Mel, S., D. McKenzie and C. Woodruff (2014). "Business Training and Female Enterprise Start-Up, growth, and Dynamics: Experimental evidence from Sri Lanka." *Journal of Development Economics*, 106: 199–210.

De Soto, H. (1989). *The Other Path: The Economic Answer to Terrorism*. New York: Harper & Row.

Drexler, A., G. Fischer and A. Schoar (2014). "Keeping It Simple: Financial Literacy and Rules of Thumb." *American Economic Journal: Applied Economics*, 6(2): 1–31.

Duflo, E., R. Glennerster and M. Kremer (2007). "Using Randomization in Development Economics Research: A Toolkit." In: Handbook of Development Economics, edited by T. P. Schultz and J. A. Strauss, 3895–962, Vol. 4, chapter 61, Elsevier.

Evans, D. S., and B. Jovanovic (1989). "An Estimated Model of Entrepreneurial Choice under Liquidity Constraints." *Journal of Political Economy*, 47(4): 808–27.

Fafchamps, M., D. McKenzie, S. Quinn and C. Woodruff (2014). "Microenterprise Growth and the Flypaper Effect: Evidence from a Randomized Experiment in Ghana." *Journal of Development Economics*, 106: 211–26.

Field, E., S. Jayachandran and R. Pande (2010). "Do Traditional Institutions Constrain Female Entrepreneurship? A Field Experiment on Business Training in India." *American Economic Review*, 100(2): 125–29.

Fitzgerald, J., P. Gottschalk and R. Moffitt (1998). "An Analysis of Sample Attrition in Panel Data." *Journal of Human Resources*, 33(2): 251–99.

Giné, X., and G. Mansuri (2011). "Money or Ideas? A Field Experiment on Constraints to Entrepreneurship in Rural Pakistan." Unpublished Manuscript. Washington, DC: The World Bank.

Heckman, J. (1979). "Sample Selection Basis as a Specification Error." Econometrica, 47(1): 153–61.

Heckman, J. J., R. J. Lalonde and J. A. Smith (1999). "The Economics and Econometrics of Active Labor Market Programs." In: Handbook of Labor Economics, edited by O. Ashenfelter and D. Card, 1865–2097, Vol. 3, chapter 31. Elsevier.

Jensen, R., and E. Oster (2009). "The Power of TV: Cable Television and Women's Status in India." *Quarterly Journal of Economics*, 124(3): 1057–94.

Karlan, D., R. Knight and C. Udry (2012). "Hoping to Win, Expected to Lose: Theory and Lessons on Microenterprise Development." Working Paper 312. Washington, DC: Center for Global Development.

Karlan, D., and M. Valdivia (2011). "Teaching Entrepreneurship: Impact of Business Training on Microfinance Clients and Institutions." *Review of Economics and Statistics*, 93(2): 510–27.

Kling, J. R. and J. B. Liebman (2004). "Experimental Analysis of Neighborhood Effects on Youth." Working Paper 483. Princeton, NJ: Princeton University, Industrial Relations Section (IRS).

Kling, J. R., J. B. Liebman and L. F. Katz (2007). "Experimental Analysis of Neighborhood Effects." *Econometrica*, 75(1): 83–119.

La Ferrara, E., A. Chong and S. Duryea (2012). "Soap Operas and Fertility: Evidence from Brazil." *American Economic Journal: Applied Economics*, 4(4): 1–31.

Li, Y., and M. Rama (2012). "Firm Dynamics, Productivity Growth and Job Creation in Developing Countries: The Role of Micro- and Small Enterprises." *Background Paper for the World Development Report 2013*. Washington, DC: The World Bank.

McKenzie, D. (2012). "Beyond Baseline and Follow-Up: The Case for More T in Experiments." *Journal of Development Economics*, 99: 210–21.

McKenzie, D., and C. Woodruff (2014). "What Are We Learning from Business Training and Entrepreneurship Evaluations around the Developing World?." *World Bank Research Observer*, 29(1): 48–82.

Restuccia, D., and R. Rogerson (2008). "Policy Distortions and Aggregate Productivity with Heterogeneous Establishments." *Review of Economic Dynamics*, 11(4): 707–20.

Sankoh, A., M. Huque and S. Dubey (1997). "Some Comments on Frequently used Multiple Endpoint Adjustment Methods in Clinical Trials." *Statistics in M 16*, 2529–42.

Schochet, P. Z. (2008). "Guidelines for Multiple Testing in Impact Evaluations of Educational Interventions." Unpublished Manuscript, Princeton, NJ: Mathematica Policy Research.

Valdivia, M. (2011). "Training or Technical Assistance? A Field Experiment to Learn What Works to Increase Managerial Capital for Female Microentrepreneurs." Unpublished Manuscript. Lima, Peru: Grupo de Análisis para el Desarrollo (GRADE).

Wooldridge, J. M. (2002). *Econometric Analysis of Cross-Sectional and Panel Data*. Cambridge, MA: MIT Press.

Wooldridge, J. M. (2007). "Inverse Probability Weighted Estimation for General Missing Data Problems." *Journal of Econometrics*, 141(2): 1281–301.

World Bank (2012). *World Development Report 2013: Jobs*. Washington, DC: The World Bank.

INDEX

Lightning Source UK Ltd.
Milton Keynes UK
UKHW012249040320
359783UK00001B/37